THE CASE AGAINST MILITARY INTERVENTION

Why We Do It and Why It Fails

Donald M. Snow

Routledge
Taylor & Francis Group

NEW YORK AND LONDON

First published 2016
by Routledge
711 Third Avenue, New York, NY 10017

and by Routledge
2 Park Square, Milton Park, Abingdon, Oxon, OX14 4RN

Routledge is an imprint of the Taylor & Francis Group, an informa business

British Library Cataloguing-in-Publication Data
A catalogue record for this book is available from the British Library

Library of Congress Cataloging-in-Publication Data
A catalog record for this book has been requested

ISBN: 978-0-7656-4755-9 (hbk)
ISBN: 978-0-7656-4756-6 (pbk)
ISBN: 978-1-315-71469-1 (ebk)

Typeset in Bembo
by Taylor & Francis Books

CONTENTS

ACKNOWLEDGMENTS

The author would like to thank his long-time friend and co-author Dennis M. Drew (Col., USAF Ret.). Denny read the entire manuscript and made many useful comments on the content and implications of various arguments I was trying to develop. As usual, he did an excellent job of untangling and simplifying some of my convoluted prose. Thanks, buddy!

INTRODUCTION

Interference in the domestic affairs of other countries by the world's states is nothing new. Such behavior is at basic conceptual odds with the principle of state sovereignty that undergirds the international system, because that principle asserts that whoever rules a sovereign, independent territory has absolute authority over its realm, a condition that interference violates. Outsiders, however, have or perceive interests in other states' business, and they act (interfere) to realize those interests whenever they feel them threatened. What matters is not whether the recipients like the interference or not, but rather whether they can do anything about it or not. Ask the Ukrainians! Sometimes the interferers succeed, and sometimes they do not. International politics has always been this way, and it likely always will be.

All interference is, of course, not the same, and as discussed in Chapter 1, its intents and means constitute a continuum from the comparatively mild, minimally intrusive to the extremely physical, highly invasive and even violent. The most extreme form contemporary interference takes is military intervention in one guise and for one purpose or another. This extreme form of interference is the subject of this book.

Military intrusion has a long and checkered history in human affairs. The focus of this book is narrower, concentrating on the American practice of military intervention. It is particularly concerned with American military incursions over the past fifty years, which have not been particularly successful, and with the prospects for future interventions, which are at least as problematical as the experiences of the recent past.

In the international system since the end of World War II, the United States has been a very active user of military force to solve its international disagreements. Writing in early 2014, Russett, for instance, observes, "Since 1950, the United

States has engaged in more militarized international disputes than any other country. China and the USSR/Russia are in a tie for second place, followed by Israel in fourth." Most of the major American engagements have been interventions into the domestic affairs of other states. Sometimes these situations involved real, ongoing shooting conflicts into which the United States intruded (Vietnam, for example), sometimes there was not prior organized domestic violence (Iraq), and in others, the United States played a role in precipitating a crisis it then sought to influence (Hawaii in the 1890s, Guatemala in the 1950s). At any rate, this country has been very busy seeking to influence other countries' politics with American armed forces.

Although some observers would doubtless contest the point, these efforts have typically been unsuccessful, sometimes in the short run, and usually in the long run. Except in the most narrow, limited sense (e.g., the short-term gain of particular domestic groups empowered by the actions of the intervener), military interventions are never embraced by host populations. There are exceptions when the intrusions are liberations from the outside oppression by other countries, and most important, when they are short (France at the end of World War II is an example), but interventions rarely meet these characteristics. Interveners, including Americans, stick around too long and wear out any welcome they may have enjoyed initially: ask Afghanistan's Hamid Karzai. As "liberation" turns into occupation in the minds of the recipients, the "three Rs"—resentment, rejection, and resistance—increasingly infect the host population. Although it may take awhile to accomplish, resistance usually prevails and the intruders retreat; any gains that may have been achieved proving to have been transitory, ethereal, and reversible.

This grim assessment should be thoroughly cautionary, and it is offered as a framework for understanding past failures and for gauging future intervention prospects. It strongly suggests that those viewing the contemplation of inserting American armed forces into another country's domestic affairs should be chastened. Such interventions are likely to be far less easy than advocates suggest (see predictions about Iraq, for instance), and it is more likely than not that whatever goals the United States sets out to achieve will not be realized. Those negative outcomes may be reached in a variety of ways, but they are relatively certain. It is really as simple as that.

This analysis rests on five interrelated theses and observations. Individually and in combination, these observations have particular relevance to potential American actions in international environments currently and in the foreseeable future. The theses and their implications pervade the pages that follow, and are worth noting as a guide to the analysis in the rest of the book.

The first observation regards whether the circumstances in which the United States has in the past and likely will be called upon in the future to act are important enough warrant American military intervention. In the realist terms that form the philosophical backbone of this work, it is a question of whether such situations rise to the level of threatening true U.S. vital interests, which is the realist yardstick for invoking the recourse to American arms. The thesis here is that such situations almost never rise to that level of importance. This is especially true in the developing world internal conflicts (or DWICs) that are the most prevalent form of contemporary violence—such situations rarely approach, much less reach, the plateau of vitality. Under the realist banner, the clear implication is that American intervention is rarely justifiable. If the vitality standard is applied, the utilization of American force in far-off conflicts would decrease dramatically.

There is, of course, a conceptual problem here, which is the subjectivity of the meaning of the term "vital." It is a difference about what is important and what is less important or unimportant. As Saunders points out in a recent *National Interest* article, virtually everyone advocating any particular course of action will assert its vitality, but doing so has a price. "Politicians' excessive invocation of 'vital national interests' to justify their varied aims diminishes their persuasiveness by breeding public skepticism," he writes. This tendency can be overcome by a thorough discussion and definition of what constitutes vitality or, as Saunders puts it, "A precise definition ... and thoughtful use of the term strengthens its meaning, impact, and utility."

The second assertion is that the circumstances in which the United States likely has and will likely be tempted to intervene at one level or another are all in essentially civil, domestic conflicts. This is true by definition of the DWICs, and it holds throughout the developing world. Aside from whether those domestic affairs affect vital U.S. interests, one major consequence is that the interests of the United States and the people of the places where intervention may be con-templated will be at variance. While some domestic elements within a particular country may share American views, many others will not and will oppose the imposition of American-backed preferences. This certainty leads to the third and related thesis.

The third observation is that these kinds of conflicts are almost always unwinnable for the intervening party, a generalization from which the United States is not exempt (we sometimes act as if we are). The reason is intuitively obvious. Internal wars are just that—conflicts between segments of a country's population divided along a variety of combinations of political, religious, social/religious, ethnic, kindred, or other bases. These wars are intensely personal and important to the internal participants, because the outcomes affect the terms of their existence. As such they are more important to them than any outsider interests are to them.

The implication is equally clear. Because of the interpersonal, intergroup dynamics of these conflicts, they can only truly be solved by the internal parties themselves. Because the interests and outcomes are so much more important to the internal parties than their interests are to the outsiders, the indigenous groups will almost always be more determined and committed to their pursuit, and their perseverance will outlast that of the outsiders. Frustrated but realizing this difference in motivation and determination, the outsiders will persevere (futilely, as it turns out), stay too long, and wear out any welcome they may have initially had. The intervener becomes part of the problem, not its solution. As Fowler, the protagonist in Graham Greene's brilliant 1955 novel on Vietnam, *The Quiet American,* explains it to Pyle, the crusading American CIA agent, "They [the Vietnamese] want enough rice. They don't want to be shot at. They want one day to be pretty much the same as another. They don't want our white skins telling them what they want."

There is one apparent exception to this description: the willingness and ability of outsiders to use severe, extreme brutality to enforce their will on their hosts. Brutality has worked historically for awhile by beating populations into submission, or in the most extreme cases, exterminating them. Genghis Khan is the historical standard; Hitler was the most recent systematic supplicant (and Stalin could arguably be added to the list, although his exterminations were mostly confined to the domestic population).

The exception is apparent for two reasons. Brutality dampens and suppresses reactions, but unless the targets are eliminated altogether, the three Rs of resentment, rejection, and resistance will inevitably return and will in all likelihood prevail in the long run. The empire of the Golden Horde was, after all, in retreat within a century (admittedly, the Mongols were truly lousy public administrators, aiding that process). At any rate, intervention's rewards are transitory. At the same time, the application of extreme brutality is so grotesque and obscene that it can only truly be practiced outside the public purview. Genghis Khan could not have prospered in the "twitterverse." Such actions are simply unacceptable and would be, should they become public (which they inevitably would), universally condemned and responded to.

The fourth observation is that the United States military is organizationally, psychologically, and physically ill-equipped and ill-suited for involvements in situations like the DWICs-style wars. The U.S. military is designed for and comfortable fighting large-scale, European-style conflicts, what are sometimes called *symmetrical wars*. Such wars require two (or more) similarly designed militaries clashing in accord with well-prescribed and generally observed rules of engagement (ROEs). No developing countries can compete in such contests, and they know it. As a result, they have adopted a style and philosophy of warfare sharply different from American preferences, and it has been generally effective in counteracting the American military juggernaut. This style is known as *asymmetrical warfare*, and, despite some adaptive efforts, the United States has no proven antidote for it. Some of the rationale and philosophy of asymmetrical war is chronicled in the bibliography at the end of this Introduction.

The fifth, and in a sense the most important, most chilling and cautionary, observation is that these kinds of conflicts and this style of warfare—DWICs—are likely to be the dominant form of violence in the world for the foreseeable future. Because of this, almost all the opportunities and temptations for U.S. recourse to arms will be in potentially quixotic situations where success is, optimistically stated, difficult to predict. More bluntly, these situations are likely to be predictably total losers—a masochist's delight. Understanding why is important national security business.

Bibliography

Bacevich, Andrew C. *Washington Rules: America's Path to Permanent War.* New York: Metropolitan Books, 2010.

Brinton, Crane. *Anatomy of Revolution* (Revised ed.). New York: Vantage Books, 1965.

Cable, Larry E. *Conflict of Myths: The Development of American Counterinsurgency Doctrine and the Vietnam War.* New York: New York University Press, 1986.

Chailand, Gerard. *Guerrilla Strategies: An Historical Anthology from the Long March to Afghanistan.* Berkeley, CA: University of California Press, 1982.

Debray, Regis. *Revolution in the Revolution: Armed Struggle and Political Struggle in Latin America.* New York: Monthly Review Press, 1967.

Fall, Bernard. *Street Without Joy: The French Debacle in Indochina.* Harrisburg, PA: Stackpole Books (Military History Series), 2005.

Galula, David. *Counterinsurgency Warfare: Theory and Practice.* Westport, CT: Praeger (PSI Classics of the Counterinsurgency Age), 2006.

Giap, Vo Nyugen. *People's War, People's Army.* New York: Praeger, 1962.

Greene, Graham. *The Quiet American.* Introduction by Robert Stone. New York: Penguin Deluxe Edition, 2004 (originally published 1955).

Guevara, Ernesto "Che." *Guerrilla Warfare.* New York: Monthly Review Press, 1961.

Gurr, Ted Robert. *Why Men Rebel.* Princeton, NJ: Princeton University Press, 1973.

Haass, Richard N. *Intervention: The Use of American Military Force in the Post-Cold War World.* Washington, DC: Carnegie Endowment for International Peace Books, 1994.

Kaplan, Fred. "The End of the Age of Petraeus: The Rise and Fall of Counterinsurgency." *Foreign Affairs* 92, 1 (January/February 2013), 75–90.

Kinzer, Stephen. *Overthrow: America's Century of Regime Change from Hawaii to Iraq.* New York: Times Books (Henry Holt and Company), 2006.

Larteguy, Jean. *The Centurions.* New York: E. P. Dutton, 1962.

Manwaring, Max G. (ed.). *Uncomfortable Wars: Toward a New Paradigm of Low-Intensity Conflict.* Boulder, CO: Westview Press, 1991.

Mao Zedung. *Selected Works of Mao Zedung,* Vols. 1–4. Beijing, China: Foreign Language Press, 1967.

Odierno, Raymond T. "The Army in a Time of Transition." *Foreign Affairs* 91, 3 (May/June 2012), 7–11.

O'Neil, Bard. *Insurgency and Terrorism: Inside Modern Revolutionary Warfare.* Washington, DC: Brassey's, 1990.

Paschall, Rod. *LIC 2010: Special Operations and Unconventional Warfare in the Next Century.* Washington, DC: Brassey's, 1990.

Russett, Bruce. "The Waning of Warfare." *Current History* 113, 759 (January 2014), 30–32.

Saunders, Paul J. "The Five Most Abused Foreign Policy Cliches." *National Interest* (online), March 1, 2014.

Shafer, D. Michael. *Deadly Paradigms: The Failure of U.S. Counterinsurgency Policy.* Princeton, NJ: Princeton University Press, 1988.

Snow, Donald M. *Distant Thunder: Patterns of Conflict in the Developing World* (2nd ed.). Armonk, NY: M E Sharpe, 1997.

——*National Security for a New Era* (5th ed.). New York: Pearson, 2014.

——*Third World Conflict and American Response in the Post-Cold War Era.* Carlisle Barracks, PA: Strategic Studies Institute, 1991.

——*Uncivil Wars: International Security and the New Internal Conflicts*. Boulder, CO: Lynne Rienner Publishers, 1996.

——*What After Iraq?* New York: Pearson Longman, 2009.

——*When America Fights: The Uses of U.S. Military Force*. Washington, DC: CQ Press, 2000.

Summers, Harry G. Jr. *On Strategy: A Critical Analysis of the Vietnam War*. Novato, CA: Presidio Press, 1982.

Sun Tzu (translated by Samuel P. Griffith). *The Art of War*. Oxford, UK: Oxford University Press, 1963.

Taber, Robert. *The War of the Fleas: The Classic Study of Guerrilla Warfare*. Washington, DC: Potomac Books, 2002 (originally published 1965).

Thompson, Sir Robert. *Make for the Hills: Memories of Far Eastern Wars*. London: Lee Cooper, 1989.

1

SETTING THE TABLE

The Phenomenon of Intervention

The central thesis of this work is that military intervention is almost always a bad idea, an observation that is especially true in contemporary times. It consistently asks the question, "Why should the United States almost always reject the temptation to commit military forces to conflicts in the developing world?" That question underlies and motivates this book. Its short answer is that such involvements are almost certain to fail, in the long run if not the short run. Failure is not always physical, in the sense of loss on the battlefield. That definition of failure is more historical in nature whereas contemporary failure is more normally measured in terms of whether such violent intrusions achieve the goals they set out to achieve. They rarely do.

Foreign forces on one's soil will almost always be resented, and likely rejected, and eventually resisted successfully. This argument gains importance because the "opportunities" for American military interventions are in internal instabilities and wars in developing countries. These developing world internal conflicts (or DWICs) resemble our most recent military misadventures and are a recurring emphasis of the text.

This assertion is hardly a revelation, especially for Americans still immersed in the wake of unsuccessful American military incursions into Iraq and Afghanistan and surrounded by crises in diverse parts of the globe from Crimea to Syria and to large parts of Africa, for which intervention is one possible U.S. policy response. An added lure to the intervention option is that it is proactive and virile, a sign that the United States remains a muscular, vital superpower, not a declining, toothless shadow of its former self that neither invites nor can demand respect. Using force is masculine and virile, while reluctance to doing so can be seen as pusillanimous. These assertions are virtually always specious.

Americans have questions and doubts about the attractiveness of using force in foreign situations. In the immediate wake of recent adventures in the countries flanking Iran, Americans are "intervention shy," a reaction similar to the period immediately after the conclusion of American involvement in Vietnam almost a half-century ago. The Vietnam hangover, as it was known at the time, gradually faded, and by the 1980s the United States was at it again with smaller incursions in places like Beirut and Grenada. By the 1990s, the pace quickened as the United States intruded militarily in the Middle East (Kuwait) and Africa (Somalia), the Western Hemisphere (Haiti), and the fringes of Europe (Bosnia and Kosovo). Stimulated by the reaction to the events of September 11, 2001, the United States engaged in full-scale, Vietnam-sized commitments in Iraq and Afghanistan. Unlike most modern U.S. politics, these actions were bipartisan, with administrations from both parties leading military adventures.

We have now returned to the post-Vietnam "square one" of how we got drawn into these adventures. The answers are complex, and their examination begins in this chapter by looking at the phenomenon of intervention, as the chapter subtitle suggests. It begins with a look at the underlying idea of political interference in its various forms, of which military intervention is the most extreme form. Interference occurs for a variety of reasons, and these motives are more or less important to states, and the importance of the interests involved are related to the severity of the interests and the consequences of their realization or denial. The discussion centers particularly on the interests associated with military intervention, since these are generally the cases where the consequences of actions are greatest. The section concludes with how the pattern of rationalization is changing both at the rhetorical and operational levels.

The chapter then turns to the historical dimension of interference. Particularly in terms of interference with armed forces, history is replete with examples of intrusion by peoples on other peoples. Historically, the most prevalent (certainly the most recorded and heralded) instances have been in order to conquer and subjugate people (the imperialist motivation). Popular histories have emphasized the successes of these efforts but not the resistance to imperialism or the eventual successes of such resistance.

The historical pattern has changed over the past century or so. Aggression and aggrandizement are no longer extolled as worthy goals, and though they are still arguably practiced in fact (e.g., 2014 Russian actions in Crimea). Interventions are now more typically justified in more benign, noble terms. The American odyssey of interference is a microcosm of the broader historical experience, and a broad overview of the evolution forms the concluding section of the chapter.

The study adds two other dimensions to illustrate why military interventions in the internal affairs of other peoples regularly fail. One dimension is indeed historical, arguing that military intrusions into others' affairs have been recurring—if underemphasized—themes throughout history, and resistance efforts against such intrusions have almost always been successful in the long run. From this perspective, what happened to the United States in its most recent misadventures are basically contemporary examples of enduring historical dynamics, not anomalies that somehow run counter to historical experience.

The historical case may not seem obvious at first. Classic imperialist motives included and often brought adventure, glory, great wealth, and access to exotic goods and experiences to the conquerors. They also brought resistance and the constant need to enforce rule over reluctant, disgruntled subjects, and that resistance usually succeeded in expelling the intruders. Conquest was always easier and more satisfying than rule. Modern interventions generally strip the intruders of the benefits and accentuate the burdens of their actions. The satisfaction has largely disappeared.

Many contemporary apologists try to argue that special characteristics of place, failures of the American will, or accidents of history have doomed what would have otherwise been successful enterprises. Although the contemporary environment does influence the dynamics of successful resistance to outside military influence, it is primarily to condense and accelerate the pace of successful expulsion of outside intruders—a quickening of historical processes of failure.

The other dimension that sets this study apart is the elaborated argument that resistance represents a basic and inexorable aspect of human nature. The ability and hence pace of interventions to produce temporary positive results may create the temporary illusion that imposition succeeds in some cases, but the underlying human response of revulsion, resistance, and repulsion of unwanted others is a basic human instinct. This may seem—and be—an unremarkable observation, and yet people have and continue to advocate and carry out interventions as if human nature is not violated by and does not reject such actions. Outside intrusion is offensive and will inevitably trigger rejection and resistance regardless of who interferes or why they intrude, a truth that is often overlooked or rationalized away. One might, for instance, recall that one reason very serious intervention advocates argued that the invasion and occupation of Iraq would be a rousing success was because the Iraqis would welcome the invading Americans as "liberators" rather than as unwanted imperialists who would not go back where they came from on their own and thus had to be resisted and eventually expelled. The gist of this second dimension is thus that outside interventions fail because that is essentially all they can do.

This second dimension changes the perspective of the "blame game" about why the military interventions in which the United States has become immersed have failed. Most contemporary critiques begin with the question of why an intervention was unsuccessful after the decision to intervene and its implementation occurred: what did we do wrong once we got there that contributed to defeat? These critiques sometimes (but not always) have an examination of whether we should have committed ourselves in the first place, but they tend to focus on unique aspects of particular application sites, not on the underlying dynamics of reaction to intervention. People argue, for instance, that Afghanistan was a bad place to intrude ourselves, because Afghanistan is a historically lousy place to try to subdue. While true enough some of the time, such a perspective misses the point that these military interventions trigger universal instincts to resist and should be avoided because they are destined to fail almost all of the time. The key question should be, "Why do we think we can overcome natural human reactions and factors?" in any particular place, the answer to which is almost always that we cannot. Looking for excuses after the fact simply misses the point.

The Idea of Intervention: Forms of Interference

One dictionary definition (*World Book Dictionary,* 1985) of *intervention* is "interference in the affairs of one nation by another." Given this broad meaning of the term, acts of interference are ubiquitous in international relations and always have been. As noted in the Introduction, interference across state borders violates the principle of sovereignty on which the state system is premised and is technically illegal in international legal terms, but it persists nonetheless.

This interference is conducted in a number of ways and for various reasons. The forms vary along a continuum of means, from the relatively limited, non-intrusive, and restrained to extremely disruptive, and even violent, methods. The means chosen in any particular situation reflect a variety of concerns and calculations, including how important it is to influence the state in which interference is contemplated and the ease or difficulty of succeeding at achieving the goals of the act: ultimately interfering is a matter of the interests of the intruding states. The most extreme form of intervention, which is the central concern of this book, is military intervention.

Although the major concern is with the use of military force to influence the actions of other states and their peoples, it is worthwhile to consider more limited forms as well. Doing so accentuates the prevalence of interference as a universal practice in the affairs of states, and the forms are sometimes linked in practice. It is not entirely unusual, for instance, for a potential intervening state to employ relatively limited, comparatively mild forms of interference to achieve its goals, and if these fail, to resort to progressively more strenuous forms, up to and even including the recourse to military intervention. At the same time, success at limited forms of interference may create an implicit belief in the efficacy of intervention and make more extensive recourse to its various forms, including force, more likely. This latter possibility seems to have been part of the American pattern of interference, especially as practiced during the Cold War, which is the subject of the last section of the chapter.

States interfere in the affairs of other states both because they feel it is necessary and because they feel they can get away with such actions. States are, after all, largely motivated and driven by what they consider to be their national interests (conditions they feel are important for national purposes). These interests often come into conflict with the interests of others, and when they do, it becomes necessary to reconcile the conflicts of interest that are represented. Since all parties want their conflicts to be settled on terms most favorable to them, one way to sway the outcome in their favor is to influence the other side to make it more receptive to their position. A prominent way to do that is to try to exercise influence within the other state—to interfere, in other words.

Whether and what kind of interference will be contemplated is partly the result of the interactive calculation of the importance of interests and how easily they can be attained. One key element is the notion of *vital interests*. These are generally defined in one of two ways, either as interests that are so important to the states that their failure to realize them would be intolerable, or as interests important enough to go to war over. The boundary between vital interests and lesser interests (less than vital or LTV) is important, because it is the point where military intervention may be contemplated.

The other key element is how easy or difficult it is to achieve a particular goal. Generally speaking, the easier it is to succeed, the more likely the attempt will be. The two elements are related. The easier attainment is, the more likely influence will be applied regardless of the importance of the issue; but the more important the interest is, the more it likely will be pursued regardless of the difficulty of attainment. When interests are considered vital, the consideration of ease of achievement may either be suspended as a consideration or false assessments may be made about that ease. All of this is most important when physical intervention with armed force is considered.

The 2014 Russian incursion into Crimea illustrates this kind of calculation. The Crimean peninsula has been considered very important to Russia since the days of the Russian Empire, to the point that it was the central feature of the Crimean War of 1853–56, when Russia tried to assert control over the territory and the other European powers resisted that annexation. Crimean port facilities are an important part of Russia's desire for warm-water ports and thus year-round access to the world's oceans, and thus the possession of secure naval bases there has long been what the Russians consider in their vital interest.

During the days of the Soviet Empire, this interest was realized, because Crimea was part of the Soviet Union. For reasons that remain opaque, Nikita Khrushchev, however, assigned Crimea to the Ukrainian Soviet Socialist Republic, and when the Soviet Union dissolved, it became part of independent Ukraine. The Russians, however, maintained their base rights in Crimea. This arrangement was satisfactory until Ukraine began to drift toward association with the European Union, raising the possibility of a hostile Ukrainian regime in control of the peninsula. At this point, a vital Russian interest seemed endangered.

It was in these circumstances that Russian president Vladimir Putin acted to gain control of Crimea. He attempted to exercise enfluence over the Ukraine by promoting pro-Russian sentiment in Ukraine to ensure a friendly government. When this ploy failed, however, he was faced with a potentially hostile regime in Kiev that might also jeopardize Russian access to Crimea. In this circumstance, he moved first to detach Crimea from Ukraine and to incorporate it into Russia.

Putin's calculations for intervention combined the importance of the issue and the ease with which it might be attained. Clearly, the Russian leader perceived a vital interest to be in jeopardy, and Russian public opinion apparently agreed. Strong actions were thus justified. At the same time, Putin calculated that his goal was attainable, since outside powers were unlikely to take decisive action to prevent the Russian takeover. Importance and attainability combined to justify the action.

One generic and concrete consequence of this general reasoning is that larger, more powerful states tend to interfere with others more than smaller, weaker states, who tend to be the recipients, rather than the instigators, of attempts to interfere with others. Larger states are likely to have more extensive interests than smaller states, and they are likely to have the means available to exercise influence, including the recourse to military force. It thus follows that larger states are also more likely to engage in interference across the board of possible actions, including the use of armed force. In contemporary international affairs, armed intervention into other states is the most frequent use of armed forces, and thus the findings of Russett and others depicted in the Introduction are not surprising: the three countries that have resorted to armed force since 1945 are the United States, Russia, and China.

Interference covers a wide range of actions that states can take to influence one another. It goes beyond present purposes to try to catalogue all the methods that states employ, but one can note that such actions form a continuum of sorts, from the least to the most intrusive and from the non-military to the military.

Non-Military/Political	Para/Semi-Military	Military

As one moves from left to right along the continuum, the actions become more drastic, active, and controversial. They also presumably reflect determinations of increasing interests at stake in different outcomes to particular concerns.

The least intrusive forms of interference tend to be political rather than military. These forms cover a wide range of possible actions that are generally limited in purposes and methods. The purposes of such actions are to influence states (normally their governments) to act in ways compatible with the interests of the interfering states. Occasionally, these attempts at influence are open and public—the U.S. Secretary of State publicly supporting a course of action in a target state, for instance. Historically, many of these actions are not open and include things like bribing officials, seeking to influence elections by providing propaganda or funds to one side or another, planting stories in the local press, spreading lies against parties who oppose the interests of the interfering state, or even encouraging internal parties to overthrow governments. The United States, for instance, has employed a wide range of these kinds of actions throughout Central America and in select South American countries like Chile in the 1970s (the American role in the overthrow of Salvador Allende as Chilean president).

What distinguishes these forms of interference is that they involve the commission of acts that are uniformly illegal in the countries being subjected to them. This illegality goes beyond international legal entreaties about interference and encompasses acts that are in violation of the criminal or civil codes of the government in which they occur. Generally, if the intrusion is revealed, it will discredit the government that initiates it and thus weaken the prospects of achieving its goals (as well as subjecting all parties to the transaction to criminal prosecution). As a result, a primary criterion for such actions is that they can be denied (known as *plausible deniability*), particularly if the actions are revealed. The extent to which a state will engage in illegal, secret means is both a measure of the importance of the issue to the initiating country and the perceived prospects of success.

In the post-World War II environment, and particularly in the heated atmosphere of the Cold War, intrusion expanded in terms of the frequency of actions undertaken, in the purposes for taking action, and in terms of the means employed. In actions directly between Cold War antagonists, this meant things like the extensive use of espionage as a tool to learn about the intentions and activities of the other side, and it also meant ratcheting the intensity of intrusive options. The most prominent of the methods employed was what is known as *covert action*. While virtually all intrusive actions were covert in the sense of being done secretly to avoid the appearance of interference and to maintain the veil of plausible deniability, Cold War covert actions raised the violent content of actions undertaken to the level of at least quasi- or semi-military methods. Two of the most prominent methods were sponsoring or materially assisting the physical overthrow of governments and even the assassination of unfriendly leaders of other countries.

Getting rid of regimes that opposed different countries' interests is not, of course, unique to the contemporary world. Assassinations with outside backing have a long if not especially rich background, but this course of action is nonetheless notable in the Cold War environment for at least two reasons relevant to this study. First, it forms a conceptual and empirical bridge between purely political forms of interference and outright armed intervention. The conceptual link, of course, is that this method introduces outside state-sponsored or conducted violence to the "kit bag" of forms of interference, an interim step on the way to open military intervention. They also represent a major step in the escalation of involvement in actual situations by states. Soviet action in Afghanistan in the 1970s and 1980s is an example. The process began with Soviet sponsorship of Afghan communists to gain power in the 1970s. When the Afghan leaders the Soviets sponsored proved incompetent and venal, the Soviets upped the ante by sponsoring overthrows of leaders and their replacement by other communists.

When these changes did not produce the stable communist regime the Soviets desired, they openly intervened in 1979, in what proved to be a predictably unsuccessful ten-year intervention and occupation.

Second, the United States became an active participant in these kinds of actions on a broad scale for the first time in its history. There was some precedent for American intrusion in the nineteenth and early twentieth century in Central America and the Caribbean, where American private commercial interests, sometimes augmented by the U.S. Marines, manipulated the political scene in places like Guatemala and Honduras, and to a lesser extent, Cuba. American active governmental involvement in covert action, however, dates largely to the 1950s in the actions of the Dulles brothers, Secretary of State John Foster and CIA Director Allen. According to Stephen Kinzer in *The Brothers*, the appetite for the use of covert action was whetted by sponsorship of the coup that overthrew Mohammed Mossadegh in Iran in 1953 and the overthrow of the Arbenz regime in Guatemala in 1954, both of which were successful in the short run. When extrapolated to Southeast Asia in the late 1950s and early 1960s, however, this precedent translated into the Vietnam War, a connection made in the last section of this chapter.

The most extreme form of interference and the form that is the central subject of rest of the book is armed military intervention. The term *intervention* can refer to any form of interference, but it is generally considered shorthand for the use of the armed forces of a country to influence, in one way or another, the politics and policy of another country. This generally means the physical intrusion of the intervener's armed forces into the territory of the host state for more or less prolonged periods. This form of interference is the most drastic form that interference can take, and it is also the most illegal in terms of its violation of sovereignty. Presumably, such extreme actions are only undertaken for particularly important reasons (to protect or promote the most important interests of the intervening state). Some of the reasons for which intervention is carried out are introduced in the next section, with an emphasis on how such rationales have changed in the contemporary environment.

The Rationales for Intervention

Armed intervention into the affairs of other states is often very controversial in the modern world, where public opinion plays an important role both in committing armed forces into harm's way and for sustaining the use of those forces. Historically, interference in the form of invasion and counter-invasion by various political entities, who would generally set up shop in conquered territories for more or less extended periods of time, was a "normal" form of political behavior, and there were no formal values or mores that prohibited it or made it arguably illegitimate. Values have changed and the rationales for interference have had to be adjusted to match those changes. The basic fact and dynamics of interference, however, remain basically the same.

Imperialism was the historic form of military intervention, although those who practiced it would not have recognized the term or concept of intervention. Rather, they pursued conquest of territory because it either seemed the natural thing to do, because it was possible, because it provided adventure and glory, because far-flung conquests promised great riches, because they wanted to overcome real or perceived dangers on their borders, or because it fulfilled some sense of destiny, to cite a few common reasons. History is replete with examples of such behavior, and one of the common themes of history is that such behavior is seen as heroic. One of the leading proponents of this explanation of warfare is the British historian John Keegan, who has stated in various works, like *A History of Warfare,* that he believes the Western notion of warfare as a conscious political act is an historical anomaly to the more historically prevalent practice of warfare for its own sake. The American analyst Edward Luttwak applies this same notion to contemporary, DWICs-style warfare, describing it as "post-heroic warfare" in a journal title in 1995. The idea that expansion was either an ignoble or illegitimate enterprise hardly ever entered traditional calculations, thereby reducing the need for conquerors to find underlying virtues that their actions produced. The excesses of imperial action, which were necessary to keep empires together, occasionally were noted (e.g., the genocide of the Mongols), but generally, the extension of domain was largely self-justifying, and most of its excesses were hidden from all but the perpetrators and their immediate victims.

The European empires that began to develop in the 1500s and only effectively ended in the latter part of the twentieth century represented the apex of the imperial justification. During the 400-plus-year period of colonial spread, the domain of European powers spread to virtually all of what is now considered the developing world, including North America, until American independence in the eighteenth century and Mexican and Canadian independence in the nineteenth century. While there is still some debate on the exact motivations that dominated imperial thought in the European colonial period, common explanations included the power and prestige of having empires (and larger empires than one's rivals) and the hope for great power and riches.

In terms of rationales, however, the European colonial period also represented a transition of sorts. While power politics and commercial success were not unacknowledged reasons to interfere in the affairs of reluctant other peoples, more noble motivations appeared necessary as well. The idea of some form of Manifest Destiny (the American version) suggested some form of higher, even divine mission being fulfilled in some cases (an argument with which those native Indian tribes who were subjugated would take issue). The most high-sounding explanations involved some form of "white man's burden," the idea that it was necessary to subjugate pagan, uncivilized people and "raise" them to the civilized standards of Western civilization. That this process included the enslavement of sizable numbers of the "liberated" was not viewed as terribly troubling until the early nineteenth century.

It is, of course, one of the anomalies of the modern era that many of the troubles and instabilities of the contemporary world are the direct outcome of the European colonial experience. At one level, these problems are further evidence of the basic thesis of this book that interventions ultimately fail in the long run, if not in the short run. More concretely, however, the great colonial "land grab" was a fairly indiscriminate form of imperialism, where territories were annexed and organized with little regard (and usually little knowledge) of loyalty structures, ethnic compositions, political affiliations, and the like. When these entities were granted independence—mostly after World War II—the result was the pattern of absolutely arbitrary, artificial states that are the primary hosts for the DWICs that represent the single greatest source of instability in the system.

The post-European colonial period has not witnessed the end of interference and intrusion by outsiders, but it has seen a change in the rationales for which they are pursued. The reasons for change have not been well studied or chronicled, but at least two contributory causes stand out as obvious candidates. One is the democratization of the major powers and the increasing role of public opinion as a factor in making decisions about the use of violence. While full-scale democratic rule is by no means universal, even autocratic regimes have to rely on public support to a significant degree, and generally speaking, publics must be convinced of the wisdom and necessity of actions, especially those involving force and potentially subjecting them to broader conflicts. Since the fascist attempts to spread domain in the 1930s and 1940s, imperial motives are not an easy sell. The other factor is the increasing transparency of international affairs. Interventions inevitably involve actions on the part of invading countries that are unattractive on television and other outlets, and electronic recording and publicity make it difficult to hide or obscure the atrocities that inevitably accompany military intrusions. In order to justify such actions at all, they must be clothed in motivations that make them seem necessary or noble. Traditional calls for "empire" do not generally meet that criterion (the Russian reassertion of sway over Crimea may be a partial exception, although it was carried out mostly without violence).

Within these constraints, potential intervening states have felt the overt need to "class up" their justifications for intruding on others. Two major strands of rationale have emerged and now dominate advocacies and explanations. One is *necessity*: the argument that if the intervening state does not act, the situation will produce unacceptable outcomes for that potential intervener. In such circumstances, intervention can be justified as an act of preemption or prevention, around which at least some legal and moral justification can be fabricated. This façade serves the dual purposes of creating internal political support for the intervention in the intervening state and for creating an argument to lessen international criticism. If the argument is convincing, it may create the democratic support necessary to sustain an operation. The Bush administration arguments regarding weapons of mass destruction (WMDs), their ties to terrorism in Iraq, and the danger of an Al Qaeda return to Afghanistan sanctuary were initially of this nature. The domino theory in Southeast Asia (the idea that if South Vietnam fell to communism, other states in the region would inevitably follow, endangering the United States) was a Cold War precursor. The underlying purpose, of course, is to make such actions selfless and necessary rather than self-serving and tawdry.

The other, and more recent, form of argumentation is what has become known as *humanitarian intervention*. In some important ways, the 1990s situations in Bosnia and Herzegovina (where the international community intervened to prevent potential genocidal acts) and in Rwanda (where the same community failed to act, resulting in a mass genocide) were the signal events for popularizing this form of action. The basic premise of this form of interference, discussed more fully in Chapter 7, is that when political groups, principally within states experiencing some form of DWIC, act atrociously toward parts of their populations, there is an international obligation to intervene and try to save the afflicted population. In other words, the justification for intervention is humane (to save innocent lives) and takes the form of a universal human obligation to come to the aid of helpless others. Intervention is, under this rationale, basically selfless and morally, rather than self-interestedly, motivated. Critiques of this form of rationale generally point out that states normally act out of their self-interest, not altruistic reasons, especially when actions as drastic as the use of military force are called for. This reluctance is often cited as one of the reasons the international community has not acted decisively to end the widespread civilian suffering in Syria.

This shift to a more benign basis for justifying intervention may be a necessary form of self-assuagement in the modern world, but it is also a change that brings other difficulties with it. Most obviously, it complicates the calculation of interference, creating the need for an intellectual justification for actions that were, in historical times, undertaken simply because it was the manly thing to do. It requires, in other words, trying to civilize behavior that is not, in many of its manifestations, very civilized at all. The major actions that form the core of intervention do, after all, include killing people, breaking things, and subjugating other humans. The novelty of humanitarian justifications is to try to demonstrate that intervention amounts to little more than putting lipstick on what is often a particularly unattractive pig.

The other problem is perceptual and involves the different perspectives of those carrying out and those receiving humanitarian interventions. The intervener in these cases is likely to feel a sense of righteousness and benevolence that the recipients either never accept as such or about which they become suspicious as the interveners linger longer than they are really wanted (which they almost always do). The Western Allies liberated France but brought the Free French armed forces with them to take over more or less immediately after liberation. The American "liberators" of Iraq from the tyranny of Saddam Hussein, on the other hand, stayed for eight years; the count in Afghanistan is more like thirteen years. Regardless of how well behaved or honorably intentioned the interveners-turned-occupiers may be, they are going to overstay their welcome and those whom they sought to save are going to resent their continued presence. The result is likely disillusionment with the experience on both sides; the deterioration of the once cordial relations between Afghanistan's Hamid Karzai and the U.S. government is a good example. It is also what a former colleague described (in a different context) as "as inevitable and as attractive as a mudslide." This observation applies to most interventions; it is particularly true and vexing in those interventions supposedly undertaken for humanitarian reasons. It is thus a rejoinder in thinking about future intrusions.

The Russian intrusion into Crimea exemplifies this change. In one sense, the Russian action seems like a classic imperial move, reasserting Russian sway in a former conquered territory over which it lost control with the dissolution of the Soviet Union, and to some extent that reason is undoubtedly part of the justification. The Putin regime, however, has gone to great length to deny naked imperialism as its motive, and has instead bathed its justification in nobler terms. On one hand, it has argued (mostly internally) that Ukraine's drift westward posed the possibility of a hostile Ukrainian regime that might threaten Soviet retention and control over Russian naval bases on the peninsula, the retention of which are vital to Soviet warm-water access to the Mediterranean Sea (an historic Russian goal). Thus, the action was a form of preemption made necessary by historical, legitimate Russian security concerns. At the same time, the population of Crimea is mostly ethnic Russian (thanks to russification actions under the czars and commissars that included flooding the peninsula with Russians and forcing native Tatars out), and those citizens argued (with some encouragement from Moscow) that they preferred to be part of Russia rather than Ukraine. As a result, the Russians were really coming to the rescue of the people of Crimea. As suggested, however, any jubilation the Crimeans may initially feel about their "liberation" is likely to cool over time with a continuing heavier Russian military presence and a growing realization that life might not be so much better as part of Russia than it was as part of Ukraine.

The landscape of intervention is thus changing, although the acts and dynamics of intervention arguably have not changed greatly across time. In order to help sort the real from the seeming changes and particularly to examine some of the more romantic connotations that attach to intervention in the past, it is useful to look briefly at the history of intrusion.

History: The Violent and Spotted Historical Experience

Groups of humans have been attacking other groups of people and invading their territory for a long time, as noted at the outset. Indeed, much of world history as it has been passed down in writing is a chronicle of these impositions. Within these accounts, there is a definite if arguably implicit bias toward the success of these incursions and the "great" empires they created: historians, like most of the rest of us, love winners. It does not matter much whether the invaders and conquerors were "noble" Romans or Englishmen or less noble "savages" like Attila's Huns or the Mongol Hordes of the Great Khan. It is their exploits that history records and schoolchildren learn: the dates of their invasions, the "great" battles, the victorious leaders, and the length of their domain are the fodder of popular history. Those against whom these invasions and impositions were perpetrated get much less ink: we do not remember many of the names of those who stood up to and resisted the invaders, how they resisted, and, until (or unless) they succeeded, when or how they triumphed. Spartacus is the exception, not the rule.

Resistance to incursion and the imposition of rule by outsiders is as universal as is that imposition, and by and large, resistance has ultimately been successful, reversing the imposition of alien rule. If humans are an acquisitive, aggressive species, humans have also shown an equal proclivity and instinct to protect themselves from unwanted outside intrusion. If the impulse to impose one's will approaches universality as a part of human behavior, resistance to and rejection of those incursions is a predictable and, in some form or another, universal response. Eventually, the resisters usually succeed, and successful resistance to intrusion (by whatever name) is as enduring a phenomenon as aggression itself. It generally has just not gotten as much historical attention.

The amateur anthropologist Robert Ardrey framed this dynamic well in a series of books written during the 1970s. His central thesis, which he called the "territorial imperative," was that humans are territory-seeking and territory-protecting creatures. Extrapolating his hypothesis empirically primarily from the behavior of primates (especially lemurs in the Madagascar and Indian rainforests), Ardrey asserted that people seek to possess territory adequate for their needs. When territory is adequate, they live in peace and harmony. When it is not, however, humans will fight either to obtain the territory they feel they need but do not possess or, if someone tries to take their needed space from them, they will fight to protect it. Human aggression and self-defense are thus both basic human instincts.

One need not accept the Ardrey formulation to observe the recurring historical theme. For reasons as various as those who possess and exercise them, humans have always intruded upon and attempted to control other people and their territory. This intrusion is hardly ever welcome among those being imposed upon, and the resentment the victims feel grows the longer and more oppressive the imposition is. At some point, the intruders recognize this resentment and, on rare occasions, respond by leaving. Much more frequently, they respond with acts of brutality and repression, which, of course, only amplifies the resentment. Resentment turns violent in more or less extensive and effective ways, and the intruder fights back. In the end, the intruders almost always lose, generally because winning (maintaining control) turns out to be less important to them than it is to those seeking to regain control of their own territory and destiny. It is the dynamics of that virtual inevitability of rejection and the dynamics of why resistance almost always prevails that is the basis of this study.

Although this book is not a history of intervention, it does begin from the premise that the history of people's incursions on others is a useful starting point within which to set the more contemporary debate about the wisdom of violently intruding on others. This framing of the subject is helpful for at least three reasons. One is that popular history has glamorized these intrusions in ways that have unduly obscured how we think of them: we know much more about the glories of sweeping through foreign lands than we do about the slaughter and inhumanity which accompanies both the conquests and the consequent efforts to retain domain. Second, popular depictions make those efforts seem a whole lot more successful and noble in purpose than most in fact were: the emphasis is generally on the conquering, not on the resistance to imperial rule or the dynamics of expelling the invaders. Third, these incursions were generally based, and much of their apparent success enforced, by what would now be thought of as grotesquely unacceptable levels of violence and brutality: the Mongols are much more remembered for the stunning proportions of their conquests than for the mounds of skulls of their slaughtered opponents that they left behind as stark rejoinders to those who might contemplate sedition against them.

This history is also useful for another reason that derives from the points just made. It is the central contention here that the history of foreign incursions was not as universally successful as is generally argued, and that such success as did occur (or appeared to occur) came in the context of circumstances that simply no longer exist. The periods of long and apparently successful subjugation happened in a very different era. Subjugation and subsequent rule by foreigners succeeded in an environment of information deprivation, where very few people (other than the direct participants) knew about the incredible cruelty, even barbarity, accompanying conquests, but more importantly, formed the necessary foundation for continued control of conquered lands. The coercive yoke has always been central to outside domination, and its tools have been force and the resort to brutal repression to intimidate the subjects into submission (or at least non-resistance). Without the levels of brutality that were present, many of the empires could not have appeared to thrive as long as they did.

Modern technology has deprived the intruders of the effective option of employing their necessary means of control. The acts that were routinely accepted as necessities to retain outside domain are no longer possible to commit outside a public eye that will not condone such actions. Imagine, for instance, the reaction of the British public to YouTube or Twitter coverage of the British imperial practice of executing those it sought to punish by forcing a victim to stand before a cannon barrel with his or her shoulders against the barrel's opening before the cannon was then fired, literally blowing the victim to bits. Such acts of brutality, which were the necessary stuff of subjugation, may still be physically possible and even contemplated, but they are no longer so readily acceptable as tools for occupying powers in the modern world. That is not the only way things have changed, but it is certainly a prominent example.

This section introduces and begins to elaborate on some historical ideas and arguments that are developed throughout the book. It begins with a general historical overview, the purpose of which is to raise doubts about the historical success or generally positive impact of attempts to extend the domains of humans over other humans. Within the historical record, there are numerous examples where the conquerors apparently succeeded, but even those apparent successes included continued resistance and had to be accompanied by brutal repression that is essentially intolerable in the contemporary context. The basic point is that intervention and the desire to increase human domain and domination have been recurring historical themes, but so too has resistance to those efforts. There are exceptions, of course, but these generally involve interventions limited in duration and with positive benefits for the occupied (Europe in 1945) or where intervention and occupation assistance were requested (Korea). In the long run, the resisters almost always prevail.

This basic assertion lays the groundwork for its extension along two lines. The first line of extension is some assessment of the conditions under which intrusions have tended or appeared to be successful. These "positive" circumstances have been more evident in historical than in more contemporary times and instances. The Roman Empire, after all, lasted for half a millennium, the "sun never set" on the British Empire for upwards of two hundred years, and even the Mongols, some of the most inept (if brutal) colonial administrators in history, managed to maintain control of their empire for a century before it began to crumble. By contrast, the most recent overt attempt at imperial extension was Hitler's Third Reich, which was supposed to emulate the First Reich's (Holy Roman Empire's) thousand years' formal existence but lasted less than a dozen years. Nobody has seriously proposed trying since. Contemporary intrusions, of course, eschew imperialist motives, but if they are lengthy or come to be unwanted by the hosts, they produce resentment, rejection, and resistance as well.

The second line of extension is what has changed to make intrusion so much more problematic than it used to be. If historical experience ultimately disfavors the interveners, it is tilted even further against them now. The venues in which intervention can now occur are in the so-called developing world, notably the DWICs. These locations are concentrated in Africa and parts of Asia, and the general status of the potential candidate states, partly as the result of European colonialism and the expulsion of the colonists from the their territories, is increasingly uncongenial to intrusion. The same factors that historically facilitated intrusion now impede the likelihood of its success. The changed dynamics accelerate the inevitable process of successful resistance and add to the inadvisability of intervention. If intervention has always been a basically bad idea, it has become even a worse one.

The historical record can be helpful in understanding these dynamics and accompanying assertions about the inadvisability of armed intrusion in other peoples' essentially domestic affairs. The governments of states—and unfortunately including that of the United States—have made decisions to intrude themselves in places like Vietnam, Iraq, and Afghanistan, despite the ample historical and common-sensical evidence that such involvements are doomed to failure. The question with which one must begin is why? The quest for an answer begins with a very selective survey of the past.

People have indeed been imposing themselves on other people for as long as history has been recorded, and almost certainly before that. In early history, the occurrence of people imposing themselves was undoubtedly not as great as it became, owing to things like the lack of many concentrations of human groups in very large territories (thus awareness of one another and opportunities to think covetously of others), limits on the physical ability of organized groups to impose themselves (military organization and sizes), and a variety of other factors. Early chronicles are limited by the absence of literacy among both the invaders and those they attacked, but as humans became more "civilized," the recorded history of mankind was increasingly about the successes and "glory" of empires as diverse as those of Alexander the Great and the early tribes of the Middle East. We know a fair amount about the exploits and extent of Alexander's forays from Macedonia, because his own publicists wrote most of the original accounts on which histories were constructed and later reconstructed (all the accounts written at the time have been destroyed). The record is far less complete or elaborate concerning those against whom intrusions occurred. The effect is, among other things, to skew the record toward the conquerors rather than the resisters.

If the hypothesis that outside violent intrusion in other territorial entities (states in the modern world) rarely succeeds is correct (and it *is* a hypothesis, not a scientific law), there can be only two logical reasons why the leaders of countries continue to defy that reality. One reason is that they do not accept the hypothesis as true, an interpretation buttressed by popular depictions of history. The other, explored later in the chapter and throughout the text, is that those who propose particular intrusions believe they are somehow exempt from the rule. Usually, the basis of such a claim lies in the notion that the particular proposed action is somehow "different" than past interventions and can succeed because it does not conform to the pattern that results in failure. This claim for exemption can be the result either of the assertion that the particular proposed site and situation are so different from others that historical processes do not apply or that the nature of the intervention is sufficiently special that historical processes are not likely to be reproduced.

Either proposition rests on the assumption that a particular proposed intrusion will not create the negative response of revulsion and rejection of the intruding other's presence, and that proposition is simply false. While the assertion that resistance is a universal response does not rise to the strict standards of a scientific law (it is not as reliable, say, as the law of gravity), a careful reading of past and recent experience suggests that it is a universal response, and that apparent varia-tions are more likely the result of perceptions by those intruded upon about whether and how their resistance will most likely succeed. The assertion of a special nature to proposed actions is suspect on the grounds that such claims are generally self-serving, based upon assessments that are more rationalizations than anything else, and also based on cosmetic rather than substantial differences that are alleged to constitute exceptions to the rule. Each proposition bears some examination.

Two patterns emerge from even a cursory examination of the history of humankind's attempts to spread domain over other peoples. One of these is that such intrusions are never welcome and will always be resisted in some form and at some time. The second follows from the first. If resistance to the imposition to intrusion is essentially universal, so is resistance to that resistance. The key element in the reaction of the invader to the truculence of the invaded has been the use of force to subdue those who resist. This application is an extension of the original application of force accompanying the original intrusion. Historically, the more "successful" intruders have been able to dampen resistance to them by showing a willingness to use considerable brutality in suppressing resistance, and the ability to act very ruthlessly and cruelly has been a hallmark of most long-term intrusions, notably the "great" empires of history. The use and especially willingness to quash resistance violently has widely been viewed as a sign of strength and resolve on the part of the intruders, and that myth has largely survived to the present.

Popular history, by emphasizing the intruders and not the resisters, indirectly contradicts this interpretation by emphasizing the successful applications of force rather than the reactions to it. The Roman Empire, for instance, was the dominant feature of what was then considered the "civilized world" for over five hundred years. This length of tenure suggests that the Romans were quite successful, and much of the history (especially that written by the Romans themselves or their later apologists) is thoroughly self-congratulatory, spending a good deal of time on the historical victories and much less on the difficulties both of establishing domain (as in Hispania) or resistance to Roman rule, despite the fact that Rome's domain was contested from the day it was established. Among the convenient mythologies that surround the whole notion of the success of the Roman Empire was the idea of *Pax Romana*. Its essence was that the imposition of Roman domain civilized and made peaceful (or at least tranquil) the savage world into which Rome spread its benign and civilizing influence. Only in the latter days of the empire, when resistance to Roman rule was increasingly successful, did chroniclers like Tacitus begin seriously to take into account those who rejected and sought to reverse Roman sway as a way to explain why the glory of Rome was becoming less glorious.

There certainly were some benefits from Roman rule: the Romans, after all, did bring Latin to parts of the world theretofore illiterate, as well as their systems of roads and aqueducts. They also brought repression and slaughter when those on the receiving end did not show proper appreciation for the Roman yoke that accompanied their presence. History only obliquely and almost certainly incompletely records and immortalizes the resisters, whether they were the indigenous inhabitants of Hispania or the Celts and others as the Romans moved through northern Europe and onto the British Isles. In a few cases, there are fairly elaborate records of resistance, such as those in Palestine between 66 and 73 AD, when the Jewish Zealots (often considered the prototype of modern terrorists) resisted Roman rule. Their ultimate martyrdom at Masada (or Metsada, depending on the vantage point of the teller) tells virtually all one needs to know about any enlightenment and civilization connected to Roman overlordship as perceived by those forced to endure it. Rome's successful reign was based largely on the overwhelming ability to suppress resistance with brutal means. When its ability to intimidate based in fear of atrocity weakened, so did its hold. Such overwhelming balances of applicable force and its brutal application are not so readily available to enforce control today. The whole notion of the Pax Romana is indeed little more than a self-aggrandizing, romantic myth that obscures a recurrent stream of uprisings and resistance that culminated in the fall of Rome at the hands of "barbarians" following the lead of Attila the Hun.

These kinds of mythology and selectivity of record were not, of course, unique to Rome. The conquests of Temujin (Genghis Khan) and his followers sweeping out of modern-day Mongolia, spreading their reign across China and then sweeping across Eurasia to parts of Eastern Europe and modern Russia, were an inexorable force that could not be resisted successfully by those who faced it. For most of the thirteenth century, the Mongol advances were irresistible, but their momentum was spent by the time Genghis' grandson, Kublai Khan, died late in the century. Resistance arose as the vice grip of the Mongols weakened, and although successors like Tamerlane (a direct descendent of Genghis) managed to extend the remnants of Mongol (by that time known as Mogul) rule over most of Asia, the Mongols' time was limited.

One of the themes of the spread of domain historically is that not all its effects were negative. The Golden Hordes slaughtered uncounted thousands of those who were unlucky enough to be in their way, but they also established a sense of order and lawfulness along their cross-Asia route that facilitated the development of trade between Europe and the Orient, which had previously been stunted by the vagaries of trying safely to traverse the routes the Mongols opened and protected. Initially, the Mongols were so overwhelming that those who physically survived their onslaught (in some cases, not very many of them did) were effectively cowed into passivity. As has so regularly been the case with those seeking to spread their influence, the Mongols eventually bit off more than they could chew. They overextended their ability to support and supply themselves and proved inadequately organized to remedy the resulting logistical difficulties.

The British Empire offers a more contemporary and culturally familiar example of the vagaries of empire and the illusion of its success. It lasted longer than Genghis' empire and spread to virtually all parts of the world. It has been the subject of innumerable accounts and histories, mostly dominated by those who built and maintained the empire and their apologists. Because Britain gradually became democratic while the empire flourished, a carefully cultivated aura of enlightenment has attached to the empire and how those who were a part of it viewed British rule. An occasional exception appeared from time to time that has attempted to puncture the myth, but until recently, without much success. The myth has always been that British rule was essentially benign and that the benefits of being part of the empire were so great that its subjects did not greatly mind its endurance.

The reality of empire was, of course, quite different, and revisionist histories (prominently Richard Gott's 2011 book *Britain's Empire*) have begun to puncture the myth of both success and benign impact. As Gott put it early in his work, "Britain's Empire was established, and maintained for more than two centuries, through bloodshed, violence, brutality, conquest, and war." That Americans, who offered the first successful resistance to and expulsion of the intruders, should buy into the myth of the British Empire is particularly perplexing. Unlike most places where the British arrived uninvited and unwelcome, the Americans, who rejected their continued presence, were not indigenous people conquered and ruled by the invaders, but basically settlers whom the original British invaders brought with them (these people were often the historic victims of British conquest themselves, such as the Highland Scots who had been displaced by English conquest and moved to America because they needed someplace to live). Yet the settlers eventually turned on their overlords, and as part of the inexorable process of history, eventually succeeded.

The myth of a Pax Brittanica rivals that of Pax Romana as romantic fiction. The British expansion was almost universally resisted wherever the empire expanded. It takes a very romantic vision of history to think of the British long-term presence in places as diverse as the Indian subcontinent or the southern reaches of Africa to the island of Ireland as anything but adversarial and apparent acceptance of British rule as anything more than a grudging admission the subjects lacked the wherewithal to expel them. As Gott points out, "they never arrived as welcome guests. ... The initial opposition continued, on and off, and in varying forms, in almost every colonial territory until independence."

British rule endured as long as it did because it was able to manage the forces arrayed against it, but always with considerable costs. Much of the empire was premised on the false assumption that it could be a profitable enterprise, which was almost never true. The costs of empire status were beginning to cause the empire to fray when World War II beggared the British treasury enough that "empire" could no longer be afforded after the fighting stopped in Europe. The process of what became successful expulsion had already begun in parts of the empire, notably the Indian subcontinent, during the interwar period. Like all the intruders before them, the British were bucking human nature, and eventually the inevitable resistance to their intrusion prevailed.

America the Intervener

Americans should not feel smug about their own exemption from these processes. Much of pre-twentieth-century American history was punctuated by the suppression, subjugation, and in some cases extermination of the indigenous Americans who were here before the Europeans arrived. The British largely took care of the problem of eastern American Indian resistance to conquest of the lands the Indians considered theirs. After the American Civil War, the concerted conquest of the indigenous inhabitants of the Great Plains and American West under the banner of Manifest Destiny was a major element of U.S. "foreign" policy. This conquest meant the subjugation and, in some cases, virtual extermination of Indian tribes and was largely completed by the end of the nineteenth century. Its success was abetted by the relatively small numbers of Indians who had to be conquered and displaced. Anyone who thinks this was a benign process should look at the detailed record. S. C. Gwynne's 2010 account of the fate of the last holdouts, the Comanches, in *Empire of the Summer Moon* is a good and sobering beginning. Much of this American belief arises from the self-perception that the United States is such a special case as to be immune from historical truths.

It can, of course, be argued that American actions under the nineteenth-century banner of Manifest Destiny in the western U.S. were a special case. The middle American plains and mountain west were, after all, largely uninhabited except by mostly nomadic and some sedentary natives (native in the sense they had migrated to North America before the Europeans), and that Manifest Destiny presented little more than populating and incorporating unused lands that were clearly part of the American geographic inheritance in the West as the country spread from ocean to ocean. As such, they were not imperial actions or intrusions in the sense of the kinds of historic instances discussed in the last section. The difference, in other words, was a qualitative matter of degree.

By the end of the nineteenth century, with what is now called CONUS (the continental U.S. of what would become 48 contiguous states) incorporated, the United States turned outward and began to act in ways familiar in the historic context. As Stephen Kinzer points out in *Overthrow,* the first overt American action of the 1890s occurred in Hawaii, where a small group of European and American immigrants with commercial interests and some governmental backing, successfully overthrew the Hawaiian monarchy of Queen Liliuokalani in 1893. In 1894, the Republic of Hawaii was formed, and in 1898, the territory was annexed by the United States. The year 1898 was a banner year in American transformation. The United States also engaged in the Spanish-American War that year, and the result was that the United States established its first, modest overseas empire with outposts in places like the Virgin Islands, Puerto Rico, and the Philippines. The latter, when it realized it had been taken over, rather than liberated, by the Americans, resisted and rebelled, a harbinger of what was to come in the twentieth century both politically and militarily (the civil war against American rule in the Philippines was arguably the first American involvement in a full-scale DWIC).

American twentieth-century interventionism is most interesting, both because it was so extensive and because it provides the backdrop for current policy considerations. As Kinzer argues, the United States truly came of age as the world's interveners and interferers during this period. In the 110-year period beginning with fomenting insurrection in Hawaii, the "Americans overthrew fourteen governments," he writes. "No nation in modern history has done this so often, in so many places so far from its own shores." Some of these interventions were relatively modest in scope, but some of the most spectacular military failures in American history, notably Vietnam and arguably Iraq and Afghanistan, are artifacts of this twentieth-century aspect of American policy.

The stimulus for the policy of intervention that has become such a staple part of the American "kit bag" of foreign policy responses was the Cold War and the cast of characters it spawned. There has always been a level of skepticism about American military intrusion into other countries' affairs. Part of the stimulus is continued in the American self-image of its legacy. It is an integral part of the idea of "American exceptionalism" that this country is somehow special, Ronald Reagan's "shining house on the hill" that serves as a magnet because of the exemplary, different nature of its behavior. In this rending, a policy of interference and intervention represents a virtually tawdry policy that tarnishes the American brand. At the same time, there has also been a thread of belief that such actions were generally futile and self-defeating. Conservative Ohio senator Robert Taft, running for the Republican nomination for president in 1948, eloquently captured the dual sources of anomaly of a policy of interventionism: "Other people simply do not like to be dominated," he said, "and we would be in the same position of suppressing rebellions by force in which the British found themselves in the nineteenth century" by adopting such a stance (quoted in Kinzer, *The Brothers*).

The heat of the Cold War confrontation swept aside these prudent inhibitions. Largely under the leadership and direction of John Foster Dulles and Allen Dulles during the 1950s, the United States embarked on a gradually expanding policy of interference in the affairs of other states, the legacy of which still lingers today. There were both ideological and operational bases of this phenomenon. At the ideological level, the Dulles brothers (especially Secretary of State John Foster) saw the world in what they viewed as highly moral, Calvinistic terms of good (represented by the United States and capitalism) and bad (represented by "godless" Soviet communism). In Dulles' narrow view, the heart of the Cold War, especially in the developing world, was over the "soul" of the new countries: would they join the righteous, capitalist West or descend to the godless evil of communism? In this battle, there could be no bystanders: one either actively supported the "good" represented by the America of Dulles' vision, or one was part of the explicit or implicit forces of evil. Good was to be extolled and reinforced; evil resisted and eradicated by whatever means necessary.

The operational imperative was largely the preserve of CIA Director Allen Dulles, who had his initiating introduction into the clandestine world as part of the wartime Office of Strategic Services (OSS). In particular, Allen Dulles had become enamored with the idea of *covert action*, semi-military actions carried out by paramilitary forces that were part of the clandestine services and whose course of action was both secret and deniable. Covert action was both less costly and tainting than direct military intervention when it worked, and initial forays into this shadowy world seemed to work, certainly enough to encourage subsequent attempts. Even when these were less successful, the appetite had been whetted and besides, the possibility of direct military intervention remained in the background as an option when other methods failed.

The ideological influence of John Foster and the operational beliefs of Allen came together quickly when both were appointed to their positions of power and trust in the Eisenhower administration in 1953. The first two marriages of ideological fervor and covert action occurred in Iran and Guatemala, where regimes committed the ideological sins of insufficient fervor as anti-communists and even threatened the interests of American corporations, the symbol of capitalism and the servants whom the Dulles brothers had served as attorneys at the New York law firm of Sullivan and Cromwell in the 1930s and immediately after World War II.

The results are familiar. In 1953, the Dulles brothers moved against the democratically elected government of Mohammed Mossadegh, the democratically elected president of Iran (he was the first, and remains the only, Iranian who can claim to have come to power through fully democratic processes). In the eyes of the Dulles brothers, Mossadegh's sins included cancelling a lucrative business contract with one of the clients of Sullivan and Cromwell (proof of his hostility to capitalism) and, even more egregiously, nationalizing the Iranian oil industry. Employing skills and associates from the OSS, Allen organized a coup that overthrew Mossadegh and allowed Shah Reza Pahlevi to return to power (he had gone into exile after Mossadegh was in power). Flush with this success, the U.S. moved quickly in a parallel exercise against Guatemalan leader Jacobo Arbenz, who exhibited the same kind of "dangerous" behavior as his Iranian counterpart, principally threatening the holdings of the United Fruit Company, also not coincidentally a major Sullivan and Cromwell client, in 1954.

These "successes" intoxicated American policy makers with the ease and efficacy of interference in other governments' affairs, and subsequent efforts were mounted against other recalcitrant developing world leaders in the balance of the 1950s. Generally speaking, these were not so successful. The attempt to engineer the overthrow of Indonesia's Achmed Sukarno failed and only managed to dampen his bubbling enthusiasm for the United States. The brothers did manage to assassinate the Congo's Patrice Lumumba, and despite concerted efforts that extended well beyond their tenure, Cuba's Fidel Castro stayed in power for over a half-century.

The least successful of the covert actions was undertaken against Ho Chi Minh, the leader of the Vietnamese independence movement. Ho presented the puzzling combination of being both the overwhelmingly popular symbol of the independence movement and a practicing communist. This combination was incomprehensible to most analysts, who argued about which characteristic was more important. John

Foster Dulles in particular was not at all concerned with this apparent incongruity: the fact that Ho was a communist was all he needed to know and trumped any nationalist credentials. When covert action failed to dislodge the Vietnamese leader, the brothers started the process that led to the overt military intervention that built in 1965 to a full-scale American military adventure in Southeast Asia.

The process of intrusion that the Dulles brothers created left two major legacies. The most obvious was that it set the precedent for American intrusion in the affairs of the newly emerging developing world in areas outside the western hemisphere, the traditional sphere of influence of the United States. This precedent, justified largely by the global nature of the Cold War competition, has continued to the present. Among the derivative elements in this legacy has been the willingness to interfere in places where the United States has few historic interests and often even less knowledge and understanding. If an opponent was a communist, merely an "immoral and short-sided" neutralist (John Foster Dulles' depiction of the unwillingness to commit to the Western side in the competition), or merely someone who opposed the interests of Western corporations, he was fair game for removal. The initial experience in Iran and Guatemala suggested that ignorance of local conditions did not matter much; subsequent experience suggested it did.

The other legacy was of policy failures and problems created by interference. The record at the time was mixed: operations succeeded in Iran and Guatemala but failed otherwise. Even the successes, however, left bitter legacies. Iran remains an obdurate foe whose citizens well remember both that the Americans overthrew their only democratic government and supported the unpopular, autocratic Shah, and Guatemala remains one of the poorest, least stable countries in Central America. These are the places covert action succeeded. The Congo has remained among the least stable states in Africa, pro-Americanism in Indonesia took a hit, and the island of Cuba remains an opponent and sore point. The failure of Vietnam is the most glaring monument to the policy of interference.

The legacies of the Cold War era remain instructive for the current environment. The most obvious legacy is to reinforce the virtual certainty that intervention will fail, in the long term if not in the short term. None of the six places into which the Dulles brothers stuck America's nose is exactly the kind of pro-American success story that they probably envisioned, and it is hard to argue with Kinzer's conclusion in *Overthrow* that "most of these operations actually weakened American security." His explanation for this result includes a lack of foresight and their ignorance of what is now called *blowback*, roughly unintended consequences that probably should have been anticipated.

All the experiences also reinforce the basic thesis of this work that intervention fails because that is really all it can do. Meddling in places about which knowledge is incomplete or altogether absent is likely to produce bad policy that may appear to succeed in the short run but is essentially bound to fail in the longer run. These conditions are true in much of the developing world and are important elements in the DWICs that have become the dominant form of contemporary conflict. How the environment got that way is the major thrust of Chapter 2.

Bibliography

Ardrey, Robert. *The Social Contract: A Personal Inquiry into the Evolutionary Sources of Order and Disorder*. New York: Atheneum, 1970.

——*The Territorial Imperative*. New York: Dell, 1971.

Aydin, Aysegul. *Foreign Policy and Intervention in Armed Conflicts*. Palo Alto, CA: Stanford University Books, 2012.

Campbell, Kenneth J. *A Tale of Two Quagmires: Iraq, Vietnam and the Hard Lessons of War*. New York: Paradigm, 2007.

Gott, Richard. *Britain's Empire: Resistance, Repression, and Revolt*. London: Verso, 2011.

Gwynne, S. C. *Empire of the Summer Moon: Quanah Parker and the Rise and Fall of the Comanches, the Most Powerful Indian Tribe in American History*. New York: Scribner, 2010.

Haass, Richard M. *Intervention: The Uses of American Force in the Post-Cold War World*. Washington, DC: Carnegie Endowment for International Peace, 1994.

Immerman, Richard H. *Empire for Liberty: A History of American Imperialism from Benjamin Franklin to Paul Wolfowitz*. Princeton, NJ: Princeton University Press, 2010.

Keegan, John. *A History of Warfare*. London: Hutchison, 1993.

Kinzer, Stephen. *The Brothers: John Foster Dulles, Allen Dulles, and Their Secret World War*. New York: Times Books (Henry Holt and Company), 2013.

——*Overthrow: America's Century of Regime Change from Hawaii to Iraq*. New York: Times Books (Henry Holt and Company), 2006.

Luttwak, Edward. "Toward Post-Heroic Warfare." *Foreign Affairs* 74 (May/June 1995), 109–22.

Menon, Rajah. "It's Fatally Flawed." *National Interest* (online), June 12, 2013.

Pfaff, William R. *The Irony of Manifest Destiny: The Tragedy of America's Foreign Policy*. New York: Walker, 2010.

Polk, William R. *Violent Politics: A History of Insurgency, Terrorism, and Guerrilla Warfare*. New York: Harper Perennials, 2008.

Posman, Jeremy. *What Ruling the World Did to the British*. London: Viking, 2011.

Russett, Bruce. "The Waning of Warfare." *Current History* 113, 759 (January 2014), 30–32.

Snow, Donald M. *Distant Thunder: Patterns of Conflict in the Developing World* (2nd ed.). Armonk, NY: M E Sharpe, 1997.

——*National Security for a New Era* (5th ed.). New York: Pearson, 2014.

——*Uncivil Wars: International Security and the New Internal Conflicts*. Boulder, CO: Lynne Rienner, 1996.

——*What After Iraq?* New York: Pearson Longman, 2009.

Tacitus (translated by Michael Grant). *The Annals of Imperial Rome* (New Impression ed.). New York: Penguin Classics, 2003.

Weiss, Thomas G. "On R2P, America Takes the Lead." *Current History* 111, 748 (November 2012), 322–24.

Welsh, Jennifer. "The Responsibility to Protect: Dilemmas for a New Norm." *Current History* 111, 749 (November 2012), 291–98.

2

THE TRANSITION

What Happened to Our World of Violence?

The organization of world armed violence has changed a great deal since 1945. The period before 1945 was dominated by large wars between the organized armed forces representing the governments of countries, an extension of the classic pattern of Clausewitzian-style European warfare. The period since 1945 has seen a transition toward internal wars between groups within states as the more dominant form of systemic violence. Among other reasons, this distinction is important for the United States, because the American military is very adept at fighting pre-1945 style warfare. It has not been as good at post-1945 variants.

In some ways, this change is a decidedly good thing for the world, if not necessarily for the American military. The first half of the twentieth century was indeed the bloodiest in human history, and a third round of global war over who controls Europe (and thus the effective international system of that century) could have destroyed world civilization as we know it. Men have fought and killed one another since, of course, but the pace, locations, and sheer bloodiness of war has generally decreased, and that has been generally a praiseworthy change. No one seriously pines for a return to the "good old days" of the world wars, except possibly in contrasting the conceptual clarity of traditional conflicts with the opacity and confusion that surrounds thinking about and conducting contemporary warfare.

The pattern of warfare has changed in important ways. These changes may or may not prove to be permanent, but they have created a different set of problems and expectations for the use and utility of military force than before 1945. It is not at all clear, however, that we have fully recognized these changes nor incorporated them into how and why we make war in the twenty-first century. The failure to adjust is one of the reasons the United States and other countries find themselves drawn into involvement in military adventures that may have made sense in the old world environment but that make much less (if any) sense in contemporary circumstances.

The effect of the past and the tendency to cling to it is that we sometimes still look at the world and its problems, for which military force has traditionally been deemed appropriate, through old lenses that do not depict adequately the world we are in today. Some of this is entirely understandable and appropriate given the era from which we have emerged. The central military reality of the Cold War, after all, was that American national security was physically threatened by the prospect of a nuclear war with the Soviet Union that likely would have destroyed both sides and possibly everyone else. Avoiding that catastrophe fell disproportionately on the military, whose job was to create and maintain the forces that would dissuade the Soviets from beginning a conflict. It was an awesome responsibility for the professional military of the time and a burden that the United States had never confronted before. The central point here is that the shadow of the mushroom-shaped cloud hung over Western society like a true sword of Damocles, and it created an awesome sense of awe and responsibility for those charged with assuring that the thin thread did not snap and send humankind to its doom.

The result of this grim context was to create a mindset that remains even if the nuclear threat is no longer so imminent. The atmosphere in which the Cold Warriors toiled was truly perilous, and it is an atmosphere no one wants to see return. The ways in which the Cold Warriors managed the confrontation physically and the absence of Armageddon coincided. Is it any great surprise that few who went through it want to take the chance that radical change might result in a return to Cold War perils?

The Cold War experience reinforced "in spades" the natural conservatism of the military. That conservative bias is prejudiced toward maintaining (or conserving) relationships that are favorable and that have produced acceptable outcomes—in this case, the national survival. The military tends to look suspiciously at changes that threaten to replace tried-and-true ways of dealing with things. The gravity of the consequences of changing and being wrong are potentially too high. A change that goes wrong could conceivably result in unspeakable disaster, and one way to lessen that possibility is to resist change.

The conservative approach suggests resisting a change to the status quo. Mutual deterrence based in huge nuclear arsenals and the absence of nuclear war have coincided, and since that is the ultimate purpose of the military exercise, why risk change to a situation that has produced a favorable outcome? Change, in other words, threatens a condition that is tolerable and may result in more dangerous, intolerable conditions. Thus, change is to be viewed with caution and suspicion, and it is to be resisted until a skeptical military establishment can be convinced otherwise.

This mentality extends beyond nuclear weapons to conventional weaponry and organization. Having faced and surmounted the potential abyss of World War III during the Cold War, there is an enormous inertial drag that undergirds how the military approaches the world in which it operates. The Western approach to military organization and warfare has been enduring, and the prospects it has confronted and overcome are representations of the "worst case" that those within the tradition never want to see arise again. Even though most military thinkers agree that the environment the military faces, including the kinds of threats with which it must deal, is different than it was a generation ago, that recognition does not translate into a mandate for radical, fundamental change either in attitude or organization. What has evolved in the past is tried-and-true. It is, in the true sense, doctrine (belief in the best way to do things). The operational problem is how to adapt that structure to the present configuration of challenges, not to construct a new model that may or may not work and that could seriously undermine the ability to respond to the older set of dire problems should they arise again. Caution and conservatism are the bywords when dealing with change.

The result is a preference for incremental fine-tuning of existing ideas and concepts rather than any drastic rethinking, reorientation, or reorganization. In the American tradition, a major driver is and continues to be the application of advancing science and technology to improve ways of making war. If there are problems that are not amenable to alteration within the given structure and set of capabilities, maybe technology can provide a capability that allows achieving goals without making basic changes in attitudes or capabilities: fine tuning the ongoing force can provide new answers without undoing basic, durable ways of doing business.

The current fixation with drone warfare provides a good example. One of the major obstacles entailed in fighting asymmetrical opponents in essentially internal wars in countries with primitive infrastructures is locating the enemy so that he can be engaged and defeated. Guerrillas, the most common form of such opponents, typically avoid contact with large, firepower-intense enemy units—the very kind of warfare the United States is best at and thus prefers. Rather, these opponents prefer to establish effective sanctuaries among friends or allies where they are effectively safe from identification and destruction.

Finding, engaging, and defeating such an enemy is not a new task. This was precisely the problem the United States faced in trying to engage and defeat the Viet Cong in Vietnam, and it was not terribly successful in doing so. Attempts to overcome this problem ran the gamut from "search and destroy" missions (sending out large, mechanized infantry units on exploratory probes to locate enemy concentrations) to Agent Orange defoliation of suspected jungle areas and roadside foliage where the Viet Cong hid. In Afghanistan, the problem has returned.

The Taliban has excellent sanctuary availability in the Ghilzai Pashtun regions of eastern Afghanistan and across the border into the frontier regions of Pakistan. Kindred tribesmen welcome and protect their presence, and the topography is so forbidding that it is virtually inaccessible even by specialized units such as Special Forces. The remaining leadership cadres of the original Al Qaeda structure have imbedded themselves in this area as well, making its penetration and destruction a tempting target for the American leadership. But how can the American military solve this problem?

The answer has been drone aircraft attacks, notably in the form of "targeted assassination" efforts against the leaderships of both the Taliban and Al Qaeda. These attacks serve some useful purposes. The most basic advantage is that they overcome the limitations of geography by permitting American lethal assets to overfly and thus ignore a hostile geography and bring the consequences of war directly to the enemy. The added benefit is these attacks can be carried out without putting Americans at physical risk since the drones are, by definition, pilotless. As assets of the United States Air Force (as well as the CIA), they are also extensions of the existing military structure—the essence of fine tuning the existing capability. Thanks to the technology of drone-photographed satellite imagery and telemetry, drones are also very effective at locating and snuffing out targeted opponents. In this sense, they are an excellent technological "fix" in the classic American tradition.

Despite the Obama administration's enamor with the use of these instruments, they also have their limits and drawbacks. Drone aircraft like the Predator may be very accurate and precise in their activities, but they are not so precise and "surgical" that they do not create collateral damage in the form of killing unintended as well as intended victims. When the intended victims of drone attacks are essentially irreplaceable, as seems to be the case with targeted attacks against Al Qaeda leaders, some level of civilian casualties may be tolerable, at least by the criteria of the Americans who do not endure them. But that is not always the case.

Drone attacks against the Taliban have had more ambiguous effects. The Taliban leaders who are "taken out" in these raids are mostly Ghilzai Pashtuns like the inhabitants who play host to them and who are the collateral damage of the attacks. There is an old Pashtun proverb that says, in effect, "Kill one enemy, make ten more." The basis of this multiplication is a deep Pashtun belief in revenge against those who do their people harm, meaning the unintended result of a drone attack may well be to make more enemies than it eliminates. The effect of drone warfare, in these kinds of cases, may be not only to allow the United States to kill otherwise inaccessible enemies, but also to alienate others and potentially make more enemies.

The point of this example is that the reluctance to "think outside the box" that is an understandable characteristic of the American military may come with costs as well. In an environment where traditional forces and ways of thinking are not clearly applicable to the circumstances at hand, it may be appropriate, even necessary, to discard old constructs and reorient what one does to a different reality. Doing so, however, is extremely difficult for institutions that have as much history and experience in a given tradition as the modern American military does. The forces of the United States and the ways in which they are used are a sledgehammer designed for the kind of heavy lifting that the Western military tradition has conditioned them to conduct. The sledgehammer was an appropriate tool for the United States when faced with a similarly oriented Soviet opponent.

What was more subtle and largely unrecognized at the time was that the nuclear weapons that epitomized the evolution of traditional warfare also signaled the effective end of the applicability of the European model for understanding and preparing for war more generally. This is a bold assertion, but one that looks much better in retrospect than it did to the military thinkers and planners more concerned with the immediate necessity of preventing another global conflict they assumed probably would look like the last two. Indeed, it probably would have been viewed as irresponsible to suggest that the old model should have been rejected and an alternative adopted because doing so might have tempted our opponents to launch a traditional war, and no responsible planner would propose taking that risk.

There has not been a major-power war since the advent of nuclear weapons, and that is hardly a coincidence. During the Cold War itself, there was certainly ample political justification for such a conflict in terms of political, ideological difference and antagonism, but nuclear weapons provided the brake upon actualizing such antagonisms. Large powers came into occasional conflict, but for decidedly limited reasons (the Soviets and Chinese in 1969 over a border dispute), before either had nuclear weapons (China and India in 1963, the various wars between India and Pakistan), or when only one side possessed an unacknowledged capability (Israel versus its opponents in the 1973 Yom Kippur War). Heavily nuclear-armed countries have never fought one another, and today the most important countries lack plausible reasons for going to war, especially in a European-style war. And yet the model persists.

A large part of the reason is that the Cold War experience is so deeply ingrained in the military tradition and process. We are no longer Cold Warriors, but the traditions and ways of thinking that suffused thinking during that period linger on the intellectual palate. To understand this residue, it is necessary to look at the Cold War itself as an ongoing influence on how we think.

The Cold War Paradigm: Context, Content, and Mindset

Depending on their ages and thus physical experiences, different readers will have varying perspectives on the Cold War. For those readers who either had not yet been born or were not wholly aware of world affairs in 1991, the Cold War is an historic abstraction with which there is no personal connection to the dynamics and the strong emotions and fears associated with it. To some others, the primary personal relationship with the long competition was with its unraveling, mostly between 1989 when communist control of Eastern Europe began to crumble and the end of 1991, when the Soviet Union physically dissolved itself. For such individuals, the fear and emotion of the Cold War is not so great, and if there is an event with which they personally associate, it is the day the Berlin Wall fell. Older readers remember larger parts, even the entirety, of the forty-five years of the Cold War experience. For those readers, the Cold War and its associated mentality are an indelible part of their reality that still, at least implicitly, guides or influences how they see the world and events in it.

The actual "Cold Warriors"—those people involved directly in arranging and managing the competition between the latter 1940s and 1991—are rapidly disappearing from the scene as central players, but a number are still influential reminders and keepers of the "faith." While the influence of these individuals and the conscious influences of Cold War realities have largely faded at the official level, many of their beliefs remain as important parameters that affect the mindsets of decision makers. Nowhere is that influence more evident or prevalent than in the area of military policy. The basic impact is to create a worldview that is more compatible with the traditional, European style of warfare than an analysis that does not begin with the presumptions the Cold War experience might provide.

If the United States is to reexamine successfully the reasons and ways that it uses military force—the need for which is the central argument in these pages—than it must start by understanding what it is about our experience that has to this point inhibited such an examination. The beginning point for such a self-examination is the Cold War—its context, its content, and the resulting mindset it has created.

The Cold War Context

The Cold War was the central international political reality of the period between the end of World War II and the demise of the competition in 1991. It dominated the relationships and foreign and national security policies of the world's traditional European-based powers through most of that period, and it was especially the central focus of American policy toward the world. At the same time, there were influences building and percolating through the period for which the Cold War was hardly relevant at all, and these would eventually come to the fore after the Cold War ended. The premises and dynamics of the Cold War were—and are—particularly irrelevant and misleading when applied to the parts of the world in which the contrary trends were occurring. Yet, it has been the implicit attempt to apply Cold War constructs to non-Cold War problems that is at the heart of so many current problems facing policy.

The Cold War, given its length and breadth, was an incredibly complex phenomenon, the details and subtleties of which go well beyond present purposes and capabilities. Instead, I will attempt to identify and briefly discuss the major dynamics that form the context of the Cold War and its influences upon the contemporary world. To this end, three major points of context are relevant.

The first contextual point is the *irony* of the Cold War competition. The central players in the Cold War were, of course, the coalition of Western, anti-communist (although both democratic and non-democratic) countries of which the United States was the leader, and the bloc of countries professing Marxism as its ideological underpinning and led by the Soviet Union and later also by the People's Republic of China. The irony arises from the leadership of this competition. The

United States and the Soviet Union had, prior to World War II, not been conscious adversaries throughout their histories (including pre-communist, czarist Russia) and had no historically based sense of antagonism as peoples. Russians and Americans had bumped into one another from time to time in places like San Francisco Bay and Alaska, but they certainly did not consider themselves enemies. Before the wartime alliance the two forged against the fascist foes, there had been the hint of an ideological competition to come, but it could hardly be said that the two peoples had any deep-seated ill will toward one another, the way that the French and Germans, for instance, had developed over their long histories. Prior to the end of World War II, some Americans harbored strong negative feelings about communism as an ideology, and "Red scares" regarding things like labor activities occurred occasionally, as did accusations about communist penetration of some American institutions (the Sacco-Vanzetti case of the 1920s is a vivid example). At the same time, some geopolitically minded right-wing thinkers (General George S. Patton was a vocal example) counseled that the Soviets would simply replace the fascists as America's major enemy and should be dispatched accordingly.

The second contextual influence was the *impact of World War II*. Prior to the war, the United States and the Soviet Union had not been adversaries, and they shared the common circumstance of being peripheral national players in global geopolitics. The lack of centrality had different origins, of course: "splendid isolationism" between the world wars meant the United States excluded itself from European politics by choice, whereas the Soviets had been placed in "quarantine" by the major powers in the hopes that, in isolation, the Russians would somehow "cure" themselves of the "disease" of Marxism.

In the end, actions by the Axis powers forced the beleaguered Western allies to bring both countries into the war as allies, aided by acts of the Axis members. The Germans invaded Russia (which almost certainly assured the Third Reich's ultimate defeat), and Japan attacked the United States. If nothing else, the old principle that "the enemy of my enemy is my friend" meant the Soviets and the Americans would join in the common effort to defeat Germany and its allies. In the process, they would emerge from the war as the only major powers who arguably had won and thus as the remaining major powers in a post-war world.

It was a situation for which neither was especially well prepared, but it was one which, for different reasons, they accepted with enthusiasm, even relish. For the Soviets, their relative position was weaker, but the new order provided an opportunity that they seized gladly. The Soviet Union had suffered the most combined damage and human loss of any Western country in the war, but it maintained a huge Red Army after the war occupying those parts of Eastern and Central Europe that it had "liberated." These areas would have communist regimes installed in them, forming the core of a communist empire that the Soviets sought to expand. The Western powers, led by the United States, sought to control or contain that expansion. The Soviet mission was evangelical, to transform as much of the world as they could in their image; for the United States, the mission became to prevent that from happening. The ensuing struggle to turn the map progressively "blue" (pro-Western) or "red" (pro-communist) became the central political theme of the Cold War.

The third contextual characteristic is the *totality* that relationship developed. As a datum of international politics for its most central participants, the Cold War was the consummate reality, the parameter and framework wherein all important actions occurred and where international success or failure was measured. The driving force that propelled the total commitment to the Cold War was the ideological divide between the communist and the "free" worlds, and it was conceived of as a zero-sum competition in which one side eventually must prevail and the other must lose. Adding fuel to the ideological fire was an evangelical spirit on both sides in which they painted one another in sharp contrasts of black and white and in which, as a result, there was a moral imperative to prevail. This moral under-pinning allowed the military aspects of the competition to be portrayed in strong moral tones in line with the American preference for good political objectives and thus to justify the enormous traditional (including thermonuclear) military machine and expenses the competition entailed. It became increasingly clear over time that a direct military confrontation would be disastrous for all concerned. Given that realization, the operational focus of the competition moved to the developing world, where the setting and constellation of problems were quite different but largely unrecognized at the time.

The wartime collaboration between the Soviets and the Americans quickly devolved into a total and encompassing opposition after they realized there was no single world order they could agree to instruct and enforce. The Americans (and their allies) demanded a world scheme in which the freedom to compete for influence would be open to all and where, because of its inherent superiority as a belief and operation system, the Western model would triumph, leaving a world of liberal democracies as its legacy. The Soviets and their allies, on the other hand, held a Marxist worldview (even if the authoritarian system they evolved had virtually no base in Marxist ideology as originally formulated) that they equally sought to spread. The two visions of the world stood in sharp, irreconcilable contrast to one another, and it was apparent that they could not coexist, either as the operating principle of international politics or within countries. Given the depth with which convictions were held on both sides, it was probably inevitable that their competition would become pervasive and total, and that is exactly what happened.

The competition became the familiar exercise of turning the map "blue" or "red." There was always a major traditional military element to the confrontation, since it was clear that on the "central front" (roughly the Iron Curtain line dividing Europe) there would be no peaceful conversion. Thus, both sides amassed enormous conventional, World War II–style armed forces on both sides of the dividing line, backed by so-called *theater* or *tactical nuclear weapons* (weapons to be used in sup-port of conventional military operations) and their huge arsenals of strategic nuclear weapons (warheads aimed at one another's homelands) to deter and, should deterrence fail, to engage in apocalyptic struggle. As it became increasingly clear what the outcome of such a war would be, the competition shifted to the "safer" grounds of the developing world, which was a less dangerous place to compete since the consequences of failing were not so great. This effective transfer did not, however, noticeably alter the military character of the two sides or how they looked at and organized military forces.

Cold War Content and Mindset

These contextual influences help define the *content* of the Cold War, and once again, it can be summarily described in terms of three elements that help explain why the Cold War was such an indelible experience and thus why its influence persists over two decades after it ended. These elements included a belief in the pervasiveness of the competition, fatalism about how it would evolve and end, and an inability to predict how it might end. These three factors were, of course, related to and reinforced one another. The Cold War was ubiquitous, and it seemed never-ending. When people speculated on how it might end, all they could conjure was through a fiery hot war, a nuclear conflagration that would destroy everything. The Cold War may have been awful, but the alternative was worse.

All three of these elements reflected the fundamental, underlying anomaly of the Cold War. In terms of the nature of the political objectives of the two sides toward one another, the Cold War was as total as World War II: a struggle where one system prevailed and the other was overthrown. The anomaly arose from nuclear weapons, which dictated that the total military means the political competition justified could not be employed to bring about the conclusive triumph. This disconnect distorted all three elements of the Cold War's content.

The Cold War thrust the United States into the role as the preeminent political actor on the world stage. This ascension required rearranging American views of its place in the world. Traditional American neutrality and aloofness from world affairs was transformed into a commitment in an "us versus them" environment in which good and evil were clearly identified. Evil-doers, in the American moralistic view of the world articulated forcefully by the Dulles brothers in the 1950s, were to be opposed both on geopolitical grounds and because of the immoral system the enemy sought to impose upon us. To shrink from the responsibility of leading the opposition to this evil was morally unthinkable.

A major political consequence that is still a pervasive part of the scene was the creation of what has been called the *national security state* in the United States. This concept was symbolized by institutions like the unified Department of Defense as the fulcrum of national security policy and a robust supporting industrial base that maintains the capability to produce enormous quantities of large, expensive weapons systems (the military-industrial complex). More conceptually, it was represented by a shift in emphasis on world affairs from "foreign affairs" (with a greater emphasis on political and diplomatic emphasis) to "national security affairs" (with a more concentrated view of problems in military terms). When the primary dynamic of relations with the world was on a Soviet Union whose main challenge to the United States was a traditional military threat, this reorientation made sense; whether it does today is not so clear.

The military establishment firmly occupied the catbird's seat within the Cold War system. To reiterate, the competition was mainly and quintessentially a military confrontation. The Soviet system did not compete successfully at the economic level with the Western system (although it took awhile to realize this), and the political appeal of communism was decreasingly attractive as well. The Soviet claim to competitiveness was almost entirely as a military colossus, an edifice that in the end had some of the attributes of a Potemkin village (false front) and the maintenance of which eventually so overburdened the economic system that cancelling the competition became the only viable option.

While the bluff lasted, however, it presented a formidable challenge that energized and created the firm basis for an American military armada of unprecedented size, strength, and prestige during peacetime. The Soviet military machine was a replica of the World War II opponent to which nuclear weapons had been added, and the United States resembled the opposition. The fact that nuclear weapons could never be turned loose on one another without risking escalation to general nuclear war was a point slow to be recognized, and it hardly affected the tenor of the arms race that was at the center of the competition. When the Cold War ended, the United States was left with a magnificent military machine ready and able to reprise World War II—but with no opposing force against which to use that machine and no real plans to convert that machine to alternative uses.

The net effect of the Cold War was to imbue the United States with a conceptual framework and military-implementing structure ready and able to organize and manage that particular, peculiar situation into which the United States was thrust in the aftermath of World War II. The Cold War paradigm was a set of concepts and capabilities to manage that competition, and it lingers to the present. The "us versus them" mentality of moral confrontation transferred nicely to the conflict with international terrorism, creating an apparent threat environment that blunted the need to adjust conceptually to the post-Cold War world. Militarily, the United States has tweaked its capabilities and doctrines to make some adjustment to a changed environment, but the core capability and mindset clearly remains.

The Developing World Subtext

While the Cold War captured the attention of the United States and the other major powers, there was a second, competing factor that intermingled with Cold War dynamics. That force has outlasted the Cold War to form the central national security task that confronts the United States now and, in fact, was the major, unrecognized (or underemphasized) operational problem during the forty-plus-year confrontation between communism and anti-communism. That dynamic, of course, centers on the emergence and evolution of the so-called developing world. The central theme of the developing world contribution to the current national security environment lies in the post-war movement of most developing countries out of colonial bondage to independence and through a process leading to their evolution as stable, prosperous members of the international system. Fractures of that process in numerous countries have led to violence and instability that represent the principal barrier to international tranquility.

The problems of the developing world are not new at all. Like the Cold War, they have roots within the Second World War. Prior to that cataclysm, virtually all of Africa, a good bit of Asia, and parts of Latin America remained under European (including American) colonial rule. In some areas, movements to remove colonial domination had arisen during the interwar period (the Indian subcontinent is a prime example), but before the colonial rulers were forced to turn their full attention to global conflict, they managed to keep the lid on these independence movements. After the war, they no longer could.

World War II served as the stimulus to decolonization in multiple ways, two of which are worth highlighting. First, the war touched virtually everywhere, meaning the indigenous people in many colonies had the war brought to their doorsteps. This meant they witnessed their mostly white rulers locked in mortal combat with other white people, thereby undercutting European claims to their superiority and exalted status. In some cases, colonial subjects were drawn directly into the war effort, as laborers, for instance, to replace European factory workers called to war. When the war ended and laborers like Kenya's Jomo Kenyatta returned to their native lands after service in England, they could not return to the docile acceptance of British rule expected of colonial subjects; instead, Kenyatta helped organize the independence movement to throw out the British and became Kenya's first president in 1964. Similar dynamics occurred across the developing world.

The war accelerated the revolutionary process against colonial rule. Colonial rule had never been consensual, but instead was based on the firm, often brutal imposition of foreign rule on native peoples, as noted earlier. Maintaining colonies was expensive business that required the outlay of considerable human and material resources. The rationale for this expenditure was the promise of physical gain and profit for the colonizer, although the latter was usually a pipe dream. More accurately, countries gained and ruled colonies because that was what great countries did, and the larger the colonial holdings a country had, by definition the more powerful and consequential it was. Before nuclear weapons provided the shorthand measure of national power and prestige, colonial empires filled that bill.

Maintaining outside rule over people who resented the imposition was always expensive, and it generally could be successfully continued only through the

imposition of harsh, brutal terms of rule that further alienated the native population—
a dynamic familiar in the current environment but conditioned by the unwillingness
or unacceptability of overt brutality among contemporary occupiers. This burden
was acceptable as long as the colonial ruling countries were stable and prosperous.
After the war, most were in dire economic straits and could no longer afford the
economic and physical luxury of empire. Something had to give.

The desire for independence intermingled with post-war colonial exhaustion
to make the decolonization process increasingly inexorable. It appeared first in eastern
and southern Asia in places like the Indian subcontinent, the Indonesian archipelago,
and the Southeast Asian peninsula. Mostly, the colonial rulers put on little more
than a token defense (the French in Vietnam were an exception) before throwing
in the towel, pulling up stakes and leaving. By the mid-1950s, the flames of anti-
colonialism had swept westward to Africa, and by the middle of the 1970s, when
Portugal became the last European colonial power to admit the futility of attempts at
continuing domination, the process of decolonization was nearly complete.

This process ran parallel to but was also intermixed with Cold War dynamics.
It clearly coexisted in time, but not in importance. To the central players in the
European-based balance of power, the Cold War was clearly dominant, and the
emergence of the developing world was but one theater in the broader competition. To people in the developing world, the difficulties of shucking colonial
rule and then struggling to establish independent orders was by far the more
encompassing task, and dabbling in Cold War politics was at most instrumental—
a way to extort resources for development. The two perspectives intersected in
the quest by the Cold War partners to extend their influence to developing
world countries and areas, whereas post-colonial governments and movements
saw these competitions as ways to increase the resources available to their movements or governments. When the interactions within the developing world
turned violent, as they sometimes did, the superpowers rushed to the aid of the
side with which they curried favor. In the extreme, they became involved
themselves directly or through proxies. These involvements were generally "safe"
in the sense that they ran minimal risks of growing to direct confrontation that
could escalate to central war between them.

The Cold War may have disappeared, but the developing world and its problems
did not. Indeed, since the two were parallel but barely interdependent phenomena,
the major impact of the end of the Cold War was to reduce Western power
interest in developing world problems, since involvement had been primarily
oriented toward countering the influence of the other rather than for any intrinsic,
altruistic motives. The problems that had been percolating in the developing
world were thus, at heart, pretty much what they were when the Cold War was
ongoing. The difference was that these problems could no longer be incorporated
into a Cold War paradigm.

The current malaise that plagues developing world areas and that has provided
the temptation—or opportunity—for the United States to involve itself with

military force is a lineal consequence of the Cold War era in which it emerged and festered. Some of these problems have their origins and evolutions in the situations surrounding decolonization and the development needs that accompanied that process. The result is the pattern of instability and violence that currently faces, and occasionally tempts, the United States.

The Colonial Legacy

To some extent, the experience of European colonial rule is encased in a romantic, even uplifting mythology that reality scarcely warrants. Part of the mythology that has surrounded colonial rule has been its motivation. Almost all of the places where colonialism was imposed were, by the material standards of the Western countries who intruded themselves upon them, backward and undeveloped. They were also non-Christian in most cases, and these dual characteristics permitted the fabrication of a falsehood that the primary purpose of colonialism was the "white man's burden," a philanthropic, moralistic mission to uplift the "natives" physically and morally by providing them with modern economic and religious systems. While some uplifting was either a side effect or even a conscious aim for some colonialists, that was hardly the heart of colonial motivation.

The motives underlying colonialism centered on two elements that had critical consequences once the colonial period unraveled. One element, which has already been mentioned, was national prestige: the larger and more geographically diverse a country's colonial empire was, the more important that country was. By that measure, a comparatively small and underpopulated country with a large navy, Great Britain, laid claim to the superpower status of its age. In the late nineteenth century, when the United States made its belated move toward colonial stature by divesting the Spanish Empire of its Caribbean and western Pacific possessions, the champions of American imperialism offered as a prime motive the idea that "a great country must have an empire."

The other, and more basic, motivation was, of course, profit. Exploration of the developing world had, after all, been partially justified in terms of creating access to the exotic riches of faraway places—the silk and exotic spices of Asia, the diamond mines of Africa, or the gold of El Dorado in the Americas, for example. The other idea that underlay this attraction was captive markets: if one occupied and controlled someplace with a valuable commodity, then that place could provide a reliable source of that commodity for the mother country. In addition, the colony would provide a convenient captive market for goods and manufactures from the European country. It was a pure form of monopoly capitalism enforced by the sword.

Populations in the colonies rarely embraced this relationship, but there was usually not much they could do about it. The relationship was humiliating and degrading, and they resented the foreign intrusion, just as they do today. The major difference was their inability to resist; colonial rule could be maintained because the colonial power monopolized the instruments of coercion and was (had to be) entirely ruthless and brutal in putting down signs of resistance and rebellion. What has changed since the colonial days is that the balance of arms has shifted toward greater equality between the intruders and the natives, and the intruders are no longer willing or able to snuff out opposition with the same viciousness as were their colonial forebears.

Another artifact of the colonial experience was the extent to which colonial rulers acted to prepare colonial subjects for independence and self-rule. Once again, sentimental mythology needs to be stripped away. Part of the "white man's burden" argument was that one of the primary roles of the Europeans was to "uplift" the savage, heathen natives, and this burden included education to make the subjects ready to assume political responsibility for their own lives and national destinies. Nothing could have been farther from the truth. The idea was to perpetuate colonial rule, not to facilitate the process of ending control. Thus, any knowledge that might encourage seditious thinking was discouraged, not encouraged. The idea of educating the natives in ways that might lead to anti-colonial actions was never a part of colonial policy—at least not until the colonial rulers had already decided to leave and wanted to "class up" their departure with a thin veneer of assistance in the transition to self-rule.

This pattern of motivation had two major consequences. The first was not to prepare colonies for self-rule. Since the purpose of colonial rule, being based in profit, was its own self-perpetuation, the indefinite maintenance of control meant stifling opposition to demands for change, including demands for colonial eviction. While limited parts of colonial populations were given a rudimentary education and a few were co-opted into Mandarin-style relationships, the implication was that keeping the natives "barefoot and ignorant" was a simple matter of self-interest. Some colonial subjects managed, despite the system, to be exposed to Western political ideas, including notions of freedom and self-determination, but such exposure was incidental and, where possible, repressed. This same general orientation extended to economic development. It was never colonial policy to create any systematic improvement in the lives of one's colonial subjects, because doing so would only whet appetites for more that might cut into colonial profits. Abject subjugation and political suppression were simply good business.

The second consequence involved the physical, geographical composition of the colonial units, a dynamic that mixed ignorance with indifference to produce explosive post-colonial atmospheres in many places. When colonies were established, the pre-existing political realities of the areas colonized were generally unrecognized by the colonists. Ethnically diverse and antagonistic peoples were aggregated into colonial administrative units either because those doing so did not know or did not care who was being placed in the same jurisdictions. In Africa, for instance, colonies were often established simply by designating a swath of shoreline and claiming territories inward with no knowledge of who lived in claimed areas. The final division of Africa into colonial units at the Berlin Conference of 1883 was done without adequate maps (due to lack of exploration) of the interior of the continent and in absolute ignorance of whose tribal units and lands were being placed in what colonies.

The outcomes, familiar in contemporary terms, included *multinationalism* and *irredentism*. These formidable terms refer to the division of ethnic groups by political boundaries, and many (arguably most) developing world countries suffer to some degree from one of these conditions or the other (and occasionally both). *Multinationalism* refers to the situation where multiple, usually incompatible ethnic groups are included within a single political unit, such as a sovereign state. Often these divisions are expressed in tribal terms and refer to tribal units that have long histories of antagonism with other indigenous groups. Virtually all of the colonies-turned-states in Africa, and almost all of the states of the Islamic Middle East are to some extent multinational. Egypt is a prominent Middle Eastern exception, but places like Sudan, Nigeria, and the Congo in Africa and Afghanistan and Syria in the Muslim world are obvious cases where multinationalism exists and is the basis of conflict.

The other condition is *irredentism*. It refers to the situation where sovereign boundaries divide members of the *same* ethnic group and where the members of that group prefer and actively work to unite their traditional lands under a common sovereign authority. While not as numerous as conditions of multinationalism, irredentist conditions can be very intractable and have major international consequences. Probably the three most prominent groups that fall into this category are the Kurds, Palestinians, and the Pashtuns, all of which have been prominent factors in ongoing or recent American conflicts. These groups are sometimes known as *stateless nations*, referring to anthropologically determined groupings (nations or nationalities) that lack a politically sovereign jurisdiction (state) of their own. This problem, like the others, existed during the Cold War but was basically unaddressed in the greater concern for preventing World War III.

The result was to aggregate usually diverse and often antagonistic peoples into colonial units. This situation was tolerable as long as there was colonial rule to manage the hatreds and even occasionally to exploit them, co-opting one particularly warlike group to help suppress the rest (a divide-and-rule strategy particularly adopted by the British). Since the purpose of colonial rule was its indefinite perpetuation, and such animosities help retard the ability of population elements to unite in political opposition to that rule, not attempting to overcome inherited differences made good political sense.

Demands for independence eventually came to the developing world, and when they became inexorable, the flaws in the colonial experience all surfaced in ways that have allegorical relevance to the current environment. The peoples who sought to throw aside outside domination were politically and economically undeveloped. They lacked both the economic base and skills to improve the lots of their populations, an ability that would have improved their viability and support if they had it. The colonial experience had consciously deprived their leaders of the education and skills to operate a political system that would have been subversive to continuing colonial rule. At the same time, when independence became inevitable, it was almost always granted to the highly artificial colonial unit that ignored pre-existing and often still-simmering intergroup animosities, adding yet another element of difficulty and potential instability into the mix. For many newly independent countries, the result was a tremendous mess. In many of those places, the mess is still there.

The Developmental Conundrum

Blaming colonial rule for the situation that emerged in the mid-twentieth century, which the above analysis appears to do, somewhat misses the point. It is true that those who fashioned and administered colonial empires did not prepare the way for a smooth transition to modernity and independence for their subjects. That is not, however, what they were trying to do, so assigning blame on that basis is unfair, amounting to criticizing them for not doing what they never set out to do. Whether colonial policies were short-sighted and should have anticipated and sought in a more enlightened way to prepare subjects for an independent future is another question and one that is less unfair. Regardless, the venality of profit-driven economic and political subjugation of the developing world failed, and the result was a confusing and complex set of dilemmas that were given less than full attention during the Cold War. They have persisted into the post-Cold War environment, and they have become a more central part of the international stage.

The problem for the newly emerging, developing countries was that they clambered onto the world stage with the deck stacked against them. They were generally desperately poor and had very little internal way to remedy that situation unless they happened to possess some natural resources (oil or mineral wealth, for instance) that outsiders were willing to extract for a price, leaving the new country with some revenues from those sales. They were politically inexperienced and lacked the educated, trained personnel to institute or to maintain governmental stability and public faith or support. Many were also beset by demographic and other divisions that made portions of the populations suspicious of other segments on ethnic, historical, or religious grounds.

At the time of independence, these deep and abiding problems were often drowned out by the general euphoria of ending colonial bondage. Even on the Indian subcontinent, the intoxication of the British departure caused the Muslim and Hindu populations to overlook their deep animosities and to accept a highly imperfect form of partition into the states of India and Pakistan. That false euphoria would last for less than a year before it first ignited in violence. Independence movements had concentrated their energies and efforts on ending dependency and had spent much less time worrying about what would happen later. In too many places, these situations have turned into endemic hot spots. Some of these have and continue to attract American attention.

All of the problems, where they occurred, were interactive. Economic under-development meant there was little underlying base for economic expansion and prosperity. A major example was the absence of a developed infrastructure—the basic building blocks of economic development. Countries lacked communications, power, and transportation underpinnings, and they also had deficient or nonexistent educational systems to train people and create "human capital." The conundrum was that the problem was circular: extreme underdevelopment meant there were no resources to finance infrastructure projects like roads, ports, power grids, or telecommunications networks, but the existence of an adequate infrastructure was necessary to attract the capital that could generate infrastructure development—a true Catch-22.

The economic problem was compounded by incompetent, and sometimes corrupt and venal political actors. Countries might be poor, and inexperienced, largely untrained political leaderships and bureaucracies only made the problem worse. In the most innocent of cases, poorly prepared leaders squandered what little wealth there was (Indonesia's Sukarno, for instance, wasted resources on a gigantic soccer stadium in Jakarta for which there were no paved access roads and built a scale replica of the White House to attract President John Kennedy to visit—which he never did). Petty corruption (e.g., bribe taking) is a long-standing tradition in many non-Western cultures, and corruption and misspending added both to poor national performance and increasingly negative public perceptions of leaders.

In countries where there were deep ethnic or other social divisions, the poli-tical struggle over the scarce economic resources available often became a further basis of internal strife, as ethnic or religious groups rewarded their kinsmen while systematically depriving others. As a result, processes that might have healed the very deep societal divisions that existed at and before independence were instead reinforced. The ethno-religious divisions within Iraq both before and since the American invasion and evacuation stand as testimony to the endurance of these kinds of barriers.

These depictions are, of course, to some extent caricatures, but they do highlight the kinds of difficulties that arose during the Cold War period and have continued into the contemporary period. What they do portray, however, is a very different set of difficulties facing the developing world than those that dominated the Cold War and around which the Cold War paradigm of international system main-tenance developed. Layering Cold War dynamics on these problems (the Dulles solution) was at best an exercise in irrelevance; at worst, it was critically distorting and destructive.

Taken individually and especially cumulatively, the net result of these devel-oping world factors is instability that occasionally becomes violent and provides a temptation for the United States to involve itself once in a while with armed force. Political instability born of inexperience, incompetence, or venality is one source of that instability, and the opposition it engenders both reinforced and intensified conditions of extreme deprivation that are themselves the source of despair. When inept or corrupt governments cannot or will not alleviate economically based suffering, instability increases. When there are additional negative influences like ethnic or demographic differences that pre-existed independence but have manifested themselves more abundantly since independence, the situation is further exacerbated. When all these factors are present in the same place, the result can be a tinderbox that explodes in violence.

These problems of the developing world existed within the Cold War context but were not treated as a separate, compelling set of difficulties requiring the same level of effort as did managing the Cold War. One consequence was that, at the highest policy levels of government, developing world difficulties did not receive an intensity of scrutiny that might cause the United States and its allies to adopt a separate paradigm—or sub-paradigm—specifically tailored to those problems, virtually none of which were solved before the Cold War ended. Instead, developing world problems were subsumed as a subset or extension of the Cold War competition, not as a separate problem demanding a distinctive set of solutions or considerations. Whether they were solvable had such an effort been made is moot, since such an effort was not made and thus never succeeded or failed. What is clear is that many of them have transcended the end of the Cold War and stand as central national security issues for the present and future. The conundrum is how to modify our view of the national security equation—our paradigm—to accommodate this changed emphasis in the world.

After the Cold War: Brother, Can You Paradigm?

The tragic situation in Syria in 2012 and the tortured American attempt to find an appropriate response to it illustrates vividly the national security paradigm in the developing world. The Syrian disaster evolved as part of the so-called Arab Spring that began in Tunisia in late 2010, spread to Egypt, Libya, and other Muslim Middle East countries in 2011, and came to a head in demands for Syrian reforms and bloody repression by the regime of Bashar al-Assad. As 2012 spilled over into 2014, the hideous death toll inflicted on portions of the Syrian population by the Syrian armed forces was documented vividly on worldwide electronic media. This coverage highlighted both the extent and savagery of the Syrian actions against its own people and created widespread international demands for the violence to cease and for Assad to step down. The United Nations dispatched observers to chronicle the worst of the atrocities and to amplify the calls for its cessation. The slaughter continued, however, with Syria supported mostly by neighboring Iran and its Cold War patron Russia, for whom Syria remained its sole remaining outpost of influence in the region.

The Syrian situation exemplified the problems of the developing world that spanned the Cold War and beyond. The territory that is now Syria has an ancient past as the center of the Seleucid Empire, but until World War I, it had been a part of the Ottoman Empire, which was undone by the war's settlement. Between the world wars, Syria was a French-administered League of Nations mandate, and it became fully independent in close to its present form in 1946. Hafez al-Assad, the father of the current president, assumed power in 1970 and held office until his death in 2000, at which time his son came to power.

The Assad family is part of the Alawite minority tribe, a Shiite group opposed by the majority Sunni Arabs of the country, and most of the current violence centers on repression of the Sunnis by the Alawites and their supporters (which include Shiite Iran). As the country drifted toward open civil war, the battle lines were increasingly drawn along ethno-religious lines and became increasingly desperate and total: the losers were likely to suffer particularly dire consequences, which partially explained Bashar al-Assad's obdurate refusal to bend to international pressures to step down. Lacking the one major fungible asset of the region (oil), Syria has always had a marginally productive economy, meaning reconciliation through economic improvements has always been problematic.

In these circumstances, the question was what to do, and the absence of an encompassing paradigm to direct actions did not help solve the impasse. There were two basic responses, reflecting the contrasting paradigmatic models available. One side, exemplified by Republican senator and former presidential candidate John McCain, called for decisive military action to force the regime from power. Reflecting distinct Cold War paradigm roots, this response called for actions such as bombing and the establishment and enforcement of "no fly" zones similar to those used in Libya, despite a very different situation on the ground. McCain and his supporters stopped short of suggesting the United States and its allies invade with ground forces, but the key emphasis was clearly a Cold War-derived reliance on the military instrument of power to solve the problem.

Chastened by the experiences in Iraq and Afghanistan, the political majority in the United States counseled against military involvement, since it believed that intervention in those two countries had demonstrated the inapplicability of American force in these kinds of internal situations. They did not, however, have particularly well-developed, convincing alternatives.

Part of the problem of American indecisiveness was the result of a deeply divided, gridlocked political atmosphere in which any proposed action by anyone about anything was likely to meet with loud, venomous opposition. At the same time, the paradigm problem meant there was no agreed general orientation—or paradigm—on which American analysts and decision-makers could consensually fall back to help frame the problem and response options. As the United States stumbled away from direct involvement and left Syria in an increasingly toxic intercommunal bloodletting between Muslims that threatened to spread more widely in the region, the lack of a paradigm remained.

The central reality from which the paradigm dilemma arises is that the same Cold War conditions do not exist in the post-Cold War world, and thus, approaches premised on Cold War realities do not obviously apply in the contemporary scene. The central threat of the Cold War—the confrontation with communism—has evaporated, and successor dynamics of discord are not isomorphic to that threat. The two, interrelated primary candidates are international terrorism and "radical Islam," a cover concept for all those who oppose the West and propose the expansion of Islam. These are not insignificant problems, but they are not of the same order of magnitude or threat potential as was the threat of communism. This lack of isomorphism has several sources and consequences.

The basic dissimilarity between the Cold War and the present is the nature of the threat facing the United States. The prospect of the Cold War devolving into a nuclear confrontation between the superpowers was sufficiently serious and of such great potential consequence that there was no question whether it should dominate the national security agenda. If the Cold War was not managed successfully, very little if anything else mattered. The Cold War focused the mind.

The post-Cold War threat, while substantial, is not so compelling. The threat levels that exist today are neither vapid nor unimportant, but they simply do not rise to the same monumental levels as did failure in the Cold War. The spread of Islamic radicalism does not, for instance, imperil the United States and Americans in the same dire, direct way that the shadow of the Soviet mushroom-shaped cloud produced a peril. Put another way, the American interests that are put at risk by terrorism or radical Islam (whatever that exactly is) are not as fundamental now as the threats were before. American survival itself was on the line in the Cold War. The nature of the current threat is not so easy to specify, but it is a real intellectual stretch to suggest that anything as primal as national existence is at issue today. The Cold War paradigm was designed for an encompassing, engulfing, and absolutely compelling threat, and it came to fit the situation. It does not fit a smaller, less encompassing threat so well. In the case of national security paradigms, one "size" does not fit all situations.

If the threat is not so compelling, neither are the solutions so obvious. The Cold War paradigm had the virtue of being applied to a familiar shape of threat for which traditional Western military solutions were appropriate. The addition of nuclear weapons certainly enlarged the nature of the problem beyond past dimensions, but the problems that those weapons posed and the means of containing them seemed more conventional. At that, the paradigm eventually got strained to the breaking point when it became evident that nuclear weapons prevented the ultimate solution of traditional Western conflicts in massive European-style warfare. That recognition itself helped convince the Soviets that the Cold War had become an unaffordable albatross and that it must be ended.

If nuclear weapons left central parts of the Cold War paradigm in some tatters, Cold War solutions even more clearly do not apply to the distinctly non-Cold War conditions that emerged in the developing world during the Cold War and which have moved to greater prominence since. Potentially actionable threats to U.S. interests are simply not of the same order as they once were. Nothing that could have happened in Iraq or Afghanistan, for instance, would have had the same potential consequences for the United States of a threatened Soviet invasion of Western Europe. In the latter case, military preparedness was clearly indicated and flowed logically from the situation and our way of organizing it. The justification for eerily Cold War–like military responses in Iraq and Afghanistan resembled the rationales for Cold War actions. Those reactions did not work, because they were answers to Cold War questions, not developing world difficulties. That they failed should come as no surprise; that we are having such a hard time figuring out why they failed is more perplexing.

The upshot of all this is that the implicit reliance on the Cold War paradigm to guide American actions in the world is flawed and will, as it has done in the past two decades, inevitably lead the United States to the wrong solutions to international problems. The American debacle in Vietnam, which remains intensely controversial four decades after it ended, should have been instructive in leading us to this conclusion. In that contest, the United States imposed the Cold War model on a situation where it did not truly fit. Because those opposing American-preferred solutions were communist, it could be and was conceptualized as a Cold War contest. The problem was that Vietnam was more than a Cold War confrontation: it was also an indigenous civil war (a DWIC) with the purpose of reuniting a Vietnam that was a single political unit before French colonization in the 1870s. The Cold War response might have been relevant to the communist–anticommunist veneer of the conflict, but it was not responsive the inner dynamic that motivated the Vietnamese themselves. For them, it was an internal civil war, a contingency for which the Cold War paradigm had no obvious specific, tailored applications. It was the war representing the developing world dynamic, for which the Cold War paradigm was inapplicable and not instructive. Since that was the more fundamental dynamic rather than the Cold War overlay, the Cold War view could not produce an outcome in which the United States did not fail.

In the wake of the Vietnam War, the United States, and especially the American military, labored diligently to discover and learn the lessons of the profoundly unsatisfactory outcome of that war. As pointed out in the next chapter, it succeeded to a remarkable degree in areas such as the nature of insurgent and counterinsurgent warfare; the counterinsurgency (COIN) strategy for which General David Petraeus took credit and applied in Iraq in 2007 is, in fact, mostly a distillation of discoveries and insights from the 1970s and before. Petraeus admits the influence of French writers like David Galula and Bernard Fall, both of whom were major critics of French efforts in Southeast Asia.

Those lessons, however, did not "stick" in official American thinking, because they were "outside the box." They were insights that could be applied to developing world contingencies, but they were hatched and incubated in an atmosphere dominated by the Cold War paradigm, which had little time or place for this direction in military thinking. By the time the Cold War had ended, most of these insights had been institutionally lost, except at the peripheries of military practice and thought. The Cold War paradigm might be a hollow shell, but it was what endured. By default, it remained the basis of thinking and planning, even if shorn of the trappings of the Cold War.

If this indictment seems hopelessly abstract, even rhetorical, an example from a recently concluded presidential election campaign may help illustrate concretely the degree to which the thinking of prominent Americans remains trapped in the essential assumptions of the Cold War paradigm. Speaking to a veterans group in San Diego in May 2012, Republican presumptive candidate Mitt Romney sought to justify his proposals to increase defense spending from its then level of about 3.2 percent of Gross Domestic Product (GDP) to 4.0 percent of GDP. The result of such spending, he exulted, would be "to preserve America as the strongest military in the world, second to none, with no comparable power anywhere in the world."

This goal was defensible, a reflection of U.S. status in the world through the Cold War and beyond. One could, and many did, quibble about the affordability and practicality of such a goal given the American economic crisis, but it was Romney's rationale for maintaining that status that revealed him as trapped in a Cold War time warp. The need for American preeminence, he asserted, was that "a strong America is the best deterrent to war that has ever been invented." Huh? American military strength may have deterred the Soviets a quarter century ago (that was certainly its purpose), but who does it deter now? Certainly it did not deter the Syrians, and one of the perils advertised for terrorists is that they cannot be deterred by any means. The deterrent argument may have applied then, but does it apply now? If it does not, what happens to the rationale for incomparable American military power?

What this analysis and example suggest is that the time is ripe for a new paradigm to replace the Cold War idiom. In the absence of such a development, the United States is likely to continue to proceed as if the central elements of the old paradigm continue to be valid. This is especially true in two areas. One is in weapons procurement, which, in the Cold War construct, leads to yet more and more expensive heavy weapons systems. How can one advocate an increase in military spending as a part of GDP other than as a kind of phallic symbol of U.S. material preeminence? The other area is determining where and in what situations the United States uses force. The Cold War paradigm suggests a fairly wide range of contingencies and problems for which such forces can be utilized and which the existence of that force can presumably deter. It is decreasingly obvious that the kinds of military force (or *any* outside military force) springing from Cold War bases can be effective in the current world environment.

A new paradigm must fulfill the basic function of providing an understanding of the national security threat environment in which the United States now exists and how and what elements of that environment provide differing levels of threats to American interests of varying intensity and importance. Such a profile existed for the Cold War, but its imperatives are not clearly relevant to the current environment. Based on that assessment, a new paradigm must provide three central elements of guidance to the national security segment of society. First, it should provide guidance and about where and in what physical circumstances the United States should and should not contemplate inserting itself with military forces. Second, this assessment should also suggest how the United States can effectively apply force, a determination with two major implications. On one hand, it should tell us where and where *not* to think force can be effective. This is a particularly poignant matter given that the United States has developed a knack for using force where it cannot succeed in a context where it lacks adequate paradigmatic guidance. Doing the "right thing" involves both knowing what should be accomplished and whether that accomplishment is possible. On the other hand, the assessment should suggest how to organize military efforts in an effective way when facing conflicts for which traditional, Cold War–extrapolated forces have not clearly been effective. Third, the determinations should, in their public representations, be vague enough and the details should be kept adequately secret so as not to tempt adversaries to take advantage of situations where they know the United States will not respond.

This is a formidable but by no means impossible task. The problems that dominate the current environment are not new. As already argued, most have their origins in the Cold War period, and the post-Vietnam retrospective and post-mortem provided us with many of the answers that are probably appropriate for a new effort. The current situation is not a "brave new world"; rather, it may be a "brave new world *revisited*" and reinterpreted. The next chapter turns to that task.

Bibliography

Apter, David. *Rethinking Development: Modernization, Dependence and Postmodern Politics.* Beverly Hills, CA: Sage, 1987.

Brodie, Bernard. *Strategy in the Missile Age.* Princeton, NJ: Princeton University Press, 1959.

Burnell, Peter, Vicky Randall, and Lise Rakner (eds). *Politics in the Developing World* (3rd ed.). New York: Oxford University Press, 2009.

Diamond, Larry, Juan Linz, and Seymour Martin Lipset (eds). *Politics in Developing Countries.* Boulder, CO: Lynne Rienner, 1995.

Fall, Bernard. *Street without Joy: The French Debacle in Indochina.* Harrisburg, PA: Stackpole Books (Military History Series), 2005.

Fukuyama, Francis. *State-Building, Governance and World Order in the 21st Century.* Ithaca, NY: Cornell University Press, 2004.

Gaddis, John Lewis. *The United States and the End of the Cold War: Implications, Reconsiderations, Provocations.* New York: Oxford University Press, 1992.

Galula, David. *Counterinsurgency Warfare: Theory and Practice.* Westport, CT: Praeger (Classics of the Counterinsurgency Age), 2006.

Gurr, Ted Robert. *Why Men Rebel.* Princeton, NJ: Princeton University Press, 1973.

Haynes, Jeffrey. *Politics in the Developing World: A Concise Introduction* (2nd ed.). New York: Wiley-Blackwell, 2002.

Jervis, Robert. *The Illogic of American Nuclear Strategy.* Ithaca, NY: Cornell University Press, 1984.

Kennan, George. *American Diplomacy, 1900–1950.* New York: New American Library, 1951.

Latham, Michael E. *The Right Kind of Revolution: Modernization, Development, and U.S. Foreign Policy from the Cold War to the Present*. Ithaca, NY: Cornell University Press, 2011.

Neuchterlein, Donald. *A Cold War Odyssey*. Lexington, KY: University of Kentucky Press, 1997.

Nye, Joseph S. Jr. *The Paradox of American Power: Why the World's Superpower Can't Go It Alone*. New York: Oxford University Press, 2003.

Rist, Gilbert. *The History of Development: From Western Origins to Global Faith* (3rd ed.). New York: Zed Books, 2009.

Schelling, Thomas C. *The Strategy of Conflict*. Cambridge, MA: Harvard University Press, 1960.

Singer, Max, and Aaron Wildawsky. *The Real World Order: Zones of Peace, Zones of Turmoil* (Revised ed.). Chatham, NJ: Chatham House, 1996.

Snow, Donald M. *Distant Thunder: Patterns of Conflict in the Developing World* (2nd ed.). Armonk, NY: M E Sharpe, 1997.

——*The Necessary Peace: Nuclear Weapons and Superpower Relations*. Lexington, MA: Lexington Books, 1986.

——*The Shadow of the Mushroom-Shaped Cloud*. Learning Materials in National Security Education Number 2. Columbus, OH: Consortium for International Studies Education, 1978.

——*The Shape of the Future: The Post-Cold War World* (3rd ed.). Armonk, NY: M E Sharpe, 1999.

3

THE INTERVENTIONIST AGE

The upshot of the analysis in the last chapter is that post-Cold War warfare is both less familiar and less manageable for the United States than warfare up to and through the Cold War. As a result, the country's military and political leaderships have been less successful in visualizing and prosecuting the new opportunities for the recourse to arms. Moreover, the new pattern of warfare appears to represent both current and also likely near- to mid-term future environments in which the United States must operate. The lack of American success suggests the need for an enhanced understanding and consequent adaptation in thought and practice. The alternative is for the country to continue suffering the kinds of outcomes associated with its most recent military experiences in Iraq and Afghanistan.

These observations may seem unorthodox and even incendiary. They require more than simple assertion to be convincing, and it is the burden of this chapter to provide evidence and argumentation in support of this position. Such discussions are further necessary to provide the basis both for making convincing the central thesis of this work that the United States cannot win these wars and that their prosecution by the United States is thus essentially masochistic, making a change in orientation and policy both desirable and necessary for the future health and prosperity of American national security.

The analysis in this chapter will proceed in steps. It begins with a partial but elaborated discussion of a point that the origins of the pattern of contemporary warfare date back at least to the decolonization process after World War II. The dynamics of these wars are ancient, because they involve deeply held human desires for self-determination expressed in one way or another across time, but the fixation with the Cold War masked these underlying human motivational factors and allowed them to be categorized not for what they were, but instead as extensions of the logic and dynamics of the Cold War. Now that the Cold War has ended, this thin but distorting veneer has been stripped away, allowing us to view these sources of international instability more clearly, if we care to and can. It is a task that we have not obviously accomplished satisfactorily to this point. When violence and instability flare up in developing world venues as diverse as Syria or Crimea, there is a residual chorus that one answer is an active U.S. military response in the form of intervention. We still do not entirely get it.

A major part of the necessary process of adjustment is conceptual. Contemporary wars clearly do not fit traditional patterns of thinking about warfare and American participation in war in basic conceptual ways. The discussion thus moves toward placing modern conflicts into traditional conceptualizations and rationalizations for making war, a process labeled here as trying to reconcile the irreconcilable. The sources of difficulty in this conceptual process include analyzing two traditional milestones for using force separately and together. One element is the level of American interests that are engaged in contemporary developing world conflict and thus the question of whether the United States needs to involve itself in these situations with armed force. The other element is the prospect of success for the United States should it become involved, a key element in the basic argument here. Traditional criteria for success do not clearly hold, and these differences are accentuated by the questionable necessity of the involvements in the first place.

With these factors established, the discussion moves to recent American experience in Chapter 4. The clearest, most dramatic instances of the problem that has and continues to face the United States is represented by the three major post-World War II engagements in which the country has been unsuccessful: Vietnam, Iraq, and Afghanistan. These three conflicts have borne strikingly similar human characteristics that helped undermine American efforts and would almost certainly do so again in American intrusion into other, similar situations. At the conclusion of the American involvement in Vietnam, the United States—and especially the military—sought to understand what had gone wrong and to rectify those conditions. The banner of those efforts was "no more Vietnams," but it was a lesson either not deeply inculcated into the American military and geopolitical psyche or one that was subsequently lost or discarded. The post-mortems of the most recent experiences in Afghanistan and Iraq need to incorporate a more profound internalization of the similar lessons those adventures produced. If these kinds of situations dominate the effective "menu" of American "opportunities" to use force in the near term, the menu options are highly unpalatable.

Decolonization and Its Traumas: The Developing World Reality

For the majority of the world's population, the fundamental reality of the last sixty years or more has not been the power balance centered in Europe and North America. Rather, it has been a largely internal struggle within political jurisdictions that has had one or both of two sequential foci: gaining independence from a European colonial world, and development of the resulting states to a position more in line materially and otherwise with the old powers of the European balance. Virtually all of Africa and a great deal of Asia had to begin by ridding themselves of the bondage of colonial rule and then try to begin the process of economic and political development.

Different states began this process at different points and faced differing levels of difficulty and their own special problems in progressing through the independence/developmental process. As a result, there are some countries that have made great progress and have come to approximate the most developed countries, whereas some countries have not. Those countries that remain at less advanced stages of progress struggle with different sets of problems, and some of these problems manifest themselves in violence that becomes an issue for the broader international community. During the Cold War, the prospect of gaining influence in how and under what political form development took largely motivated the communist world, which sought to export its own developmental model to the new states. Denying that inroad motivated the West, and especially the United States, to become involved as well. What is notable is that their motivation was largely instrumental—gaining Cold War advantage—rather than reflecting an inherent empathy with developing world problems. When the Cold War ended, the level of developed world interest in the developing countries receded, as noted earlier.

The process of change in the developing world is long, complex, and beyond present purposes to discuss in great detail here. The dynamics that underlie the phenomenon, however, are basic to understanding the pattern of instability within the international system, since it is countries at various points in the developmental process that exhibit the most instability and provide the conditions wherein America occasionally finds itself tempted to become engaged. The Cold War model does not apply very well as a framework for understanding what is going on in the developing world, and the extension of the lesser included case (the idea that if one accounts for the worst possibility, one has also prepared for lesser problems) is a particularly bad fit.

The heart of this developmental process begins with the dynamic of self-determination of the peoples of the developing world. For countries that entered the second half of the twentieth century under colonial rule, the first step was to rid themselves of colonial domination and suppression—decolonization. This process was only a partial form of self-determination in many cases because of the nature of the colonial jurisdictions granted independence. Shrouded in the glow of ending foreign domination, independence movements often initially overlooked or ignored that national self-determination masked more primal desires for self-determination based on group loyalties within the new units that would have to be worked out later. Once Nigeria achieved independence in 1960, for example, it realized that there remained desires for autonomy and self-determination among its various subgroups, dominated by the Hausa-Fulani, Yoruba, and Ibo tribes but containing many more ethno-tribal groupings to which individuals felt primary loyalty. Many of these differences remain contentious and the underlying reality within highly conflicted societies today.

Independence, in other words, removed some problems but allowed other difficulties to emerge. Newly independent governments were often inept and squandered or pilfered the scarce resources that could have brought some calming improvement in people's lives, and the road to development was rocky at best, with relatively little outside assistance beyond what one Cold War side found necessary to promote its own influence or to deny influence to its opponent. The dialogue between the most developed world and the new countries came to center on the extent to which the old countries (including most of the former colonial masters) had been responsible for creating the mess in which the new countries found themselves, and thus what the European powers "owed" the developing world in compensation for the poverty and underdevelopment that they inherited at independence. With their attention more riveted on the Cold War competition, the countries of the European balance tended to relegate this debate and developmental efforts to secondary importance as long as the Cold War competition continued. If the worst case could not be avoided, lesser cases did not matter much. Even if one realized (as former colonists tended to do more than the Americans) that the lesser included case was a fiction, the resources were not clearly available to remedy the problem.

When the Cold War imploded, the central competition (the worst case) collapsed with it. The implications of that basic change were initially difficult to accept and even harder to turn into changed policies and postures. Through most of the 1990s, for instance, a good bit of effort was expended on the possibility that the Russians might revert to communism and that the former Soviet satellites in Eastern Europe might destabilize or morph into some dangerous new status, and these fears provided an adequate rationale to "keep the powder dry" and avoid any fundamental change in the national security approach of the United States and its allies.

The problems of the developing world were only slightly affected by the end of the Cold War. The internal dynamics of developing world misery had been placed at the margins of international concern during the Cold War. If anything, the end of the Cold War only added to that marginalization, as the Soviet Union no longer existed as a player in developing countries and the United States cut back its meager emphases now that there was no Soviet influence to counter. The implosion of the central competition did not, however, have much positive effect on meeting the needs of developing countries nor alter the process of their incorporation into the international mainstream.

The 1990s represented a decade wherein the United States reassessed its continuing international role. It was now *the* remaining superpower—what Secretary of State Madeleine Albright famously described as "the indispensable nation"—in an unrivaled power position in the world. The initial momentum of economic globalization revived the American economy and its centrality in the world economic system. The "peace dividend" meant the United States spent less on military defense, but its reductions in expenditures were far more modest than those of others, and the net result was that the American military advantage was actually enhanced.

It was also an introspective period. As it became increasingly clear that the Cold War threat would not soon be replaced by some ominous new form of competition, the question of where and under what circumstances the United States would contemplate the use of armed force arose. Implicitly, this meant a pivot of attention to the developing world without explicitly admitting this was the case. With no new principles to guide the transformation, the United States selectively "dabbled" in world instability. It intervened and got burned in Somalia, it avoided and its president later regretted not bringing an end to the slaughter in Rwanda, and it became involved without serious incident in Haiti and the Balkans (Bosnia and Kosovo). Although most of these occurred under the banner of "humanitarian intervention" (actions designed to relieve human suffering), it is not entirely clear that any real devotion to humanitarian concerns was the motivation. As the century ended, America was in the throes of the paradigm problem introduced earlier.

The terrorist attacks of September 11, 2001, appeared to clarify the new threat situation. The terrorist threat emanating from the Islamic Middle East and symbolized by Osama bin Laden and Al Qaeda, provided as close to a focus to American national security policy as had been conceptualized since the Soviets disappeared, and it was used to justify efforts such as those in Iraq and Afghanistan. It was, however, more of a cosmetic alteration of Cold War containment than a thorough reworking. The negative reaction that has come to typify opinion about the Iraq and Afghanistan adventures suggests that the new overlay was incomplete and imperfect.

The Cold War Paradigm in the Developing World: A Bad Fit

There are two lenses through which self-determination in the developing world could be viewed as it was unfolding: the Cold War and the developmental paradigms. Each view contained relevant elements, but each was also limited in its total ability to organize a thorough understanding around which to fashion policy. Of the two, the Cold War paradigm was probably the least applicable; it was also the dominant view in Washington and other capitals and the framework within which policy was tailored. In terms of the developmental process in the developing countries themselves, their choice was pretty clearly unfortunate and failed to resolve problems the developing world is struggling with now. In a world fixated with the central clash between the thermonuclear behemoths, the emphasis was understandable and probably inevitable. We are still paying for it.

The two paradigms appealed to different constituencies in the United States. The Cold War paradigm appealed primarily to the emerging Cold Warriors, and more specifically to members of the new policy community that saw international affairs in national security terms. These newly minted geopoliticians included most of the membership of the enlarged professional military establishment and like-minded realists for whom the failure to foresee the slide to World War II was primarily attributed to liberal wishful thinking and the consequent failure to prepare adequately to deter or more easily defeat the fascist threat. The appeal of the Cold Warriors included their "hard-headed," even more "manly" understanding and willingness to commit and sacrifice in a clearly hostile world defined primarily in stark, military terms.

The proponents and constituents of the developmental paradigm paled in comparison, especially during the early Cold War period when the apparent absence of sufficient anti-communist zeal was sometimes associated with "softness" in resolve against the communist menace. The systematic expression of ideas of economic and political development were relatively new and were mostly confined to academic circles, where a variety of social scientists (economists, sociologists, and political scientists) wrestled with the problem from their own particular disciplinary perspectives. While the effort they engaged in was intellectually quite impressive, it remained largely isolated to the ivy-covered walls of academic institutions and a few supporting, but less than central, governmental agencies that provided sustaining, but never overwhelming, financial support either to develop or implement the ideas the academics conjured. Moreover, the institutional setting contributed to the isolation of the developmental perspective from the political mainstream. Development, particularly when put forward as an alternative to the realist-based paradigm of the Cold Warriors, seemed soft, even effete in the face of the hard-steel menace of Soviet communism. In a head-to-head competition for broad political support, the proponents and defenders of the developmental perspective never had a realistic chance.

Each paradigm did, however, have some descriptive and thus prescriptive merit, depending on the situation to which it was applied. For the central confrontation between the Soviets and the Americans, the Cold War was clearly the more appropriate framework. The central Cold War clash was a geopolitical competition defined operationally in military terms, and to treat that aspect of world affairs in any other way would have been potentially disastrous and thus largely irresponsible. It would also have been largely irrelevant, as the only halfway attempt to apply the developmental perspective to the Cold War setting in the late 1940s demonstrated. When the Marshall Plan was first proposed in 1947, it was offered to all the war-torn countries of Europe, including those sliding into the communist bloc. The Soviets rejected the offer out of hand on behalf of themselves and the newly communist states on the grounds that American aid would be a kind of Trojan horse that would have facilitated subversion of their new empire. The United States took the rejection as clear evidence of the intractability of communist opposition to a peaceful world. Both were undoubtedly correct in these assessments, but the failure also showed that the developmental paradigm did not apply to the Cold War environment.

The developmental perspective was largely devised to deal with problems of the developing world, and it was in this setting that it was most clearly applicable. The problem that developmental theorists grappled with was how to transform societies underdeveloped in Western terms into modern, stable, Western-style states. This effort included political, economic, and social dimensions that clearly interacted: a stable and growing economy supposedly would lead to political and social stability, for instance. These were the difficulties facing emerging countries in one way or another, and it was for them that the developmental paradigm was constructed. It suffered, however, from three debilitating and ultimately insurmountable difficulties.

The first difficulty was that an understanding of the developmental process was—and still is—a work in progress. There was no firm, systematic understanding about how traditional societies emerge from the cocoon of underdevelopment into a condition of developed stability on which the developmental thinkers could build. Instead, the advocates operated to a large degree from the seats of their pants, devising ideas and schemes and then attempting to test them where they could. They could not confidently predict success in any of their ventures, because the process was so new and indeterminate. The inability to say with confidence that "this works" undercut their appeal and compromised their claim on scarce economic resources that were necessary to apply their schemes. Developmental schemes that might work but might not could hardly comprise a foolproof, compelling appeal. This problem continues to the present.

The second difficulty flows from the first: developmental proposals suffered from a lack of enthusiasm, conviction, and material support from the policy community. It was a circular dilemma: the developmental advocates argued that they needed adequate—read large—investments by the policy community to allow their schemes to reach successful fruition, whereas those with the resources argued in return that large investments could not be justified until their results could be demonstrated. The United States' long and basically penurious track record on developmental assistance (the United States ranks near the bottom of advanced countries on commitments to developmental assistance as a percentage of GDP) serves as testimony to the struggle the developmental advocates have faced.

The third difficulty is that the developmental paradigm had to compete with the Cold War paradigm in the political arena for support. This was, as already suggested, not a fair fight, particularly in the context of the paranoia and fear that gripped the Cold War world. The thrust of the Cold War paradigm's appeal was that it offered hard, tempered-steel protection against a predatory enemy who posed an imminent threat to national survival. Those advocates who argued the developmental perspective offered academic possibilities about how to make the world better and thus how to limit future, largely undefined dangers. Is it any surprise, under the circumstances, that the warriors in their crisply fitted uniforms and brandishing their metaphorical swords prevailed over the academics in their rumpled tweed jackets and pipes?

Applying each paradigm had different effects on developing world policy. In the end, neither perspective was wholly adopted as the approach the country would take toward the developing world. Instead, there was a hybrid strategy incorporating parts of each. It involved a two-track approach, the aim of which was to blunt the appeal of expansionist communism (the Cold Warriors' goal). On the one hand, the major criterion for developmental assistance was Cold War based: what countries were most threatened by the communist menace? Once chosen, the developmental paradigm could be applied, but with financial limits that were largely determined by Cold War considerations: the countries with the greatest perceived geopolitical significance got the most money. Because of a general lack of enthusiasm for the developmental paradigm, the amounts were inadequate to make much difference except in places where maximum efforts were made, such as South Korea.

The geopolitical, Cold War paradigm thus basically won out as the prevailing model. As a global matter, the outcome was probably inevitable and certainly justifiable within the context of the time. When the Cold War ended, however, most of the developmental problems of the formerly colonial world remained largely unsolved, at least partly because they were not addressed systematically in a world dominated by the Cold War paradigm. Things had, of course, changed. Oil had transformed the Middle East into a global hot spot quite independent of Cold War considerations, and the process of economic globalization was beginning to affect other parts of the world, notably in Asia. There still remained, however, significant parts of the world where the developmental process had not played out to any satisfactory conclusion. These places also were sources of instability and occasional violence in the post-Cold War world, as they had been before. The Cold War paradigm had not provided solutions to these situations beyond artificially classifying them in terms of the blue-red map struggle. With the veneer of the Cold War paradigm stripped away, the United States had no adequate framework through which to think about these conflicts. What it did have were some influences that further complicate the picture.

Reconciling the Irreconcilable: Contemporary Warfare and the American Military Culture

The Cold War was a tremendously powerful influence on the way the United States, and especially its military, views the world, what one can call the American military culture. This influence should not be surprising. Prior to the Cold War, military concerns were not prominent in American thinking about the world, and the American military establishment was a mere fraction of its size—and especially prestige—today. The Cold War was the forge in which attitudes about the American way of war, with roots in the earlier past, were cast into an enduring legacy.

The Cold War, like World War II, was a total conflict, and it bred the mentality and preeminence of total war as the enduring standard for American force. *Total wars* are, by definition, wars that are very important, even essential to the national interest, which is why the country can and must apply the totality of its resources to prosecuting them. An Axis victory in World War II might not have threatened American survival, but it would have left the United States intolerably isolated in a very hostile world environment. The possibility of nuclear holocaust added the pressing element of national survival to the concerns with and seriousness about total war. Wars in the developing world are not, *from an American perspective*, like that.

Developing world conflicts are scarcely, even arguably never, that important to the United States. During the Cold War, the United States fought twice in situations where important interests were alleged to be involved. In Korea, the United States successfully prevented the takeover of the Korean peninsula by a hostile regime, an objective important in its own geopolitical terms and because a hostile Korea so near the Japanese archipelago (Korea has sometimes metaphorically been referred to as "a dagger aimed at the heart of Japan") would have been intolerable to our closest post-war Asian allies. Relatively few people doubted whether Korea was worth fighting over (although many argued over how we conducted the war). At any rate, a favorable outcome was important to the United States. The same reasoning was applied to Vietnam. The situations appeared similar, in that a hostile communist North Vietnam was attempting to unite all of Vietnam by conquering and annexing anti-communist South Vietnam (an entity the United States helped create). Within the time frame of the early 1960s when the United States progressively committed to the defense of the Republic of Vietnam (South Vietnam), the defense of intervention had a Cold War, vital-interest base: under the "domino theory," if South Vietnam fell, others in the region would also fall like a row of dominos, and the result would be intolerable for the United States, if in less obvious ways than in Korea.

These two conflicts are both prototypes and legacies of the Cold War's influence on the present. Korea was the United States' first limited war of the post-World War II environment, but it was also, with the exception of the first Persian Gulf War (Operation Desert Storm) of 1990–91, the country's last conventional war in terms of conduct by the U.S. and its opponents. The United States did not exactly prevail in the sense of vanquishing and destroying its foe, but it also accomplished the goal of preventing a united, hostile Korean peninsula. Vietnam, on the other hand, was a limited war for the United States (although it was total for our opponents). It was largely fought conventionally by the United States and unconventionally by the opposition, and by no measure did we do anything but fall short in the effort. Unfortunately for the United States, more recent U.S. military involvements have been much more like Vietnam than Korea (the initial campaign against Iraq in 2003 is an exception), and those dynamics appear to hold for the foreseeable future.

The Cold War physical and conceptual experiences have two important legacies for thinking about the use of American military force in the future, and each legacy is cautionary and bedeviling. Both are artifacts of the American preference for total war and the legacy of the intellectual underpinning of the Cold War in the international relations theory of realism. The first is a distinction regarding the importance of particular war possibilities. It essentially asks if war is worth fighting and is an assessment often divided into *wars of necessity* and *wars of choice*. The American tradition of total war preference emphasizes involvement in the former, while the current environment provides many more examples of the latter. The other distinction is the *winnability* of wars, and it asks if particular wars can be fought successfully. The question raises concerns both about whether the United States can prevail in particular situations and defining what prevailing means in those situations. The distinction can be put more simply: the first asks whether the United States *should* use armed force, while the second asks if the effort can succeed. DWIC involvements do not unambiguously generate positive answers to either question.

Wars of Necessity, Wars of Choice

The legacy of the Cold War mindset influences thinking in the post–Cold War world in two important and ultimately debilitating ways. The first is about the worth of fighting particular wars. It is an important question that includes both an assessment of how important particular engagements are in terms of American national interests and how well those interests can be portrayed as "good" objectives to the American people.

The common means of categorization is between wars of necessity and wars of choice. It is a commonsensical distinction. Wars of necessity are, as the name implies, conflicts in which the country *has* to engage, because the consequences of not doing so would be intolerable. The determination of intolerability means that wars of necessity must involve the country's most important, or vital, interests.

In a true war of necessity, the imperative to participate and potential unacceptable possible outcomes are so obvious that there is little dissent surrounding American commitment. The objectives, in other words, meet the criteria of "good" political objectives as introduced in Snow and Drew (*From Lexington to Baghdad and Beyond*), and there is a strong consensus both about entering the war and sustaining its conduct. In the American experience, wars of necessity have generally been total wars, a commonality that follows from the definition: if a war must be fought and won, then it makes sense that the country would commit all the resources at its disposal to prosecute it. Wars of necessity are those philosophically favored by political realists, whose convictions include a limitation on the use of force to situations where vital interests are engaged. The connection between necessity and total war, however, is limited in a nuclear-armed world where war avoidance can be a greater necessity than pursuing objectives through war.

In concept and appeal, wars of necessity are much easier to argue and gain support for, but they are also far less numerous in the contemporary world, where opportunities to engage in wars of choice are considerably more abundant. In contrast to wars of necessity, wars of choice are situations where the United States may *choose* to involve itself with armed forces, but where the conflict and its outcomes do not *impel* it do so. Wars of choice are generally associated with less-than-vital (LTV) interests, matters where the outcome might inconvenience or disadvantage the United States but in ways that are not intolerable. In terms of the nature of American commitment in wars of choice, these wars tend to be limited in terms of both political objective and military conduct. They also tend not to meet as many of the criteria of good objectives as do wars of necessity. They are thus more likely not to elicit great public enthusiasm, and support is likely to erode if they become protracted and their outcomes problematic, which experience shows they often do.

The post–World War II period offers primary examples of the dominance of each kind of war. The Cold War, had it ever gone "hot," would clearly have been a war of necessity, because American survival was clearly imperiled. There are no obvious examples of unambiguously necessary wars in which the United States will likely become a part in the contemporary world. A fundamental revolution in Mexico (an overt takeover by criminal, drug-related elements) might result in an outcome intolerable for the United States that would impel an American response, but it would not necessarily have strong apocalyptical implications. The current American worst case, conflict with China, is implausible on grounds of self-interest (why would either want to destroy the other given their economic ties?) and because such a conflict would almost certainly become nuclear if pressed to its logical ends. These same objections can, however, be raised about World War I, where the rejoinders did not prevent war, so they are not absolute inhibitions.

At least from an American vantage point, the most numerous recent opportunities to fight have been in wars of choice in the developing world. As the name implies, wars of choice are opportunities for involvement in conflicts where there is meaningful choice for the United States in terms of the consequences of becoming or not becoming involved. In most developing world conflicts, the stakes for the United States do not engage fundamental American interests. Since most of these conflicts are essentially internal in nature, they are extremely important to the indigenous participants, for whom participation is clearly a matter of necessity and where negative outcomes can have literal life-and-death consequences. They are, in other words, total wars for the internal participants, whereas they are limited wars for the United States. This difference in motivation has major negative consequences for the willingness of the United States to pursue its interests with adequate rigor and sacrifice compared to that of the internal factions. This very important distinction is rarely ever portrayed when a commitment is being contemplated or argued, either because it is unrecognized (the kindest possible interpretation) or because those making the justification do not want to advertise the difficulties of success given the modesty of interests involved (the less charitable interpretation).

The trick for engagement in these kinds of wars is convincing the American public and their elected representatives that these engagements are necessary when they are not. This attempt can occur in two different ways. One is to try to inflate the importance of intervention to the point of vitality of interest and thus necessity. The Iraq War is a primary example: overthrowing Saddam Hussein might be a desirable thing to do, but in and of itself, it was hardly necessary for the United States. Necessity could be argued only if the Iraqi regime harbored dangerous intents and matching capabilities toward the United States, and this rationale was provided by allegations of the Iraqi weapons of mass destruction (WMDs) threat and ties to terrorist enemies of the United States (neither of which, of course, subsequently could be demonstrated). The other way is to argue that the criterion of necessity/vital interests (the realist standard) is too restrictive and that there needs to be provision for action in situations analytically somewhere between necessity and choice. This line of reasoning has been most clearly associated with the neo-conservatives who were important during the George W. Bush administration.

Because wars of choice are less popular among the American populace, the trick for supporters of involvement in these situations is to perform a kind of sleight of hand to convince the American people to support involvements that they are not really prone to supporting. The recent experience of the United States in these kinds of wars has been that it may be possible to accomplish this deception in the short run, but for it ultimately to succeed, it must be possible to end involvement fairly quickly, before the American people realize that the effort is not really necessary. The George W. Bush administration, for instance, apparently thought it could topple the Hussein government in Iraq, engineer its replacement, and depart in a matter of months. When this calculation proved incorrect and the commitment became protracted and open-ended, questions of worth were raised. Involvement in wars of choice thus raises the question of winnability in a different way than wars of necessity.

The Question of Winnability

It goes without saying that winning in any activity as profound as war is important. The degree of importance, of course, depends on just how significant the stakes are. The seriousness of winning takes on particular salience since the major cost of war is precious human life. Thus, winning is the traditional measure by which war is finally accounted.

Unfortunately, the meaning of winning in war is not as simple as it might appear at first blush. Victory in war has at least two important dimensions: prevailing on the battlefield and accomplishing the political objectives for which war is engaged in the first place. In traditional wars, the two senses are sequential: victory on the battlefield is the necessary precondition for asserting or imposing the political conditions on the opponent. This relationship between the two forms of victory stands at the heart of the Clausewitzian calculation that has dominated the European tradition of interstate warfare for at least two centuries, but it is not so clear that the relationship is as valid in contemporary, developing world conflict.

Many modern, internally based wars sever the connection between military and political aspects of victory, particularly when these wars invite outside intervention by major powers. These kinds of wars, which include the three major contests in which the United States has not prevailed, divorce military from political success, because the indigenous forces that outsiders like the United States encounter cannot possibly "defeat" those outsiders in any conventional military sense. They instead become asymmetrical wars in which the military objective for those opposing Western intervention adopt different military criteria of success than the traditional goals of vanquishing the enemy (destroying it as a means of resistance) held by the interveners. For the indigenous force, success means not failing—remaining a viable opposition until the outsiders become frustrated and leave. In this outcome, neither side exactly wins or loses in traditional military terms, but one or another of the indigenous forces generally ends up accomplishing its political objectives—the other sense of winning.

These kinds of distinctions are traditionally alien to Americans, for whom victory and defeat are clear-cut, discernible conditions. The determination of winners and losers for Americans is akin to the outcome of athletic contests, where the final tally is recorded on a scoreboard and the winner is the one who scores the most points. This sports mentality does not hold in contemporary wars between highly mismatched foes. The only analogy I can conjure is with one of Americans' least liked spectator sports, soccer (football to most of the world). In a soccer game between two highly mismatched opponents, the less talented side may well play entirely defensively, hoping for a scoreless tie. This outcome is the best that such a team can expect (unless it gets lucky and more or less accidentally scores a goal), and the supporters of the less advantaged team consider a 0–0 draw a great success. American fans have a very difficult time getting enthusiastic over a scoreless contest in which one side does not seriously try to win by scoring goals and cannot understand when that outcome is applauded.

The question of winnability has two sometimes imponderable aspects. One of these is predicting in advance whether one will prevail or not in a particular war. In a sense, the ability to predict victory is not so important in a war of necessity, since the nature of the situation indicates one must try regardless of likely success. Ironically, the ability to predict winning is terribly critical when the outcome is less important, because the outcomes of involvement in wars of choice matter less in terms of political objectives being achieved. As a result, traditional victory, particularly if it can be accomplished quickly and reasonably painlessly, is the palliative to dampen criticisms based in the worth of the enterprise.

The other aspect of winnability is whether one knows in advance what it takes to win in particular circumstances. In total wars, prediction is sometimes easier, because totality means that all the resources countries have will be placed on the line. The most capable is likely to prevail, because not only does it have the most but it is also motivated by the necessity of prevailing and will thus continue the fight even in the face of adversity. An often-stated example is the realization by many in Japan that, after it failed to sink the entire American Pacific fleet at Pearl Harbor, it could not possibly defeat the United States in an all-out, prolonged struggle of society against society.

The ability to predict victory is compromised significantly when one faces an opponent who fights in unfamiliar ways, or at least in ways for which one does not have adequate doctrinal bases for defeating that enemy. If potential opponents in developing world countries would stand and fight in the European tradition (as Saddam Hussein's armed forces attempted in the Kuwaiti desert), there is no question who would win, thereby increasing the popularity of potential involvements. The problem is that the opponents Americans face in developing world settings understand this dynamic, and so they refuse to fight in ways that assure their defeat. That is the nature of asymmetrical warfare, and until the United States devises a way to defeat an opponent who refuses to fight on our terms, confidently predicting victory in advance will amount to little more than sophistry. The simple fact is the United States has not devised a reliable method to defeat asymmetrical opponents militarily and especially politically; until we do, predicting victory is a chimera.

Winning, and being able to predict winning, is important, but it comes with a contemporary conundrum. We are able to predict with some precision who will win and who will lose in total, traditional wars, but these are the very kinds of wars we dare not fight and which are consequently the least likely military adventures in which we will find ourselves. On the other hand, we have so far proven woefully unable to predict positive outcomes in contemporary developing world contests that are the most likely opportunities and where a confident prediction is most necessary, since the reasons for fighting are the most questionable. This conundrum comes into particularly clear focus when one combines the two dimensions of importance and likely success.

Conjunction: Necessity, Choice, and Winnability

Public support is critical for political democracies to succeed at war. The only obvious exception to this generalization is if warfare can be conducted so rapidly and decisively that there is no opportunity for negative opinion to arise. One of Clausewitz's more famous formulations was what he called the "trinity," and it consisted of three parts: the army (armed forces in contemporary times), the government, and the people. His argument was that for war to be prosecuted successfully, all three of these elements must support the effort. If one comes into opposition, the effort will fail. The critical element is the people's support, both because the population affects how decision makers (the government) act and

Worth	Winnability	
	Winnable	Not Winnable
Necessity	Cell 1	Cell 2
Choice	Cell 3	Cell 4

because they provide the soldiers and resources on which the army depends. Popularity, and thus support, rests on a delicate combination of the perceived need to be fighting particular wars and the perceived likelihood of success.

These distinctions are complex and not entirely intuitive, but they are important to the conduct of military operations. To capture and provide a vehicle for unraveling these distinctions, the two dimensions are presented in a 2×2 matrix form, which produces four possible combinations, each of which is worth exploring.

An examination of the cells of the matrix will clarify the distinctions. The upper left quadrant (Cell 1) is winnable wars of necessity. This combination is the gold standard among candidates for military involvement: it represents the situation where military action is both needed and will succeed, and thus it represents the combination most likely to have and to sustain public support. As a result, the public will recognize that need and its support will endure, since it is leading toward victory. Advocates of particular wars will generally always try to depict military engagements as necessary and winnable, a claim that they will try to make lively and convincing by demonizing the opponent's intents and the perils it poses (Saddam Hussein's WMDs, for instance) and emphasizing the gap between that opponent's military might and our own. Because wars outside this cell are always going to be less popular, opponents will question both whether a war with a particular opponent can be or is worth conducting. The more ambiguous the placement of the war is on either dimension, the livelier the debate.

Cell 2 represents the most difficult situation, and one the United States has not historically experienced. There can be situations where a military action is absolutely necessary to support the vital interests of the country, but where conducting such a war will almost certainly result in defeat. In these cases, the country faces a severe dilemma. If resistance is predictably futile, it faces unpleasant options. One is to engage in a quixotic defense (e.g., the Poles in the face of the German invasion in 1939) where defeat is preordained and post-war retribution may be increased because of resistance. The second option is simply to put up no resistance and accept defeat (e.g., Austria in 1938), hoping for the best from the outcome. The only obvious situation in which the United States has faced this combination was during the Cold War, when Americans debated "better dead than red" (fighting and losing) or "better red than dead" (not fighting and accepting defeat but surviving). Happily, the Soviets faced the same outcomes, and deterrence prevailed.

There is, however, a third option that represents the dilemma facing the United States in the developing world. If a potential American opponent recognizes the certainty of losing to American force but is unwilling to accept an unfavorable outcome, the option may be to change the rules of engagement so that defeat is no longer certain: the asymmetrical warfare option. The objective of changing the rules by which a war is fought is to change the calculation of winning away from certain defeat to attainable success. In the process of doing so, of course, the same calculation for the superior military force (the United States, in this case) is also changed negatively. One of the central problems with which this book is concerned is that the United States has not always recognized that, in the process, *its* calculation must move from winnable to at least potentially unwinnable. The operationalization of this option is explored in the next section of this chapter.

Winnable wars of choice are depicted in Cell 3. For the United States, war situations that fall into this category have tended to be small, isolated situations where America's most important interests were not at stake, but where whatever interests were involved could be attained easily enough that getting involved would not cause a major public controversy. The best recent examples are American military participation in the "humanitarian interventions" during the 1990s in the Balkans and Haiti. In these situations of choice, the United States was not impelled into action by some geopolitical necessity but out of a concern for humanitarian tragedies. While levels of active support for these missions were tepid at best, the costs in lives and treasure were modest enough not to fuel active opposition. The danger in situations like these is miscalculation of the prospects and ease of success. Since core American values are not engaged in these war opportunities, public opinion can easily and quickly turn on them and make them unsustainable.

If an involvement in a war of choice turns out to be less easy than anticipated, the result can be a Cell-4 situation. For the policy maker, this is the nightmare scenario, since it is almost certain to bring negative popular reactions, including possible ballot box retaliation. Unlike Cell-2 situations, unwinnable wars of choice will generally attract gathering opposition, especially since, in the American case, the inability to win is not physically losing, but rather failing to prevail. It is a subtle distinction that can be lost on those who must support the effort—the public. For the public, such an effort can be akin to cheering a scoreless soccer tie—frustration and senselessness.

The danger of involvement in Cell-4 scenarios is evident in two kinds of situations that have faced and frustrated the United States in the twenty-first century. One is the contemplation of involvement in contemporary humanitarian disasters where there would be considerable opposition to an American (or allied) intrusion. The most obvious examples are Arab Spring–inspired events like Libya and Syria. Although each is complex and to some extent idiosyncratic, they share widespread attacks and atrocities perpetrated on civilian population elements opposing the regime. The Libyan case was the more attractive for intervention: American allies like France and Italy were highly dependent on Libyan oil and thus had arguably vital interests in the outcome, and Libyan geography and demography made it possible to interfere effectively with Qaddafi's armed forces from the air, rather than forcing intervention by ground forces, including likely casualties to the interveners. In those circumstances, humanitarian concerns were enough to permit action, which could be effective without putting "muddy boots" on the desert sand. In Syria, on the other hand, the government controlled considerably more armed force than the Libyans, and a military intervention would have almost certainly have required putting forces on the ground in situations of uncertain outcomes and certain casualties. In that situation, the winnability factor did not favor intervention.

The other, and more prescient, example is involvement in situations that may appear to be important and winnable, but prove otherwise. The wars in Iraq and Afghanistan were not, of course, advertised as Cell-4 cases in advance of American intervention, but as Cell-1 cases. Both were portrayed as wars of necessity involving vital American interests (Iraq's alleged WMDs and cooperation with terrorists, the Afghan government's provision of sanctuaries for Al Qaeda), and American military prowess was deemed so great that the question of prevailing was not a major stumbling block to gaining support for operations. As these operations dragged on in their distinct ways, perceptions of them gradually slid diagonally downward from Cell 1 toward Cell 4. Wars that are not unambiguously Cell-1 engagements are the major prospects for American developing world involvements in the future, and so the discussion moves to the most prominent examples of that dynamic in the past.

Lesser *Unincluded* Wars of Choice: DWICs as Asymmetrical Wars

Many of these distinctions come together in assessing involvement in DWICs, the central concern of this book. These conflicts span the bridge between the Cold War and the present, and unfortunately, the organizational lens through which they tend to be viewed is the Cold War paradigm. This construct was of dubious applicability when it was first employed to organize Cold War–era thinking about DWICs, and it is of even less relevance outside the Cold War context. Particularly when an American intervention is contemplated, these conflicts are or become asymmetrical wars, for which Cold War–force assumptions are dubiously applicable. In the realist sense, they are also fairly unambiguously wars of choice, although their champions deny the designation.

The Cold War–force model is an inappropriate framework for thinking about or contesting DWICs militarily. Because the internal factions that fight these wars do not use Western forces or methods, DWICs tend to be different from the European-style warfare on which the Cold War paradigm is premised. These conflicts are certainly smaller than World War III on the northern European plain would have been, but they are also so structurally different that they can hardly be thought of as lesser included cases to which the Cold War military model can be applied. DWICs are *not* lesser included forms of conflict, they are a distinct genre that the Cold War construct does not help one understand. They are *unincluded* problems in the Cold War construct, and treating them as lesser included cases has been a major source of misunderstanding and frustration for intervening outsiders like the United States anticipating a very different fight than they actually encounter.

The motives underlying outside intervention in DWICs also do not conform to Cold War paradigm standards. The paradigm's central fixation was a classic war of necessity, where the problem was how to win such a war and thus make it a Cell-1 rather than a Cell-2 prospect. Nuclear weapons ultimately invalidated this calculation so that war avoidance became the most acceptable strategy, thereby rendering the concern moot. The issue in the outcome of a DWIC to an outsider like the United States will hardly ever rise unambiguously to a level of national necessity. It does, however, have that level of importance to the internal participants. Champions of intervention will argue the necessity of their actions, but these assertions will hardly ever be universally accepted, and support for interventions will inevitably erode with time and the absence of clear progress.

DWICs are clearly different than the classic conflicts for which the Cold War paradigm was designed, and trying to overlay the paradigm on these situations has led to the frustration of bad policy outcomes. DWICs are lesser "unincluded" in terms of the Cold War framework, and applying its criteria to these conflicts distorts analysis and thus leads to inapplicable decisions. The Cold War paradigm was intended to frame policy to a world where the major problem was a potential World War III. The contemporary environment thankfully lacks such a likely danger. Instead, it is a world where DWICs are the major operational problem, and thus it is imperative to understand these conflicts as what they are, asymmetrical wars, and to adjust the lens of policy to fit that reality.

DWICs as Asymmetrical Wars

The synonym for asymmetrical warfare is *unconventional warfare*. It refers generically to situations where the various parties to conflict do not fight in the same way or for the same purposes. Asymmetrical warfare is unconventional militarily in that both (or all) contestants do not organize or fight in the same way: they follow different rules or conventions, in other words. Politically, the various actors often fight for different reasons and outcomes, particularly when outside interveners are involved.

In the first half of the twentieth century, the dominant method of warfare was the clash of large, similarly organized state-based military machines fighting to establish domain over one another. All sides employed roughly the same rules of engagement (ROEs), and the basic military purpose was to overcome enemy hostile ability. These wars were symmetrical or conventional, in that both sides fought the same way for the same reasons. By the end of the last century, the United States military had come close to perfecting these conventional approaches and was both its strongest practitioner and advocate. Its superiority was so great that it made little sense for any opponent to challenge the Americans within this framework.

Symmetrical approaches, not surprisingly, favor those who are best at it, which in this case generally means the strongest. The aphorism for this phenomenon is Napoleon's observation that "God favors the big battalions." For those who are disadvantaged under the prevailing conventions, conforming to those rules may create such a severe handicap as to preclude the possibility of success. If one is unwilling to accept these consequences, a logical response is to ignore the existing rules and to adopt means by which one has a chance. Someone who reaches that conclusion is unconventional because he violates existing conventions, and the resulting clash is asymmetrical, because both sides do not fight according to the same conventions.

Stated this way, the term *asymmetrical warfare* is clearly much newer than the dynamic it describes. The instinct to resist the imposition of outside force is as old as imposition itself, and the resisters have devised different ways to organize their resistance. Those methods have almost always meant abandoning the conventions of the conquerors and adopting methods at which they could succeed. Some argue that Sun Tzu's *The Art of War*, written over three thousand years ago as a manual for Chinese warlords, was the first blueprint for asymmetrical warfare.

Asymmetrical warfare is a methodology, not a series of methods. The concepts underlying asymmetrical approaches are premised on the idea that the weak can only compete with the stronger if they reject conventions and attack the enemy outside the rules the stronger prefers and at which he will prevail—which is why the stronger prefers playing by the "rules." The means (or methods) by which the weaker reframes the contest will, to some extent, be idiosyncratic, depending on situations that exist. Experience with past situations may help influence the methods in any particular case, but each will also be special depending on circumstance. Adaption is a key element in the methodology of asymmetry.

This "customizing" aspect of asymmetrical approaches creates difficulties for the symmetrical warrior, as it is supposed to do. It means no two asymmetrical conflicts are exactly the same. Because of this, it is hard to prepare in detail for any given encounter with a particular opponent, either tactically or strategically. Since a major purpose of doctrine is to provide guidance about what to do in likely situations, the result is uncertainty in preparation for and execution of military tasks, the absolute bane of military leaders. Reducing uncertainty is, after all, one of the primary functions of having rules and conventions of behavior, and it is thus unsurprising that conventional warriors particularly dislike asymmetrical warfare and hold its practitioners in disdain.

Asymmetry also extends to and intimately affects the balance between military and political objectives in warfare. Conventional wars in the European style are classically "military" in nature: the purpose is to overcome opposition hostile ability by defeating its armed forces as preface to imposing one's political will on that opponent. Military action precedes and is, to a large extent, independent of the political purposes for which it is undertaken. The military leader evaluates his actions in terms of their impact on the enemy's hostile ability; it is the politician's job to sort out political effects after the fact.

Typical DWICs reverse, even invert, the balance between military and political concerns. Internal foes in asymmetrical wars may seek to defeat one another's hostile ability, but if they face an outside intervener like the United States, they cannot hope to accomplish this goal. The object of the conflict becomes the outsider's *cost-tolerance* (willingness to continue resistance despite the costs of doing so) which, if successfully overcome, will cause the outsider to conclude continued prosecution is either futile or not worth the cost and leave. As a result, those faced with American military might have chosen a strategy of attrition to wear down American resolve in situations of debatable vitality to the American intruders. That military resistance has the directly political intents both of attacking American support for the war and of mobilizing expanding natural resistance to a foreign military presence on their soil. The resisters cannot hope to drive the intruders physically from their lands, so they seek instead to convince the intruder his continuing presence is so unwelcome as not to be worthwhile. The indigenous opponent can continue to pursue this objective as long as it avoids decisive defeat: militarily, it can win by not losing. The intruder, however, must destroy the opponent and its physical ability to resist: it can only win by physically winning. Thus, outcomes are asymmetrical as well.

The result is a kind of "double whammy" for the outsider, who must decide how to achieve objectives for which he has no foolproof formula for success in situations where it is not altogether clear whether what he is doing is worth the trouble. His task may simply be impossible. He is trying to impose his solutions in an environment where he cannot possibly succeed. He is an outsider whose efforts will be resisted on those grounds alone, and his objectives may well not be those of the people on whom he seeks to impose them. Great efforts have been expended to surmount this arguably insurmountable combination within the American military community, and the result has been very much a love–hate relationship with DWIC involvement.

COIN: The American Response

Within the developing world, the most common military forms of DWICs have been variations of asymmetrical warfare. Efforts to try to deal with this problem have fallen in the generic category of COIN, an abbreviation for counter-insurgency adopted largely to describe the ideas associated with General Petraeus and attempted in Iraq (after the American invasion spawned an insurgency against the occupying Americans) and Afghanistan (where the United States joined the government to resist Taliban insurgents). The idea of COIN is by no means newer than insurgency; the problem is that except in special circumstances, instances of its successful application are very limited.

The United States has a long and spotted history of involvement in asymmetrically fought internal wars. The country was born partially as a result of the DWIC of its time, in which many of the successes of the revolutionary cause were won when the American warriors fought asymmetrically, borrowing their methods from the indigenous Indians. When the Continental Army stood and fought its British counterpart, it generally fared poorly. When the Americans reverted to what one British general at the time called the "dirty little war of terror and murder," they succeeded. Among other things, their successes egged the British into adopting brutal means of suppression that only made matters worse. These dynamics were introduced in Chapter 1.

Nearly all the subsequent American experience has been as a counterinsurgent. The United States employed COIN approaches to subduing many of the Plains and Southwestern Indians (where they succeeded largely because there were too few Indians to defeat them), and in places like Cuba and the Philippines. Marines engaged in COIN in Central America during the early twentieth century, and during World War II, there was some exposure to this form of warfare in the Asia-Pacific region (see, for instance, Hilsman's account of working with anti-Japanese guerrillas in Burma in *American Guerrilla*). Vietnam was America's true baptism by fire with COIN.

The COIN concept has never been truly embraced by an American military establishment rooted in conventional, European-style warfare. The conventional campaigns of World War II remain the holy grail of each of the core services, as Carl Builder pointed out in 1989 in *The Masks of War*. Concern for asymmetry has been assigned to the fringe elements of the services: mounted cavalry against the Indians and the "light infantry" Marines and Special Operations Forces (SOFs) in more contemporary times. The problem of massive, European-style conflict in Europe (World War III) remains at the core of the values, structure, and doctrine of American forces, at which they are peerless. In the present, however, there are no remaining symmetrical forces facing the United States for which that emphasis is clearly relevant. Instead, the present and foreseeable future are dominated by asymmetrical DWIC opportunities, at which the U.S. military has not proven itself especially adept and for which its preferred approach is not clearly applicable.

This situation is not entirely the military's fault. The military has been averse to DWIC involvements at least intuitively because they recognize their own limitations and the impossibility of prevailing in circumstances where, as argued here, intervention is doomed. The military may help create the conditions for failure when it is inserted into situations where it is unwelcome, and its continued presence may well make the situation worse, but these negative processes are the result of political decisions, not military actions per se. The military may make itself more or less of an irritant by the way it occupies, but the heart of rejection of occupation results from the decision to intrude and stay. The only clear way to relieve the irritation is to withdraw the military from the situation, another political decision. It is not at all clear that the military can overcome the problem of rejection while it remains in occupation.

Yet trying to improve the unimprovable condition of occupation resentment is exactly the task the military is given in DWIC interventions. Essentially all the literature on COIN—up to and including the Petraeus manual—ignores this dynamic and emphasizes military techniques for defeating insurgents as if the outsiders were a benign or neutral factor, which they are not. A common thread is the curious proposition that by doing more (becoming more intrusive), the outsider may "solve" the problem—hence the "surges" in Iraq and Afghanistan. It is more likely that the greater the outsider presence, the more resentment it creates. Upping the ante simply causes the dog to chase its own tail harder.

Many in the military intuitively grasp the fecklessness of being forced into these impossible roles. The result has been a deep ambivalence within the American military toward DWIC involvements. This sentiment is deepest in the Army, which bears primary responsibility for DWIC intervention implementation. Some of this resistance is along predictable, self-interested lines: officers from the traditional European-style warfare specialties like armor and field artillery are more opposed that those whose specialities expand where COIN is emphasized. SOFs are the obvious example. In some ways, such sentiments reflect nostalgia over a glorious past that is no longer part of the present.

Part of the ambivalence and reluctance to embrace the DWIC intervention role and its COIN implications is also the realization that these missions and strategies are simply losers. Given the illusion of successful COIN and the star quality of its leading apostle, General Petraeus, its prominence seemed supreme until recently. The failure of COIN in Afghanistan and skepticism about the strategy among prominent figures like Vice President Joe Biden helped tip the scale away from the concept. The eclipse of Petraeus' star quality for unrelated reasons seems likely to assure the ascendancy of anti-COIN forces within the Army for awhile. Until it can be clearly demonstrated that there is some variant of COIN that successfully solves the problems of resistance discussed here, that is a good thing.

The Changing Problem of Violence

The dominant forms of warfare have changed greatly since the end of World War II. The second global confrontation of the last century was the climax of European-style warfare between the large, highly organized and diversified forces of states clashing over conflicts of national interest. That form of warfare was the signature face of war in the European-dominated international system of the last three centuries. The exhaustion of the core European states in World War II eroded that dominance; the potential deadliness of thermonuclear war completed its obsolescence. There has been nothing like it since.

Internal conflict between factions within states fighting in other ways has also been an enduring form of warfare. Historically, at least some of that violence has featured partisan groups seeking to repel outside intruders and occupiers. At the same time, factional disputes among domestic groups have also been a major cause of violence. Largely stimulated by geographic imperfections arising from decolonization, this has gradually become the dominant form of contemporary systemic violence. Cold War concerns masked this emergence; it is clear to see with the Cold War veil removed.

Internal wars are very different than traditional European-style wars along a wide range of characteristics. Most important for present purposes, they cannot be "solved" by the application of conventional force in traditional ways. DWICs are indeed asymmetrical, both abjuring conventional modes of warfare and creating rules and purposes designed to frustrate conventional efforts. Paradigms to cope with one form of violence do not transfer to very different problems. DWICs are indeed unincluded anomalies for the Cold Warriors.

This chapter has introduced some of these changes and changing dynamics and discussed why applying traditional constructs does not result in favorable resolutions. To this point, the discussion has been general and abstract. Chapter 4 applies the generalities to the most recent American efforts to apply Cold War constructs to unincluded situations.

Bibliography

Aydin, Aysegul. *Foreign Policy and Intervention in Armed Conflicts*. Palo Alto, CA: Stanford University Press, 2012.

Builder, Carl. *The Masks of War: American Military Styles in Strategy and Analysis*. Santa Monice, CA: RAND Corporation Publication Series, 1989.

Clausewitz, Carl von (translated and edited by Michael Howard and Peter Paret). *On War*. (Revised ed.) Princeton, NJ: Princeton University Press, 1984.

Gallagher, James J. *Low-Intensity Conflict: A Guide to Tactics, Techniques, and Procedures*. Mechanicsburg, PA: Stackpole Books, 1992.

Haass, Richard N. *Intervention: The Uses of American Force in the Post-Cold War World*. Washington, DC: Carnegie Endowment for International Peace, 1994.

——*Wars of Necessity, Wars of Choice: A Memoir of Two Iraq Wars*. New York: Simon and Schuster, 2009.

Hentz, James J. *The Obligation of Empire: United States' Strategy for a New Century*. Lexington, KY: University of Kentucky Press, 2004.

Hilsman, Roger. *American Guerrilla: My War Behind Japanese Lines*. Washington, DC: Brassey's, 1990.

Kaplan, Fred. "The End of the Age of Petraeus: The Rise and Fall of Counterinsurgency." *Foreign Affairs* 92, 1 (January/February 2013), 75–90.

Kinzer, Stephen. *Overthrow: America's Century of Regime Change from Hawaii to Iraq*. New York: Times Books (Henry Holt and Company), 2006.

Lacquemont, Richard A. *Shaping American Military Capabilities After the Cold War*. Westport, CT: Praeger, 2003.

Millett, Allan R., and Peter Maslowski. *For the Common Defense: A Military History of the United States of America*. New York: Free Press, 1994.

O'Hanlon, Michael E. *Defense Strategy for the Post-Saddam Era*. Washington, DC: Brookings Institution Press, 2003.

Peters, Ralph. *Fighting for the Future: Will America Triumph?* Mechanicsburg, PA: Stackpole Books, 2001.

Polk, William R. *Violent Politics: A History of Insurgency, Terrorism, and Guerrilla Warfare*. New York: Harper Perennials, 2008.

Sandstrom, Karl. *Local Interests and American Foreign Policy: Why International Interventions Fail*. London: Routledge, 2013.

Shafer, D. Michael. *Deadly Paradigms: The Failure of U.S. Counterinsurgency Policy*. Princeton, NJ: Princeton University Press, 1988.

Snow, Donald M. *Distant Thunder: Patterns of Conflict in the Developing World* (2nd ed.). Armonk, NY: M E Sharpe, 1997.

——*Uncivil Wars: International Security and the New Internal Conflicts*. Boulder, CO: Lynne Rienner, 1996.

Snow, Donald M. and Dennis M. Drew. *From Lexington to Baghdad and Beyond: War and Politics in the American Experience*. Armonk, NY: M E Sharpe, 2010.

Sun Tzu (translated by Samuel B. Griffith). *The Art of War*. Oxford, UK: Oxford University Press, 1963.

Van Creveld, Martin. *The Transformation of War*. New York: Free Press, 1991.

4

MODERN MAYHEM

The American Experience in Vietnam, Iraq, and Afghanistan

If the dynamics introduced in the last chapter were merely abstract and academic, their implications would not have large national security impact or import. Unfortunately, that has not been the case. The United States has been the world's leading military intervener of the last century, and it is American intrusion into the domestic instabilities of developing countries that has contributed significantly to the U.S. position as the global leader in employing force over the past sixty years.

These intrusions have continued through the Cold War period and beyond despite their often spectacularly failed results. This is neither to suggest nor to advocate that the United States should cease all interference in what goes on in foreign countries; such an advocacy would be both naïve and subversive of American pursuit of its national interests. Rather, it does suggest that an examination of American investment of military resources for protracted periods in the internal affairs of other states triggers dynamics that virtually assures its failure. This conclusion is strongly supported by the cases examined in this chapter and should serve as a major—even preclusive—warning for the future.

Thanks largely to its intervention in DWICs, the American track record in major conflicts since World War II is not particularly envious. Of the five engagements in which the United States has committed major military resources for prolonged periods of combat and in which it has sustained significant casualties and expended considerable resources, only one has been an unquestionable success in the traditional American sense (Operation Desert Storm in Kuwait). The war in Korea also qualifies as a successful action, because it succeeded in accomplishing the limited goal for which it was undertaken: liberating South Korea from the North Korean invasion and restoring sovereignty to the country. The memory of Korea is, however, tainted. It was a limited war that did not result in the surrender of the enemy, an expectation that was a holdover from the world wars, and for a time, the United States appeared to adopt the total goal of reunifying the Korean peninsula, an outcome it did not attain and a goal from which it retreated. Kuwait and Korea were, however, the successes.

The United States has not succeeded in its other three major endeavors in Vietnam, Iraq, and Afghanistan, lowering considerably our "batting average" at war. Each of these conflicts was advertised, in effect, as a winnable war of necessity, and each failed to live up to that billing. Each appeared to represent a much more important enterprise at the time it was being proposed than it turned out to be. The domino theory in Vietnam, on which the necessity of American involvement was premised, turned out to be true but largely irrelevant. The "fall" of Vietnam to communist control did play a role in the sequence of communizing other parts of Southeast Asia (Cambodia and Laos), but it is difficult to discern the geopolitical disadvantages these events created for the United States, especially in the longer term. The Iraqi adventure was premised on the necessity of removing a malevolent regime providing potential aid and succor to terrorists who had supplanted communists as the *threat du jour* after 9/11. This threat proved to be both false and inflated, and the successors of the Iraq regime (a process still unfolding) appear not to be particular improvements over the Saddam Hussein regime which they replaced, at least from an American viewpoint. The net effect was to replace one set of villains with another. In Afghanistan, the suppression of Al Qaeda's sanctuaries in that country was a laudable and arguably necessary goal, but once that was partially accomplished (Al Qaeda evicted but not destroyed), the subsequent implicit goal of support for a less-than-praiseworthy Afghan successor government has proven questionably desirable and attainable.

Clearly, none of these wars proved winnable, which is probably most important to Americans. There are arguments about whether each one could have been won if "proper" actions had been taken. Most of these arguments are made by disgruntled veterans who believe their efforts were somehow shackled by irresolute politicians, a self-serving argument. In essence, these wars were not won because they could not be won, and the reasons have little to do with levels of political support for what was done or not done to conduct them. More firepower would have prolonged the losing in Vietnam, as it has done in Afghanistan, but that is beside the major point. Each of these wars was effectively a masochist's delight, where the United States intruded itself into a situation for which its military might was not and could not be decisive and where, as a result, the longer it continued to flay itself in a quixotic cause, the greater the pain it inflicted on itself and everyone else—with no reasonable prospect of success.

Some readers may maintain that any comparison between these three unsuccessful experiences is misleading and inappropriate, because each represents a unique set of circumstances. To some extent, such a criticism has merit, in that the exact shape and nature of the problem and its solutions in each of the three cases was indeed different. In looking at each individual case, some attempt will be made to examine those differences. At the same time, however, the underlying dynamics of the three were sufficiently alike that one cannot help feeling he or she has seen this movie before when attention shifts from one to another.

All three, for instance, had strong civil components, with population elements that deeply distrusted one another and sought to gain power at the expense of other groups. Although the bases of division were different in each of the three cases, the common dynamic was to create a desperation and depth of importance that made each a total war for the internal participants (a normal characteristic of civil conflicts). In each case, the United States intervened because it thought it had an important interest in the outcome and because it felt, incorrectly as it turned out, that its intervention could be decisive in influencing the outcome. Underlying the intrusion was the fact, however, that American motives were less deeply held than those of the internal combatants. These were limited wars for the Americans and total wars for the indigenous forces, and it is a simple truth that the motivation of total war is more important than the motivations of limited conflicts. The result in each case was an enigma, in that the clearly most powerful military force in the war (the United States) was also the strategically less moti-vated side. In each case, human factors, including a greater stake in the outcome, helped a lesser force negate the impact of the greater force. This does not mean that individual American soldiers, sailors, and airmen did not fight skillfully or earnestly, but that what happened was more important to the other side than it was to us. The answer to that dynamic was not more firepower or better tactics or logistics. Rather, it was a cause as vital to us as it was to them.

American intervention changed the nature and physical dynamics of each war, but ultimately it probably did not change the final outcome of any of them. What American military intervention accomplished was the prolongation of processes that would have worked out faster without it. Without American physical intrusion in 1965, the unification of Vietnam under communist rule probably would have occurred in late 1965 or early 1966; with American interposition, that unification was delayed until 1975. The end point has not been reached in Afghanistan, but the latest solution of ongoing Afghan civil violence might con-clude with one side or the other triumphant (it is hard to say which). Whatever the outcome is, it will have to wait until the Americans are gone. Iraq inverts the details. There was no overt violence against the Saddam Hussein regime before the American invasion, just simmering hatreds among various groups that the regime had been able physically to crush. The American conquest and occupation unleashed dynamics that had been suppressed. As a result, the outcome (whatever it may turn out to be) will take longer, because the American action required the over-throw of the Saddam Hussein regime; without that action, it is pure speculation whether or when violence would have broken out.

What is true about American intrusion in each case was that it was able to freeze the outcomes *as long as American forces were in place.* Leslie Gelb and Richard Betts observed this dynamic in a 1979 Brookings Institution Press book, *The Irony of Vietnam: The System Worked*. Their central argument was that American military power was sufficient to retard and prevent the North Vietnamese triumph as long as American forces were in the field blocking an unfavorable outcome, but that once the Americans left, internal dynamics took over that produced an outcome the Americans had fought to avoid. In Iraq, the American occupation masked the furious posturing for dominance among Iraqi factions, but the United States presence was simply a palliative, not a cure. Once the last Americans have left Afghanistan, the struggle between the Taliban and the Afghan government will be decided, unaffected by the artificial crutch provided by the Americans. Effectively, this means that American blood and treasure delays the inevitable in these situations, but it could not change those outcomes.

There is an internal American political dynamic that comes across in each case as well. Each war looked like a better idea at the time than it does in retrospect. Because each represented a response to the current ideological threat in place at the time, the idea of intervention initially seemed attractive, based in the language of a necessary response to a grave threat. In each case, there were dissenters from the decision to go to war both inside and outside the U.S. government, but these voices were effectively suppressed or ignored. Ironically, in each of the three cases, there were entirely accurate assessments of the futility of each adventure available before they were undertaken, but those analyses were uniformly rejected as inaccurate, appeasing, or defeatist in the face of commitments of necessity in which the United States could and would prevail. Those within the Kennedy and Johnson administrations (Paul Kattenburg, for instance) who argued the principle dynamic in Vietnam was Vietnamese nationalism were shown the door by the majority, and the same was true in Iraq and Afghanistan. Dissents about throwing an artificial, fractured Iraqi state into a predictable chaos and unwanted ending were drowned out in the shrill cries for blood led by the Bush administration's neo-conservative foreign policy makers. The subtle, virtually unrecognized and unacknowledged pivot of the American effort in Afghanistan from the discrete objective of punishing Al Qaeda to taking sides in the virtually perpetual civil struggle occurred almost without notice, even if a mere cursory survey of Afghan history reveals the folly of outside interference in internal Afghan affairs.

There is abundant detailed literature on each of these conflicts that need not be condensed here, but it is helpful to look at each situation, raising concerns that may be helpful in establishing benchmarks for future American actions. These include whether the United States could or should have known what it was getting into before it became involved, what role internal American elements, including the military, played in forming the "conventional wisdom" that made involvement appear to make sense, and the lessons that could or should have been learned from the experience. These are somewhat different for each of the three experiences.

Vietnam

In some important ways, the Vietnam War was the most understandable American misstep. It was, after all, the second Cold War occasion where the United States had intruded with major military force in a developing world conflict, a situation which was thus arguably unique and without precise precedent or analog. The kinds of criteria outlined in the last chapter were not part of the analytical tool bag at the time. Even if such criteria had been established, the country might still have plunged into war given its own naïve understanding of such situations and its assessment of the times in Cold War terms.

Vietnam was, of course, by no means the first time the United States had intervened in the internal affairs of another state, including military invasion, occupation, and even assumption of the reins of government. Such practices were, if not exactly common, not uncommon either. Between the world wars, the United States had interposed itself frequently into the small republics of Central America and the Caribbean under the banner of the Monroe Doctrine. These adventures were sometimes extensive, as in American overlordship in Haiti for two decades (1916–35). Most were relatively non-controversial (at least for Americans), because they represented limited incursions with relatively small costs in treasure and American lives. The U.S. Marines developed particular experience in these affairs that exhibited itself in a Marine attitude toward Vietnam distinct from the Army.

Vietnam was clearly depicted as a Cell-1 involvement when it was proposed. It was clearly viewed as a war of necessity, an extension of the central conflict between the communist and non-communist worlds to the Southeast Asian peninsula. As such, it was seen a major test of the containment line that had already been breached by the communist assumption of power in China in 1949 and the attempted expansion of the communist world by the North Koreans. These two Asian precedents elevated the symbolism of the attempt to unite the two halves of Vietnam to a much more important place than it might otherwise have occupied. At the same time, the obvious disparity between American military power and the comparatively limited, even primitive military capabilities of the North Vietnamese adversary made American decision makers confident that they could prevail against a "third rate" power like North Vietnam. From the vantage point of early 1960s decision makers and military leaders, involvement in Vietnam seemed both imperative and likely to succeed.

There were, of course, dissenters from this view who saw a very different situation and outcome, and they turned out to have been much more accurate than the purveyors of prevailing wisdom. At the core of the disagreement, there had been division about the nature of North Vietnamese communist intentions. That disagreement went back to the immediate post-World War II liberation of Vietnam from Japanese occupation and the subsequent attempt by the French to reestablish colonial rule, a desire and action very much opposed by the vast majority of Vietnamese. The controversy centered on Vietnamese communist leader Ho Chi Minh.

Ho Chi Minh was an enigma to the West. The son of a schoolteacher (among whose students was South Vietnamese president Ngo Dinh Diem), Ho went into exile in France after World War I and spent part of the interwar years in Chinese prisons. While in France, he helped found the French communist party and returned to Vietnam as the leader of the resistance to the French reimposition of colonial domain. He also posed a quandary to Western, including American, leaders.

The problem was how to think about the Vietnamese leader. Was he the leader of the Vietnamese independence movement, a kind of Asian George Washington, or was he a communist subversive intent of furthering the worldwide communist movement to take over the world? Immediately after the war, Westerners tended to view him primarily as a nationalist figure and thus supported his bid for Vietnamese independence. As the Cold War emerged and evolved, the prevailing view shifted, and Ho was considered more and more a communist leader. By the time the overt conflict to unite the two Vietnams under communist rule began to surface, the nationalist mantel had given way to the view that Ho and his supporters were a simple extension of the international communist conspiracy that should be thwarted. John Foster Dulles was the poster child of this position.

The enigma was that Ho Chi Minh was *both* a nationalist and a communist. This combination was unfathomable for Westerners who believed someone had to be one or the other. The closest analogy was Yugoslav leader Josip Broz Tito, the communist who had led the resistance movement against the Nazis in World War II and had emerged from the war as the popular, yet communist, leader of his country. While Ho Chi Minh was compared to Tito in some circles, Tito's open and very public defiance of the Soviets seemed to set him aside as *sui generis* and thus stifled comparisons with the Vietnamese leader. The Cold War ideological nexus made it impossible to think of someone who could bridge the political gap between communist and nationalist, and Americans gradually came to think of Ho more as a communist than a nationalist. This perception was to help obscure that the revolution he was leading was also both communist and nationalist. As a consequence, while the Americans were fighting communism in Vietnam, many of our Vietnamese opponents were instead fighting for national self-determination, a motivation that proved more durable than ours. Wars to gain national independence from someone trying to deny that freedom tend to be very important and total in nature; wars to avoid a part of the political map changing colors tend to be more geopolitical and limited.

The dynamic of national self-determination was recognized by some who, like Kattenburg, argued that going to war against national self-determination was futile. That sentiment was drowned out by the drumbeat of the Cold Warriors, who saw Vietnam as a much more serious and direct threat to American interests than those who saw the instability in Southeast Asia as a nationalist manifestation. Those who argued nationalism was the primary dynamic tended to be anti-war, either because they believed the outcome was none of our business, futile to pursue, or because the threat was much more localized than the Cold Warriors portrayed. The opponents were ultimately shouted down as wooly-eyed, even cowardly idealists by the more militaristic Cold Warriors, who tended to portray the effort as a patriotic crusade and thus to paint opposition as less than patriotic. As the war dragged on and opposition spread, these positions became increasingly hardened and polarized; to some extent, they endure to contemporary critiques of the Vietnam experience.

If there was legitimate question about whether Vietnam was a war of necessity or choice, there was also question about whether the United States knew how to fight and win it. At the outset, the American military establishment viewed the war in almost completely traditional European military terms, believing that the application of superior American firepower could and would break the North Vietnamese and their Viet Cong allies. This initial judgment was vindicated in the first large American encounter with North Vietnamese regulars in the Ia Drang Valley. That battle, captured in Harold G. Moore and Joseph Galloway's book (later turned into a motion picture) *We Were Soldiers Once … and Young*, was ultimately decided when U.S. airpower overwhelmed a North Vietnamese force that out-numbered the Americans engaged on the ground ten to one. The misleading lesson was that American firepower could prevail, and it proved an incorrect assessment. The real lesson, hardly considered at the time, was that the war was so important to the enemy leadership that it would bear any level of sacrifice to achieve it, a level of determination that Americans simply lacked.

What the North Vietnamese leadership learned from and applied after the Ia Drang battle was that the Americans could not be confronted and defeated on American terms—massive, firepower-intensive encounters where American bulk and raw power could simply overwhelm their opponents. Rather, the North Vietnamese and their allies reverted to the asymmetrical warfare method of the time, Maoist-style mobile-guerrilla warfare, a style which the Americans had not seriously considered previously despite the fact that it was a method of warfare used successfully by the Viet Minh predecessors of the Viet Cong to defeat the French a decade earlier. The American military establishment continued for a long time to ignore this style as irrelevant: firepower would prevail. As the war dragged on, some modifications of ROEs evolved and the American military effort took on more of a counterinsurgency tone than it originally had, but a core constituency within the leadership of the military, wedded professionally and psychologically to conventional warfare, never fully accepted the notion that the opposition in Vietnam represented a basic change in the kind of warfare that would dominate the environment and toward which the U.S. military had to adapt.

This opposition has endured. There is still a level of opinion within the military that the reason the United States lost in Vietnam was not because we were fighting the wrong war in the wrong way, but because we did not try hard enough to prosecute the war on our own terms. The principal whipping boys in this argument are weak-kneed politicians who would not allow the military to give a maximum effort, instead forcing the military effectively to fight "with one hand tied behind its back." In this view, we failed to prevail not so much because we could not win given the situation and the way we fought, but because we did not try hard enough. This belief persists in some quarters to the present.

The question of winnability pivots on whether the United States understood the war in Vietnam and thus what it would take to succeed. Within the Kennedy and Johnson administrations that paved the decisional road to war, there was only sporadic resistance in the early going. One particularly interesting and instructional example is that of Roger Hilsman, a Kennedy confidante who was an official in the State Department at the time the decisions to go to war were made. During World War II, Hilsman had led Burmese guerrilla forces resisting the Japanese occupation, a set of experiences he highlighted in his book, *American Guerrilla*, and he had learned something about the dynamics of this form of asymmetrical warfare in the process. Assuming that the Vietnamese resistance to an American interposition would employ the same kinds of dynamics, he opposed an American intervention on the grounds it would fail. He was sacked for his efforts.

The voices that counseled caution and prudence in the early 1960s were isolated cries in the wilderness and went unheeded in a Cold War atmosphere where military braggadocio and patriotism were conflated. Vietnam was a Cold War challenge, and it could only be met one way—with military force. When one looks back with the 20/20 clarity of hindsight, the warning bells had rung, but hardly anyone heard them over the steady beat of the war drums. The full impact of the folly was only fully accepted when the last Americans abandoned the embassy in Saigon and the South Vietnamese government formally surrendered on April 30, 1975. At that point, the United States had unequivocally lost the war in the political sense that the war was over, none of its political objectives had been achieved, and the opposition had realized its objective of a unified, communist Vietnam. It was the same result that would have occurred probably sometime in 1965 had the United States not intervened and delayed that outcome of the internal struggle for eight years. The irony is that all of the reasons for going to war in the first place, notably those associated with the domino theory and its projections about other regional countries that would fall if Vietnam did, were true, and, in the long run, hardly mattered at all. The Khmer Rouge rampage ensued in the mid-1970s in Cambodia and the United States watched helplessly as the Chinese-backed Khmer Rouge slaughtered one-third of the country's civilians until the Soviet-backed Vietnamese intervened, took over, and ended the carnage. The Pathet Lao communists prevailed in Laos, but the dominos stopped tumbling there. It is hard to argue how or if the United States is particularly worse off as a result, other than that the residual resentment over the war caused the United States to lag behind other capitalist countries investing in a Vietnam that has maintained communist political tyranny but abandoned Marxist economics.

The lesson of Vietnam was obvious at the time but rapidly faded when the Cold War ended. In the wake of America's most negative military adventure (at least until then), the near-universal cry was "no more Vietnams." The slogan had both political and military implications. Politically, it was expressed in a determination to avoid American physical immersion in similar situations elsewhere along the containment line. Ironically, the clearest statement of this political determination came from the staunchest anti-communist among Cold War presidents, Richard Nixon. His "Nixon Doctrine" declared that when friendly regimes were threatened in the future in places that were not absolutely vital to American interests, the United States would provide physical assistance in forms like military aid, training, and equipment, but that American ground forces would not join the fray and thus involve the country in another potential Vietnam-style fiasco. Militarily, a post-Vietnam generation of mid-level military officers worked frantically to understand the asymmetrical warfare dynamics that had resulted in defeat and to devise appropriate strategies and tactics to deal with these situations in the future. In addition to strictly military advice, one of the most basic aspects of this advice was to exercise considerable caution about becoming involved in a future Vietnam-type "briar patch." These lessons appeared to alter American assessments of importance and winnability in developing world situations.

The Vietnam experience also had a deadly conceptual impact on the Cold War paradigm and support for it. The paradigm's vitality had rested on two bases of consensus: agreement on the nature of the communist threat and the impelling need to counter it, mainly through unconditional support for the American military as the primary instrument for dealing with the threat. The negative outcome of Vietnam undercut both premises.

Conceptually, Vietnam was the first overt extension of the paradigm's anti-communist mandate to a DWIC. The problem, of course, was that Vietnam was an expression of national self-determination that happened to be led by a communist. In the fanatical evangelism of the Cold War, leaders like the Dulles brothers ignored the nationalist aspect and focused solely on the communist thread. The result was to distort the situation and thus to mount an inappropriate response involving vital U.S. interests that were not in fact engaged. The pervasiveness of the paradigm for application to all situations became questionable.

More obviously, Vietnam undercut critical support for the crown instrument of American Cold War policy, the military. After Vietnam, support for the military plunged, not to revive until the 1980s. Nothing exemplified this erosion of support more than the need to suspend conscription and install an all-volunteer force: Americans were no longer willing personally to bear arms in the name of a lost and discredited cause in Vietnam. The blame was only partially fair: the military did fight most of the war inappropriately and resist call to change its ways, but it was also saddled with an impossible mission in which it could not succeed. At the time, the latter hardly mattered to a disillusioned population.

Unfortunately, the lessons so painfully learned were themselves abandoned or forgotten in the post-Cold War environment. I will speculate on some of the reasons why in Chapter 5, but the reasons include that the lessons were learned by the middle levels of the officer corps below flag rank (general or admiral) but not so clearly at the highest levels, where an attachment to the traditional European structure and employment dictates was not so thoroughly questioned or modified. At the same time, the end of the Cold War created a euphoria in which much seems to have been forgotten. When terrorism raised its ugly head as the new foe, the United States was ready to charge ahead as if Vietnam had never happened.

Iraq

After a comparatively uneventful decade following the collapse of the Soviet Union in 1991, the United States returned to national security activism after the terrorist attacks in New York and Washington, D.C., on September 11, 2001. The 1990s had been a more ambiguous and introspective decade, as the country adjusted to the meaning of a non-Cold War national security environment and searched for worthy successor threats. Finding none of comparable consequence, the country had the luxury of "sweating the small stuff" in minor internal conflicts in the Balkans and elsewhere. These involvements were, by and large, innocuous and relatively painless encounters for the United States which suggested, among other things, that not all intruding in less developed countries' internal politics resulted in disaster for the United States. Vietnam was receding in the country's rearview mirror; by the time a new Republican administration took office in January 2001, the Vietnam trauma had all but disappeared from decision makers' memories.

The Al Qaeda terrorist attacks shocked the system out of its torpor. Terrorism experts here and abroad had been warning of the likelihood of large-scale terrorist violence for over a decade before the 9/11 attacks. Incidents like the first attempted assault on the World Trade Center in New York in 1993 and Timothy McVeigh's lone wolf assault on the Murrah Federal Building in Oklahoma City in 1995 gave some credence to their entreaties. Still, these isolated incidents seemed idiosyncratic enough or were carried out on foreign soil distant enough not to raise major storm flags in the popular mind.

Osama bin Laden and his compatriots punctured the reveries and unleashed a furtive, sometimes flailing response in which paranoia became an active ingredient. Americans, including most of their leaders, did not comprehend the full import and dimensions of the new, terrible threat posed by international terrorism; most importantly, they had little idea what was coming next. It was a perfect setting for overreaction to flourish, and it did.

The American military adventures in Iraq and Afghanistan were the largest manifestations of that reaction. The two events were separated in time, motivation, and actual relationship to the 9/11 events, but they became linked in the popular mind both because of their proximity to the terrorist events and because those who promoted them actually created links between 9/11 and those countries. What Iraq and Afghanistan also shared was a link to Vietnam that might have been better recognized in less emotional, more reflective times. They were both intrusions into the internal politics of unstable developing world countries.

Moreover, the United States had no reasonable prospect of success, and a large, basically conventional American military campaign was effectively an exercise in trying to force a large round peg into a small square hole.

The factual linkage between the two involvements and their relationship to 9/11 is, in fact, tenuous, tied primarily by their justifications as parts of the "war on terror." Even this link is suspicious. The initial American response in Afghanistan beginning barely a month after 9/11 was a direct action aimed specifically at those behind the attacks who were hiding in government-protected sanctuaries on Afghan soil. That link largely dissolved after the attempt to punish Al Qaeda operatives in Afghanistan failed when the terrorist fled into Pakistani exile and the Americans stayed in Afghanistan anyway. In Iraq, the linkage amounted to no more than a series of what turned out to be untrue or unsubstantiated allegations linking the Saddam Hussein government to the terrorist threat. Other than those charges, the only concrete connection is that preparation for the Iraq invasion caused the Bush administration to withhold or withdraw military assets from Afghanistan in the late months of 2001 that might have allowed Operation Anaconda to succeed in crushing Al Qaeda on the spot.

The war in Iraq may well go down in history as the most controversial military action in the American experience at war for a number of reasons on which I have commented elsewhere (see especially Snow's *What After Iraq?*). Three bases of controversy, however, stand out because they help define the uniqueness of this American adventure and because they point to the folly of the exercise—the common thread of the three unsuccessful American wars.

The first point is that the Iraq War began with a blatant, illegal, and basically unprovoked act of military aggression on a scale and of a nature unprecedented in American history. So depicted, it was also a clearly illegal act in which the United States joined its victim as the only members of the United Nations to break its Charter obligations and invade another member (Iraq set the precedent when it invaded and conquered Kuwait in 1990).

At the time the war clouds were building and the Congress was acting to authorize the Bush administration to take action against Iraq, questions of the illegality (and arguably immorality) of the invasion, conquest, and open-ended occupation were hardly raised outside of a few isolated academic circles. When these concerns were articulated, they were drowned out in a loud, emotional chorus of anti-terrorist jingoism. How much damage was done to the historical American claim of "specialness" in international affairs remains to be determined by historians. It was not the first time the United States had aggressively attacked someone: the Plains Indians are a nineteenth-century testimony to occasional American aggressiveness, even viciousness. Iraq, however, raised the scale in the American experience.

The egregiousness of the U.S. action was made worse—at least in retrospect— by the suspicious justifications for starting it in the first place. This second point is that the American case to the Congress and the public was based in two familiar and largely discredited claims of the Iraqi WMDs program and the regime's link to terrorist organizations like Al Qaeda. These allegations were reinforced by dark imputations that Saddam Hussein might provide WMDs to Al Qaeda. Of these two accusations, the WMDs charge was the less implausible. The Iraqis had an active WMDs program in the 1980s, had used WMDs against Iraqi Kurds and the Iranians in the latter stages of the Iran-Iraq War of 1980–88, and had refused full international inspection of suspicious facilities until the virtual eve of the invasion. When unsubstantiated claims were made about suspected Iraqi WMDs activities, they at least had some ring of possible authenticity. Subsequent exhaustive searches in occupied Iraq were unsuccessful in finding any positive evidence of the existence of such efforts.

The terrorist link never made much sense. Particularly in regard to Al Qaeda, there was no basis for kindred feelings of sympathy beyond some shared dislike for the Americans. The kind of Sunni dictatorship that the Hussein regime represented and Al Qaeda were implacable foes locked in a deadly competition for power in the region; they were not potential bedfellows. Knowledgeable observers knew of this antipathy and dismissed the connection out of hand. Only a state of virtual hysteria over terrorism and a woeful state of public ignorance made such an accusation plausible to the novitiate in the bizarre world of Middle East politics.

There is a more subterranean set of motivations that more convincingly explains why America made war on Iraq. It centers on the so-called neo-conservatives, a group of visionary, right-wing national security analysts, many of whom have close ties to Israel. These *neo-cons*, as they are known, were relatively minor players in the administration of the first Bush but rose to senior positions of power and influence under the second Bush. These advisors shared a visceral hatred of Saddam Hussein and a virtual obsession with his overthrow. Most of them believed the United States had blown a golden opportunity to topple the Iraqi dictator in 1991 and saw in the anti-terrorist frenzy a renewed opportunity to rectify the situation by tying the Iraqis to 9/11. To this end, the neo-cons championed the bogus charges surrounding the alleged Iraqi WMDs program, while semi-privately arguing that once Saddam was overthrown, he might be replaced by a model political democracy that would serve as a beacon for change in the authoritarian Islamic Middle East and, not entirely coincidentally, be less threatening to Israel.

Saddam Hussein was, of course, a reprehensible dictator, but that fact alone hardly makes him a special candidate for overthrow in a world where there are numerous rulers of the same ilk. The removal of Hussein would hardly be bemoaned much anywhere, however, and thus was not an event that could be easily opposed. The vision of a democratic Iraq, on the other hand, was a silly pipe dream the inability of which to realize doomed the American effort from the beginning. To the neo-cons, it hardly mattered. When American forces poured into Iraq on March 19, 2003, Saddam was doomed and the core of their mission was achieved. When the occupation went sour, others could be blamed for the predictable failure to achieve the impossible—a familiar refrain from Vietnam to be repeated in Afghanistan.

This leads to the third point, which is how the Iraq War should be classified in terms of necessity and winnability. What may distinguish Iraq from other military misadventures is that not only was Iraq a clear war of choice that ultimately could not be "won" in any meaningful, acceptable sense of success, but that these characteristics were clearly discernible before the first shot was fired. There were no viable excuses for not knowing what would happen in Iraq.

The Iraq effort was not, of course, advertised as an unnecessary loser by those who proposed it. Action against Iraq was justified as a necessary theater in the war against terrorism, a compelling but false assertion made apparently more sentient by the extremely volatile environment of the aftermath of 9/11. The argument that attacking Iraq represented a vital interest had to be made plausible in the face of prima facie evidence to the contrary. Iraq was, after all, a developing country halfway around the world from the United States with a population one-tenth that of this country. Its only visible asset and claim to importance in the world was its possession of vast and largely unexploited oil reserves (which had been denied to American oil companies since Hussein came to power in 1978). How could anyone suggest a country like Iraq could pose such a threat to the United States that it required a full-scale American military action against it (a war of necessity)?

The answer was two-pronged, based in the nature of the Iraqi threat and the relative ease of achieving it. The case for necessity was publicly tied to the WMDs/terrorism link, and its imputation was clear: something had to be done about Iraq because it was part of the broad and pervasive terrorist threat to the American heartland. Whether or to what degree leaders who formulated this argument believed it is not, and may never be, clear, but it was an argument that carried the day with the Congress, which authorized the president to proceed as he deemed appropriate against this threat. The unstated goals of toppling Saddam Hussein cherished by the neo-cons, or even the darker imputation that what the United States really wanted was Iraqi oil, probably would not have been adequate to "seal the deal" on an American invasion.

The second, and equally fallacious, assumption was that the goal could easily be achieved: Iraq would be completed successfully before the potential critics had a chance to mount their objections. This second prong of the argument had both military and political components, and the calculations of success were both completely, yet predictably, wrong.

An action of the exact dimensions, and especially duration, of the eight-and-a-half years of American combat exposure was never suggested at the time, and had an accurate vision of what would actually transpire been widely held, there would have been critically less support for the enterprise. What the planners saw was a conventional blitzkrieg that would topple the regime, followed by a very brief period of adjustment during which time a new regime came to power and the Americans could exit in triumph hardly bloodied. Secretary of Defense Donald Rumsfeld was the clarion of this view, proclaiming in May 2003 after the conventional military campaign had overwhelmed Iraqi resistance that substantially all American forces would be out of the country by Labor Day. This assessment combined two fantasies: how the Iraqis would accept the occupation and the ease with which a successor government could be formed that could institute stable, representative government in the place of the dictatorship.

The naivete of these assumptions was breathtaking. In 1991, President George H. W. Bush had vetoed an invasion and occupation of Iraq on the grounds that the result would become an unconventional, guerrilla resistance that would create an open-ended commitment for the United States. He was, of course, entirely correct at the time; among those who publicly agreed with him was his son, George W. Bush. That judgment was amply confirmed in the Iraqi reaction to 2003 occupation, a contingency that caught the American military off-guard and unprepared, presumably having forgotten the first President Bush's prescient prediction. As it evolved, the only dynamic that made the asymmetrical war waged against the Americans manageable was that it was carried on by various internal factions which were enemies of one another and thus could not cooperate in efforts against the Americans.

The political solution was also doomed from the beginning. Its dimension—Sunni Arabs versus Shia Arabs versus the Kurds—is well known now, and was to even the casual student of Iraq at the time. Iraq itself is an artificial state cobbled together of territories historically dominated by each faction, and they have never developed a modus vivendi among them. Authoritarian rule in which one faction physically dominates the others has been the de facto solution to Iraqi political differences, and Saddam's Sunni dictatorship was the manifestation the Americans toppled. Doing so certainly interrupted Sunni tyranny against the Kurds and Shiites, but the idea that the result could be a peaceful reconciliation and transition to democracy required an absolute suspension of credulity. The inability of a Shiite-dominated post-occupation regime to establish itself as legitimate among the Sunnis and Kurds was the predictable outcome of a reshuffling of the Iraqi power deck by the American occupiers.

Any assertion of American success in Iraq ultimately comes down to a judgment about the stability and viability of post-occupation Iraq, and there is scant positive evidence that the outcome will be what the United States says it wants. Since the Americans withdrew the last combat forces in December 2011, the Iraqis have regressed to the kind of communal bickering that has always marked Iraqi politics. The current objects of Iraqi disagreement are about the form of Iraqi governance and oil revenues.

What is particularly disheartening about Iraq is that the falsity of claims and the inability to realize results was abundantly clear in advance. It was probably easier to engage in self-delusion on the military level than it was on the political level.

The American military had smashed a larger and more capable version of the 2003 Iraqi military in the Kuwaiti desert over a decade before, and as long as the Iraqis fought a conventional defense, a successful outcome was pretty much ensured. The notion that Iraq could somehow be transformed from a brutal dictatorship to something like a model democracy was much more difficult to sustain given Iraqi history.

Both assessments of likely success turned out to be predictably false, and essentially all the complications that flawed the outcome were well known and advertised in advance. The military aspect was undermined by the false assumption that Iraq would mount a conventional defense, and when that failed, they would capitulate and accept American domain. The assessment was half-right, but it was the half-wrong aspect that doomed the effort. Iraq did mount a token conventional defense that was easily overcome by the American juggernaut, but the Iraqis clearly understood that would be the case. As a result, when the Iraqi armed forces were disbanded (one of several vitally unfortunate American decisions), the former military simply slunk away and reorganized as guerrillas to resist the American occupation (a contingency for which the American military demonstrated only the slightest concern). George H. W. Bush predicted this form of Iraqi reaction twelve years earlier, and there was no shortage of analysts (including the present author) who agreed. Administration planners required a short, decisive war, and accepting the conventional "shock and awe" dismantling of Iraq's armed forces at the end of the fray was the only vehicle for such a conclusion. It was also incorrect, and the residues of the very predictable Iraqi resistance to the American occupation are still evident throughout the country.

The idea that the removal of Saddam Hussein would stabilize the very volatile politics of Iraq is virtually unfathomable. For years, Iraq had been widely acknowledged as the quintessential artificial state, the existence of which in its present form says much more about European geopolitics than any political realities on the ground there. The animosities of the major groups within the Iraqi polity toward one another were equally well known among all those with even a passing understanding of Iraq. As a result, there was no shortage of analysts who pointed out in advance of the invasion that it would likely not only lead to a protracted, asymmetrical resistance but that the end result would likely be a less, rather than a more, stable Iraq politically. The present author was a small voice in that chorus. The critics were largely ignored by the Bush administration. Those critics were also basically correct in their assessments, and had their warning been heeded rather than shunted aside, the long and painful Iraq experience might have been avoided.

Iraq was proposed and defended as a war of necessity which the United States could win. It was neither. American interests have certainly not been realized in Iraq. If indeed there is any clear international beneficiary of the war, it has been Iran, since it has infinitely more influence with the current Shiite regime than it ever could have with its Sunni nemesis, Saddam Hussein. Increasing Iranian influence was certainly not what the United States had in mind in 2003, but it was an entirely predictable outcome. Despite this setback, the United States has not been irreparably harmed by an unwelcome outcome: Iraq was clearly a war of choice, not necessity. Militarily, Iraq began as a conventional war, the kind at which the United States excels, but it became an asymmetrical war, the kind at which the United States is far less proficient. As a result, the military ledger suggests not a defeat in any traditional military sense, but not a success either.

Afghanistan

American military action in Afghanistan is the story of a good idea gone wrong. Although it is all too seldom described in this manner and sequence, the American involvement in that bleak, forbidding, and unforgiving land is really the tale of two conceptually separate missions, connected only in the sense that they are joined by the American decision, for whatever reasons, to remain there after the first mission. The first mission was noble, understandable, and justified, but it failed. The second, follow-on mission grew from the first but is quite distinct both in terms of its purposes and viability. Its nobility and justification are also less unequivocal. The first was brief, occupying the last three months of 2001; the second has dragged on ever since.

The two Afghanistan "wars" need to be separated and evaluated individually. The first mission was a direct response to the terrorist attacks of 9/11 and their aftermath. The heart of that mission was to uproot, capture, or kill the leadership of Al Qaeda that had planned and executed the horrendous attacks. The mission had to be carried out on Afghan soil, because that was where the attack was planned and from which it was directed. Moreover, the Taliban government in power at the time had granted sanctuary to their former allies in the struggle to evict the Soviets (both the Taliban and Al Qaeda have roots in the Afghan *mujahidin* resistance to the Soviet occupation from 1979 to 1989). That sanctuary had included a safe haven for the terrorist organization to organize and operate, including bases for terrorist training facilities. Osama bin Laden and the cadre around him who had executed the attacks were known to be in Afghanistan during and after 9/11. The United States insisted that the Afghans surrender the Al Qaeda perpetrators to American custody; the Taliban refused to do so for a variety of reasons, including the Pashtun code of *Pashtunwali*, which dictates treatment of guests, the specifics of which did not include surrendering them for arrest. In this situation, the American choices were stark: either accept the Taliban refusal, or engage in an act of violence to extricate Al Qaeda from Afghanistan in the face of Afghan government resistance. The U.S. government, of course, chose the latter course.

Deciding to interfere in Afghanistan was uncontroversial, even if it was also technically a direct violation of the sovereignty of a UN member state. The international community, as shocked and offended as the Americans at 9/11, raised no objection, tacitly arguing the action essentially an act of reprisal and provided it international legitimacy. The American public and its elected representatives likewise acquiesced, even applauded, the bold move to assault and punish the 9/11 perpetrators.

This first mission also met the requirements of a good military action. Its objective was clear, unambiguous, overwhelmingly morally justified, and apparently attainable. Attacking the Al Qaeda terrorists was clearly a necessary act, not a response of pure choice, particularly in an uncertain atmosphere where the fear of follow-on attacks seemed real. The only real question, hardly mentioned at the time, was the attainability of the objective and thus whether it was a Cell-1 (necessary and attainable) or Cell-2 (necessary but unattainable) event in the taxonomy introduced in the last chapter.

On paper, it looked like a Cell-1 action. Operation Anaconda was symbolically named after the South American snake that wraps itself around its victim and slowly strangles it to death (the name also graced the original Union plan for defeating the Confederacy in the American Civil War). The idea was that American and associated forces would surround Al Qaeda forces in the rugged eastern Afghan mountains (Tora Bora) and would gradually tighten the perimeter until a strangled Al Qaeda was finally brought to justice. All of this could have been accomplished by the end of 2001, and had it been, there almost certainly would have been no further American involvement in Afghanistan.

The mission did not, of course, succeed. The exact reasons for its failure are still in some dispute, but include faulty intelligence from unreliable and possibly hostile Afghans purportedly aiding the capture (some of whom, it is alleged, may have led bin Laden and his cohorts through the snare to safety) and the famous withholding of key American forces who had been diverted to planning for the invasion of Iraq in 2003. Whatever the causes, the opposition evaded the noose imposed around it and escaped safely to the Pakistani side of the Durand Line (the official border between Afghanistan and Pakistan, but a frontier not accepted by the Pashtun tribesmen who live on either side of it). By the end of 2001, this clearly supported and supportable mission had failed, and the only reasonable anti-Al Qaeda role for American forces was to prevent their return. Whether that was a compelling reason to stay was never entirely discussed or decided. Nonetheless, the Americans did, and the second mission was, by default, engaged.

The initial assault was made easier by the fact that the Taliban were locked in a civil war with other Afghan factions and thus could not divert military resources to try to interfere with the American effort against Al Qaeda. Thus a link was established between the two involvements in the form of an ongoing civil war in Afghanistan. A violent struggle for power (or, just as often, to ensure no one else gains considerable power) is an endemic Afghan condition, usually fought along tribal and clan lines. The Taliban had come to power in 1996 as the result of a similar movement against the hopelessly corrupt, inefficient Afghan coalition government that was an outgrowth of the end of the Soviet occupation in 1989. The Taliban had gained power on a pledge to be honest reformers, but their conduct of office offered little improvement over the government they succeeded, and their bizarre, even atrocious social policies (especially those directed against women) helped spawn a new round of resistance and civil war. It was certainly nothing new in the Afghan experience.

The opposition in 2001 was known as the Northern Alliance, and it consisted mostly of a coalition of tribal, non-Pashtun ethnic groups largely from the northern and western parts of the country, opposed by the Ghilzai Pashtun tribally led elements from the mostly eastern part of the country that supported the Taliban. As is normally the case in Afghan internal struggles, the rebels were as much concerned about denying significant power to the central government (a historical Afghan theme) as anything else. Also as usual, the coalition was weak and changing, and despite the lack of support enjoyed by the Taliban, was basically a standoff before the American arrival.

Prior to 9/11, the United States had essentially no stake in this ongoing struggle. The United States had no formal relationship at all with Afghanistan before the middle 1950s, and after that, it was basically confined to a small and sporadic foreign assistance effort toward the Afghans. Who ruled Afghanistan and how they ruled were not top American priorities. Interest piqued during the Soviet occupation, not so much because of any inherent interest in Afghan welfare as out of a fear that Soviet control would give them a strategic foothold near the Persian Gulf. Moreover, assisting the opposition could create trouble for the Soviets, a much more important interest than anything arising from a devotion to Afghan well-being. As evidence, when the Soviets left, so basically did the Americans as well.

The gist here is that there was no compelling reason based in prior experience for the United States to take sides in the struggle between the Taliban and the Northern Alliance. An indirect interest arose over the attempt to suppress Al Qaeda. Since the Taliban provided protection for the terrorists, their destabilization or overthrow removed a barrier to the American assault on Al Qaeda. Since overthrowing the Taliban was also the Northern Alliance's aim, a marriage of convenience emerged, and American air and Special Operations assistance helped tip the internal war in the insurgents' favor.

The relationship could have, and arguably should have, ended there, but it did not. After it was clear that Al Qaeda had escaped to Pakistan, there was essentially no longer a terrorist threat in Afghanistan. Since eradicating the Afghan landscape of terrorists had been a byproduct of the more basic objective of punishing and destroying the terrorist organization, it was, in a sense, accomplished. The only reason for the Americans to stay based in the original objective was to assure that Al Qaeda did not *return*. A regime in Kabul hostile to the terrorists might help keep them out, but beyond that, there was no compelling reason for the United States to underwrite, promote, and nurture a new Afghan political order—and especially one that flew in the face of a long Afghan tradition of weak central governments.

It is from this chaos at the end of 2001 that the second, ongoing American objective and action evolved. This mission has always been obscured behind the gauzy film of a continued concern over the return of Al Qaeda, which has now been essentially absent from Afghanistan for well over a decade. At heart, however, the Afghanistan War has become a contest to promote governance of that country by the regime that emerged from the 2001 civil war—a war in which the United States had essentially no non-Al Qaeda stake.

Supporters of the war do not, of course, like to have the issue framed in this manner. Why the United States would engage in the longest war in its history to ensure the continuation of a regime in a country of such low salience to the United States as Afghanistan is not a question that even the staunchest defender of the mission would like to answer directly. Thus, official defenses of "staying the course" and leaving behind a viable, stable anti-Taliban government are ultimately justified in terms of the first mission: we are there to make sure the Taliban does not win and invite Al Qaeda back.

That explanation suffers from predictable objections. The most obvious objection, of course, is that there is *no* Al Qaeda threat in Afghanistan: those Al Qaeda terrorists who remain from the original organization are mostly in Pakistan. Thus, if the primary American military objective is suppression of the terrorists, then the action should be concentrated on Pakistan. Indeed, the heart of that mission is the campaign of Predator drone attacks against suspected Al Qaeda hideouts in Pakistan, a highly controversial effort that has the United States at considerable odds with Pakistan over violations of Pakistani sovereignty. The war against Al Qaeda, in other words, has very little to do with Afghanistan and has not for a long time. The only connection between Al Qaeda and the American effort is the prospect that Al Qaeda might return if the Americans fail. This is an arguable proposition.

Another part of the reason the Al Qaeda explanation suffers is because there are hardly any Al Qaeda left anywhere. The drone campaign may be controversial on a lot of grounds (some of which are explored in Chapter 5), but it is hard to argue it has not been effective in killing off Al Qaeda members, and especially leaders. American officials regularly trumpet the extent to which the Predator campaign has thinned the ranks of the terrorist enemy, but they uniformly fail to draw the link to the effort in Afghanistan. Stated simply, the more effective the Predators are in killing off the terrorists in Pakistan, the less need there is for American presence in Afghanistan to counter dead terrorists. There are plenty of terrorists left in the world, including Al Qaeda spinoffs, but they are not in Afghanistan.

This discussion sets the stage for assessing the current effort in terms of the criteria of necessity and winnability. While it is hard to argue that the first campaign in late 2001 was other than a war of necessity, it also turned out to be a failure. The question is whether that outcome was the result of placing American forces in an unwinnable situation or because the mission was bungled. The consensus is the United States, in President Obama's often-used phrase, "took its eye off the ball" by diverting forces from Anaconda to Iraq: a bungled effort. Imagine what the military history of the last decade would be like had they not done so.

What about the second mission? This phase of American involvement is only cosmetically an extension of the original, necessary mission against Al Qaeda. Since Al Qaeda's departure from the country, the heart of the war is a civil contest between the Taliban, which returned to Afghanistan in 2003 after seeking refuge in Pakistani Pashtunistan, to resume the civil struggle. In the interim, the government of Hamid Karzai, a Durrani Pashtun warlord from the Kandahar region, has won support from Afghan clan leaders associated with the Northern Alliance and had also won the blessing and support of the United States and its NATO allies who are part of the International Security Assistance Force (ISAF) in the country. The war that has been going on and of which the United States has been a major (and growing) part ever since is a direct consequence of the renewal of that civil conflict. It is not an extension of the war against terrorism, although it is often described and defended as such. The United States, once again, has taken sides in an internal developing world civil war in which it has little stake. The only thin, tenuous connection between the original and the current missions is the greater likelihood that a triumphant Taliban would allow Al Qaeda to return than would the current government.

The mission so described does not obviously constitute a war of necessity for the United States. The claim to necessity revolves around the Al Qaeda consequences of the "wrong" side winning, and that raises two questions that must be—but have not been—satisfactorily answered. The first is whether even a Taliban government could not be persuaded not to embrace its old allies. Al Qaeda has become very unpopular among Pashtuns in Pakistan, and it is not at all certain that the Afghan Taliban might not throw Al Qaeda under the train if they could get some American guarantees of non-interference or even assistance in return. Making such an offer might be hard to swallow, but it would be a lot less painful than the price of continued interference. Moreover, even if the Taliban did not agree to keep Al Qaeda out of the country, that refusal does not mean the United States would not simply extend the drone campaign from Pakistan to a Taliban Afghanistan ruled by people we oppose and whose objections to our actions would not be particularly troublesome to us. The first question amounts to asking if there are no other ways to keep Al Qaeda out of Afghanistan than a prolonged American presence, and the answer would appear to be that there might be.

The second question is how much of an Al Qaeda threat remains anyway. If reports on the drone attacks are to be believed, the original Al Qaeda "herd" has been pretty thoroughly thinned over the past decade and virtually has no living leadership associated with the old cadre that was in Afghanistan. Even were they to return, it is not clear how potent a force they would be, especially in light of a continued Predator barrage against them.

It is very difficult to conclude that the ongoing campaign in Afghanistan is anything more than a war of choice. Beyond the Al Qaeda question, there is no doubt the United States would, on humanitarian grounds alone, prefer not to see the return of the Taliban and its bizarre, barbaric (at least from our perspective) practices. In context, we have and continue to allow governments who are not much of an improvement to continue in office without contemplating or mounting major military actions against them (Syria and Myanmar are particularly glaring examples). At the same time, the Karzai government and its probable successors are no great shakes either, annually being rated no worse than the second most corrupt national government on the planet on the Corruption Perceptions Index (CPI) of Transparency International. Will Karzai's successors be an improvement? They may be, but don't bet on it.

The other dimension is winnability: can the United States prevail in its program to ensure that the Karzai government or its successor triumphs in the current civil war and can establish the kind of stable central government that the United States insists is needed? At the military level, the prospects seem dubious. The United States has intervened in and attempted to order the politics of a country that has throughout history successfully avoided others doing exactly what the United States is trying to do. No American policy maker would admit that American motives are as harsh and cruel as the Mongolian Hordes, or British colonizers, or the Soviets, of course, but the effect has to be much the same from the view of the rural Afghan villagers and warriors who bear the brunt of the occupation and resistance. Afghans do not like foreign invaders; nobody does, but the Afghans are legendary for their ability to resist and throw out such intruders. We do not think of ourselves as conquerors, occupiers, or colonizers, but it is almost entirely delusional to believe many Afghans do not. The unpromising dynamics of successful intervention in other peoples' internal struggles quite aside, the idea that the United States can be a decisive factor in Afghanistan flies directly in the face of literally thousands of years of history.

Achieving the political goal of a stable Afghan political system featuring a strong, competent central government is also fanciful. The present regime in Kabul has had over a decade to establish itself as a positive—competent, non-corrupt—governing force, and it has basically failed. The anecdotal evidence is overwhelming that many rural Afghans do not want to be liberated by the government, because the government will steal them blind if that happens. Moreover, the history of an independent Afghanistan, which goes back roughly to the same time the United States gained its independence, has consistently been one of resistance to a strong central government. There has also been a strong rural–urban cleavage in the Afghan population, and one of its clearest manifestations has been a distrust of central government in the rural areas. Afghanistan has rarely had such a political system, and most Afghans prefer a highly decentralized, more confederal form of governance through something like the *loya jurga* system of periodic conferences among tribal elders. Once again, it is more a product of American arrogance than Afghan reality to think we can impose a different system on them. The conclusion must be that Afghanistan is an unwinnable war of choice, precisely the kind of conflict the United States should avoid.

Unpalatable Menu Choices

The problem facing the American national security policy and execution should be becoming clear by now. Shorn of the organizational and conceptual security blanket of the Cold War but without a successor paradigm to guide its actions, the United States has floundered twice since the end of the Cold War into major military actions that were unfortunate and ill-advised. In Vietnam, it misapplied its principles with the same outcome. All have failed or are, certainly in a political sense, in the process of reaching conclusions that do not meet American expectations expressed in the political objectives for which they were undertaken. The records of the two post-Cold War forays are not identical, and neither is the same as Vietnam. What draws them together is they were entirely predictable American failures. Recognizing why they did not and could not succeed is the key to avoiding repetition of the same mistakes in the future.

All were, or became, unwinnable wars of choice. There would have been no war in Iraq in 2003 had the United States not started one, and the fact of American instigation is the unique contextual setting of that situation. If the goal was to disassemble the old Iraq and replace it with something better, it was partially a success: the Saddam Hussein regime fell, but the process of creating a better successor remains, charitably, a work in progress. Less charitably, Iraq is in the process of moving from a Sunni dictatorship to a Shiite autocracy or breaking apart into separate Sunni, Shiite, and Kurdish states. Anyone who finds this evolution surprising simply has not paid attention to the region's history. Where it will lead is anyone's guess; that it will not end up the way the United States hoped is probably as close to a given as we have.

Afghanistan is built from the same fabric. What might be called the American Afghan War Part I (the campaign to capture Al Qaeda) was at least an arguable war of necessity that could have been won had it been competently led and conducted. It was not, and so it failed. The greater problem and lesson surrounds the American Afghan War Part II, which has pursued the feckless goal of creating a stable, strong, anti-Taliban central government in Kabul, a goal the Afghan people either do not share in principle or at least do not desire under the current, American anointed and blessed regime. Vietnam, by contrast, was at heart a war of nationalism where the United States ended up on the wrong side of the Vietnamese desire to be united as one country, quite regardless of the ideology of the liberators.

These kinds of morasses occur when a country, in this case the United States, involves itself in unstable developing world internal conflicts (DWICs) with armed forces. The underlying dynamics of these situations—particularly when outsiders like the United States become involved—are quite similar and lead to similar outcomes. This statement of the dynamics is intended to be cautionary, because in all three situations, there is no indication that the United States understood the complexities and vagaries of the situations into which they intruded and believed that American military power could be decisive in ways and directions that proved incorrect.

The next chapter examines the reasons for these mistakes in more detail, but that analysis can be previewed from the experience examined here. One common theme has been to treat individual situations as sui generis, because the atmospherics were different and apparently special. Vietnam was a Cold War communist battle fought in steamy mountainous jungles; Iraq was about over-throwing and liberating an Islamic population from a brutal dictator; and Afghanistan was a war of liberation fought in the bleak high mountains of the top of the world. There was, however, one common element in all three that explains a lot: all three wars began as localized conflicts in which an outsider stuck its military nose, and in all three, the internal inhabitants came to resent that intrusion. This is nothing new in history, even if it is a dynamic shrouded in differing cloaks. The Montagues and Capulets of Shakespeare not only preceded the Jets and the Sharks of *West Side Story*, they both reflected the same kind of theme as Ovid wrote about in *The Metamorpheses* in the form of the tragedy of Pyramus and Thisbe. What was different in each case were the atmospherics: feuding clans in Verona, street gangs in Manhattan, or rival next-door Romans. Those different settings did not hide the common themes of us-versus-them hatred and tragedy.

Those who reject the commonalities emphasize the uniqueness of each event and thereby distort the meaning. The answers to common failures in the three wars are often attributed to a lack of adequate U.S. military effort, but that argument overlooks two points. The first is that these were, for the United States at least, limited wars in which escalation may have changed the very nature of the wars: direct military action against Hanoi during the Vietnam War is an example. The other point is that such solutions reflect distinctly Western, American pre-dilections about how war is fought. The Western, Cold War–forged answer is to up the ante, mainly with more firepower, at which the U.S. excels, even if such a response is inappropriate and nonproductive. As a caricature of this attitude, Lt. General Thomas McInerney (USAF, Ret.) opined on December 16, 2010, in an article for FoxNews.com that the secret of success against Afghanistan was "attacking the Taliban ... more aggressively with powerful additions to our kill chain." Despite the unfortunate imagery of "kill chains," the problem is that what he suggests almost totally misses the point about what the war in Afghanistan is about.

The analysis to this point has been on how the contemporary condition has been reached. It does leave the United States with an "unpalatable" set of menu options for confronting the problems that lie out there in the world. Those options are difficult in large part because almost all of them are much more akin to Vietnam/Iraq/Afghanistan than they are to Desert Storm. The nature of the bleak prognosis of involvement in such situations also needs further explanation.

Bibliography

Barfield, Thomas. *Afghanistan: A Cultural and Political History*. Princeton, NJ: Princeton University Press, 2010.

Berman, Larry. *Johnson's War: The Road to Stalemate in Vietnam*. New York: W. W. Norton, 2013.

——*No Peace, No Honor: Nixon, Kissinger, and Betrayal in Vietnam*. New York: Touchstone, 2002.

——*Planning a Tragedy: The Americanization of the War in Vietnam*. New York: W. W. Norton, 1983.

Builder, Carl. *The Masks of War: American Military Styles in Strategy and Analysis*. Santa Monica, CA: RAND Corporation Publication Series, 1989.

Campbell, Kenneth J. *A Tale of Two Quagmires: Iraq, Vietnam, and the Hard Lessons of War*. New York: Paradigm, 2007.

Chandrasekaran, Rajiv. *Imperial Life in the Emerald City: Inside Iraq's Green Zone*. New York: Alfred A. Knopf, 2007.

Coll, Steve. *Ghost Wars: The Secret History of the CIA, Afghanistan and Bin Laden, from the Soviet Invasion to September 11, 2001*. New York: Penguin, 2004.

Crews, Robert D. and Amin Tarzi (eds). *The Taliban and the Crisis in Afghanistan*. Cambridge, MA: Harvard University Press, 2008.

Diamond, Larry. *Squandered Victory: The American Occupation and the Bungled Effort to Bring Democracy to Iraq*. New York: Times Books, 2005.

Ewans, Martin. *Afghanistan: A Short History of Its People and Politics*. New York: Harper Collins, 2002.

Gelb, Leslie, and Richard K. Betts. *The Irony of Vietnam: The System Worked*. Washington, DC: Brookings Institution Press, 1979.

Glantz, Aaron. *How America Lost Iraq*. New York: Jeremy Tarcher/Penguin, 2005.

Haass, Richard N. *Wars of Necessity, Wars of Choice: A Memoir of Two Iraq Wars*. New York: Simon and Schuster, 2009.

Hashim, Ahmed S. *Insurgency and Counter-Insurgency in Iraq*. Ithaca, NY: Cornell University Press, 2006.

Herring, George. *America's Longest War: The United States and Vietnam, 1960–1975*. New York: McGraw-Hill, 1995.

Hilsman, Roger. *American Guerrilla: My War behind Japanese Lines*. Washington, DC: Brassey's, 1990.

Johnson, Robert. *The Afghan Way of War: How and Why They Fight*. Oxford, UK: Oxford University Press, 2011.

Jones, Seth G. *In the Graveyard of Empires: America's War in Afghanistan*. New York: W. W. Norton, 2009.

Kattenburg, Paul. *The Vietnam Trauma in American Foreign Policy: 1945–1975*. New Brunswick, NJ: Transaction Books, 1980.

Krepinovich, Andrew F. *The Army and Vietnam*. Baltimore, MD: Johns Hopkins University Press, 2986.

McInerny, Lt. Gen. Thomas. "The 'Surge' Afghanistan Needs." *FoxNews.com*, December 15, 2010.

Moore, Lt. Gen. Harold G. (Ret.), and Joseph L. Galloway. *We Were Soldiers Once … And Young: Ia Drang—The Battle That Changed the War in Vietnam*. New York: Harper Perennials, 1993.

O'Neill, Bard E. *Insurgency and Terrorism: From Revolution to Apocalypse* (2nd ed.). Washington, DC: Potomac Books, 2005.

Packer, George. *The Assassin's Gate: America in Iraq*. New York: Farrar, Straus, and Giroux, 2005.

Polk, William R. *Understanding Iraq*. New York: Harper Perennials, 2006.

Pike, Douglas. *PAVN—People's Army of Vietnam*. Novato, CA: Presidio Press, 1986.

Pollack, Kenneth. *The Threatening Storm: The Case for Invading Iraq*. New York: Random House, 2002.

Rashid, Ahmed. *Descent into Chaos: The United States and the Disaster in Pakistan, Afghanistan, and Central Asia*. New York: Penguin, 2009.

Record, Jeffrey. *Dark Victory: America's Second War Against Iraq*. Annapolis, MD: Naval Institute Press, 2004.

Ricks, Thomas. *Fiasco: The American Military Adventure in Iraq*. New York: Basic, 2006.

Snow, Donald M. *Cases in American Foreign Policy*. New York: Pearson, 2013.

——*What After Iraq?* New York: Pearson Longman, 2009.

Snow, Donald M., and Dennis M. Drew. *From Lexington to Baghdad and Beyond: War and Politics in the American Experience*. Armonk, NY: M E Sharpe, 2010.

Sorley, Lewis. *A Better War: The Unexamined Victories and Final Tragedy of America's Last Years in Vietnam*. New York: Harvest, 2007.

Summer, Harry G. Jr. *On Strategy: A Critical Analysis of the Vietnam War*. Novato, CA: Presidio Press, 1982.

Sun Tzu (translated by Samuel B. Griffith). *The Art of War*. Oxford, UK: Oxford University Press, 1963.

United States Army and Marine Corps. *Counterinsurgency Field Manual (U.S. Army Field Manual 3-24, Marine Corps Warfighting Publication 3-33.5)*. Chicago, IL: University of Chicago Press, 2007.

United States Marine Corps. *Afghanistan: Operational Culture for Deploying Personnel*. Quantico, VA: Center for Advanced Cultural Learning, 2009.

Westmoreland, William C. *A Soldier Reports*. New York: Dell, 1980.

5

STICKING YOUR GUNS IN OTHER PEOPLE'S BUSINESS

One reason the United States has blundered its way into places like Vietnam, Iraq, and Afghanistan is because it has lacked a proper framework within which to organize the decision process about intervention. The United States lacks a successor framework or paradigm to the Cold War model that is specifically designed for situations quite unlike those that faced the country in its confrontation with Soviet-led communism. Further, the United States lacks a full appreciation of the human dynamics of developing world conflicts. More specifically, it lacks an appreciation that American interference, no matter what our intentions may be, can and often does make matters worse and make more likely a negative outcome for the United States than a less aggressive stance might produce.

These kinds of revelations run counter to the American self-image of itself in the world. Americans are quintessential "do-gooders" whose most fundamental instinct is to help those less fortunate. That spirit is captured in the historic offer on the Statue of Liberty to "give me your poor, your huddled masses yearning to breathe free" awaiting immigrants in New York Harbor. That poem captures two essential self-depictions of Americans that extend to the developing world: a bond with and desire to help the less fortunate and a road map to salvation through freedom and self-determination. The bond is further strengthened because the United States shares the decolonization experience with these parts of the world, since the American Revolution was an eighteenth-century prototype of decolonization in the second half of the twentieth century.

These instincts were both complicated and reinforced by the coincidence of the Cold War and decolonization. The complication came from the inability to separate the two phenomena as almost entirely independent problems for which common solutions were not applicable. Of the two problems, the Cold War was overwhelmingly more immediate and compelling, and so the paradigm for its management was properly given top conceptual billing, at the expense of developing an independent plan for organizing efforts regarding the emerging problems of the new developing world. The American view and attitude toward the African-Asian world became an extension, even an overlay, of Cold War politics in a very different physical setting.

In essence, the developing world became a theater of the Cold War competition, where an evangelical communism and an equally proselytizing Western ideology clashed in a red-blue map exercise driven both by geopolitical and idealistic goals. The heart of that competition was communism versus anti-communism, whereas most of the problems that faced the emerging countries were internal, dominated by the needs for development and reconciliation of diverse populations as the means to national development and stability. The Cold War overlay barely addressed these problems, focused as it was on the red-blue map competition. The victim was any serious attempt to develop a conceptual framework that specifically applied to actual conditions in these parts of the world. As a result, when the Cold War ended, there was no distinctive, obviously valid framework through which to view the problems of the developing world.

The Cold War emphasis did, however, provide some reinforcement to the American predilection regarding its place in the world. The Statue of Liberty's greeting does include the desire of less fortunate people to be "free," and to most Americans, freedom is equated with an emulation of American political and economic values. From this presumption flows the idea that what other peoples want (or if they do not realize what they want, need) is to graft something like the American system to theirs. In a general sense, this presumption is at least arguably defensible, but it is not the basis for an overarching paradigm for the developing world. Trying to clone the principles of "one man, one vote" democracy is not, for instance, an immediate solution to the political problems of Iraq. In that country, it has had easily as many shortcomings as virtues, since the effect of adopting a U.S.-style system has been to transfer Sunni powers of domination to the more numerous Shiites, a nice change if one is Shiite, but not necessarily the balm to soothe all national wounds. The advocacy of a strong central government in Afghanistan is a similar example.

The further legacy of applying the Cold War paradigm to the developing world is a predisposition toward personal activism to solve problems that arise. In the Cold War sense and context, it was necessary to be ready and willing to take active measures to ensure the other side did not reap damaging advantage. In a developing world context where there is no obvious "other side" (terrorist organizations being a partial exception), the rationale for activism is dramatically reduced. A paradigm specifically designed for the developing world would likely reflect more restraint; by default in an environment where no such alternate worldview exists, Cold War activism remains the impulse.

The vacuum created by an inaccurate worldview for dealing with the developing world becomes obvious when the standards introduced in Chapter 3—the importance and prospects of successful activism—are applied. Just how important are instabilities in the developing world to the United States? More specifically, how important are those instabilities when they are manifested in violence and when an American response may also require the application of U.S. armed force? Where the intervention of the United States may seem warranted by events, what are the likelihoods of success, and at what cost? How does a low level of probable success affect the calculation of possible involvement? Does the virtual certainty of success elevate the attractiveness of involvement regardless of importance? Do we understand how our involvement will alter the situation and make different outcomes more or less likely and difficult?

All of these are questions for which the United States does not have current accepted answers. Each question involves a range of possibilities, not a simple either/or, yes/no set of responses. The importance of involvement is, of course, another way of asking whether involvement would represent a war of necessity or a war of choice. In the Cold War, such involvements were elevated to involvements of necessity by Cold War considerations. Vietnam is the clear case in point: the outcome of a power struggle over who ruled that part of Southeast Asia had relatively little importance to the United States as such, and were it viewed in that light, the answer would almost surely have been that any involvement was one of choice. Since Americans are more clearly drawn to situations where they feel they are forced to fight, the situation would almost certainly have been seen as not important enough to fight over. But that was not how Vietnam was viewed. As a theater of the Cold War and a test case in American resolve in the red-blue map contest, a favorable outcome seemed vitally important, making it appear an involvement of necessity.

Without the overlay of the Cold War, most developing world crises do not obviously involve the most important, vital interests of the United States. The only geopolitical overlay with some conceptual links back to the Cold War involves the contest with terrorism, and it is no surprise that both the wars in which the United States has been involved since the early 1990s were advertised as wars of necessity arising from the war on terrorism. The other basis of American interest in extreme, violent developing world conflict has been humanitarian, the desire to alleviate great human suffering. Modern electronic mediation of events provides the incentive in the often gory depiction of human suffering at the hands of obnoxious regimes (Syria and Libya are recent poster children), and the question of importance depends critically on the level of interest the United States has in alleviating world suffering and inequity.

That calculation is affected by the potential for success. Winnability is a slippery concept, because of our marginal understanding of the military dynamics of DWICs and our dismal record in predicting outcomes or incorporating skeptical views into the decision process. Nobody who made positive recommendations on the War in Afghanistan Part II had any idea that the contest would drag on without definitive result for over thirteen years, but it has. Since the United States (and, in fairness, nearly everyone else) has devised no satisfactory methodology for fighting or predicting the outcomes of such conflicts, the effect is to make judgments on an ad hoc, seat-of-the-pants basis. We engaged in a very limited form of involvement in Libya, because the situation permitted it; we avoided direct military action in Syria because conditions seemed nowhere nearly so propitious. Adhocracy can also be pragmatism and is not entirely a bad approach; it is not, however, an entirely satisfactory planning tool for measuring and deciding on policy toward a very complex, highly differentiated world environment.

These kinds of factors form part of the problem of dealing with the use of military force in the developing world. There is yet another dynamic, hinted at in the preceding pages, that is particularly critical and damningly cautionary. That is the human factor in DWICs and the impact that outside intervention has on those conflicts and the prospects that an outside intervener like the United States can influence positively the outcomes of these situations. This dynamic is critical and normally overlooked or underappreciated. It cannot be if a successful paradigm is to be constructed.

The Temptation: Civil Disorders with International Consequences

Instability and latent or ongoing violence is widespread in the developing world, but the United States is not equally drawn to all instances of such instability—at least to the extent of being tempted and occasionally succumbing to the temptation of active military involvement. Rather, there is a subset of situations with some geopolitical base to which the United States is drawn. Those circumstances are, as the section heading states, civil disorders with apparent international consequences.

The idea of "international consequences" is the key here, but it is an admittedly vague concept stated so simply. Getting to the core of what it means, especially as a factor that may create international interest or, in the extreme, action, is somewhat like peeling the layers off an onion until one arrives at the core.

At its most preliminary level, *international consequences* refer to civil disorders, the effects of which are not confined to the country in which they are occurring, but indeed spread across borders into other countries where they produce impacts of concern. Disorders that remain contained within the boundaries of a particular country will, in only very exceptional conditions, create an international or American interest. The ethnic slaughter in Rwanda in 1994 is something of an exception, but much of the international angst and reaction occurred well after the murders ended in the form of trying to bring the perpetrators to justice and to help rebuild and recover from the disaster. An uprising in Tibet against continued Chinese rule of that territory, on the other hand, is unlikely to produce much international reaction. When the Tibetans periodically rise in some opposition to their Han Chinese overlords, in general their actions are fairly quietly suppressed. The international reaction is usually limited to some verbal hand-wringing and vows of support for the Dalai Lama. Internal disorders that remain parochial and do not produce horrific violence generally remain on the peripheries of international concern.

Cases of purely internal conflict are becoming increasingly rare, for at least two interconnected reasons. On one hand, the amount of global information available, and the inability of regimes to entirely control the observation and reporting of events means that even the smallest and most internationally insignificant happening will be brought to the attention of the global "village." Fifty years ago, the technology was not available to publicize disorder and its consequent violence everywhere; it is today. Since disorder almost inevitably includes human suffering, the result will be international awareness of the consequences of disorder and some international public condemnation. The case of Boko Haram's terrorist kidnapping of young Nigerian girls is an example. This leads to the second observation: those who have a stake in the outcomes of otherwise completely internal disorders often think of international concern as a tool to aid their particular causes. Riot police wading into a crowd of demonstrators can create enough bloodied victims to elicit international condemnation that may affect the outcome of the uprising; manipulating events by stimulating violence that receives international media coverage may thus be a way to increase sympathy and make success more probable.

If virtually all internal disorders now have some international repercussions, they are not equally important to the rest of the world. The United States does not, for instance, dispatch the Marines to every capital in which rioting breaks out, even if some Americans may be caught up in the violence (if enough Americans are placed at great-enough risk, that calculation may be reversed, of course). Just as in George Orwell's depiction of the pigs in *Animal Farm,* some international repercussions are clearly more equal than others. The next layer of the onion is how one places priority on the international importance and consequence of particular internal disorders: which ones get our attention?

The experience of the last sixty years or so suggests one way to draw a distinction. There are two kinds of situational calculations that have produced some form of reaction by the international community (and more specifically the United States) to otherwise internal disorders: geopolitical and humanitarian concerns. This distinction is easier to make and apply in specific incidences in the abstract than in reality. In almost all situations, there are elements of each present: even the most horrible manmade or natural humanitarian disaster has some repercussions that seep across international borders, and internal situations with principally international security implications usually contain a prominent dollop of humanitarian concern as well. The two kinds of concern were prominent in different post–World War II periods, although they are both reasonably prominent in the contemporary world.

Geopolitically interesting situations have been associated most prominently with internal conflicts in which the outcomes may have an effect on power balances and thus the security of states beyond the borders in which a particular conflict may occur. The most obvious kinds of situations of this nature occurred during the Cold War, when one side (usually the government) was supported by the United States and the other (usually those seeking to overturn the government) was assisted by the Soviet Union or China. In these conflicts, a victory for the regime or its opponents could have consequences in red-blue map terms for the country involved and possibly beyond the border into nearby countries. Interest in Vietnam is a clear case in point: victory there determined whether that part of the Southeast Asian peninsula turned red or blue on a Cold War political map, but it was further assumed by the domino theory that the victor would be able to use success in Vietnam as a platform to influence similar events in places like Laos, Cambodia, Thailand, and beyond. This rationale proved at least partially true in that the first two dominos fell, but it was also partially false (the most consequential "domino," Thailand, did not fall and considered the imputation that it was just another domino insulting) and largely irrelevant in broader geopolitical terms.

The mantel of ideologically based geopolitical motivation disappeared with the end of the Cold War but returned in the current millennium in the form of opposition to terrorism, depicted as a "war" on terrorism. The outcomes of civil conflicts in geopolitical terms are now often assessed in terms of whether particular outcomes will result in the creation of regimes sympathetic to terrorists. That has been the clear rationale for American involvement in the second phase of the Afghanistan War and is the current reason for a concern over internal unrest and disorder in Yemen, a desperately poor, desolate hunk of desert on the Arabian Peninsula with virtually no importance beyond its strategic placement near naval choke points going into the Red Sea.

All geopolitical motivations are not directly or entirely ideologically driven. Philosophies of governance and alignment on issues can be factors outside a specific ideological framework but have geopolitical imperatives. Who (if anyone) rules Somalia, for instance, is important at least partially because it would be geopolitically beneficial to almost everyone to have a government in Mogadishu that could control the actions of pirates operating from Somali bases. Location can thus provide a geopolitical base, as can the regional prominence of particular places and whether particular countries possess things that others want or need.

Disorder in some places is geopolitically interesting simply because of location and their relative weight regionally and beyond. The world, for instance, has not been able to avoid altogether an interest in the instability in Egypt since the Arab Spring spread there in January 2011. Egypt is the largest of Arab states in population and sits at a strategic junction between the historic Near East and Africa. It has been a place over which people have fought for millennia, because the Nile River Valley has long been a fertile granary for the region and beyond. Moreover, it has been, at least since the 1970s, a comparatively moderate, moderating force in the regional competition between Israel and its neighbors. A tranquil and stable Egypt (internally and thus internationally) is clearly in the geopolitical interest of people within and outside the region.

Location and size are thus not inconsequential concerns in determining levels of interest. Another major form of international consequence is the possession by developing states of commodities that others want or depend upon. These commodities are rarely finished goods or services, but normally natural resources. Of all these, the most obvious and internationally motivating is petroleum energy, since its interruption and, in the worst case, withholding, can have direct and dire international consequences. Baldly put, countries with lots of oil—and nothing more—are internationally interesting far beyond their salience by any other measure.

Iraq may be the quintessential case in point. Iraq is, in one sense, a model of the bases of internal disorder. It is, as already suggested, a totally artificial state that was the mistaken delusion of the British foreign office that probably should never have come into being in its present form at all. Its history has been rocky and conflicted: Sunni and Shiite Arabs at one another's throats and exploiting one another and separatist Kurds far more interested in living in a place they call Kurdistan than in a union with the fractious Arabs. Rule and a semblance of apparent stability have existed generally only when some of form of tyranny has been imposed by one group on the others. The Iraq War of 2003 removed the Sunni from that command role, and after an eight-year period of feckless occupation intended to nurture tolerance and support for democracy among the feuding factions, "one man, one vote" Iraq appears headed for a period of unstable Shiite autocracy that will almost certainly result in a new round of internal violence with an uncertain outcome, as events in 2014 seemed to presage.

At the risk of appearing crass, hardly anyone who does not live in or near Iraq would care about any of this—at least not enough to try to do something forceful about it—without oil. Iraq is a fair-sized country with a population of around 30 million: a medium-sized country by regional standards. It is wedged between Shiite Iran and Sunni Saudi Arabia, both of which seek to maximize its own and to minimize the other's influence in the country. This international consequence is of interest beyond the region almost entirely because the Saudis, Iraqis, and Iranians have the largest conventional petroleum reserves in the world except for Canada's tar sand deposits.

Without oil, there would be minimal interest in what happens in Iraq. The interest the rest of the world has in Iraq comes from Iraq's possession of some of the world's largest and most accessible reserves in Shiite Arabistan (the southern part of the country) and in the shadows of the Zagros Mountains in Kurdish territories. The oil is abundant, it is of high quality (relatively low sulfur content), and it is easily accessible (comparatively close to the surface) due to limited exploitation. Iraqi oil is a treasured commodity, and among those with the most rapacious appetites have been the Americans, who were denied any access to Iraqi petroleum during Saddam Hussein's rule. Some observers (the present author included) have suggested this exclusion had more to do with American motivation to invade the country than is publicly admitted.

Remove petroleum from the Iraqi geopolitical equation, and international interest in internal unrest in the country quickly subsides. Fighting would likely still exist between the various factions, and there would be levels of atrocity: Saddam Hussein's 1988 use of chemical weapons against rebellious Kurds in Halaba is a demonstration of that likelihood. The atrocities in Iraq, however, pale beside those in a place like Rwanda, where over a half-million people were slaughtered. Iraq has oil; Rwanda does not. When the United States started the Iraq War in 2003, exploitation of North American shale oil and gas was no more than a vague prospect, and Iraqi oil was a coveted resource (the United States government disingenuously denies this motive). In 2014, shale is the centerpiece of American energy policy. Would the United States invade Iraq today?

Geopolitics has waxed and waned as a motivator. It was the prime consideration in terms of international interest during the Cold War with communism as the motivating force, and it has been the major influence since 9/11 and its consequent focus on terrorism. During the 1990s, there was an ideological lull, and humanitarian motivations became a more prominent factor for determining the extent and level of interest created in internal developing world disorders. Although there has been no event of the drama and finality of the fall of Soviet communism, there are some reasons to believe the geopolitical motivation of anti-terrorism may be losing some of its intensity. Whether this change will result in a revival of interest in humanitarian concerns remains to be seen, but that is certainly a possibility.

The humanitarian criterion for interest derives from a concern with the atrocious things that people within countries do to one another. Man-made (as opposed to naturally caused) disasters have been particularly prevalent in developing countries that were artifacts of demographic imperfections in colonial empires. As already noted, colonies were often established with little knowledge or care about the political composition of the territories they aggregated into colonial units, and when these units were granted independence pretty much within the bounds of colonial designations, the result was often a crazy quilt of simmering hatreds among sub-groups that had not been reduced during colonial rule. When the veil of suppression was lifted, one of the new freedoms was to resume intergroup animosities, often vividly in blood.

Most of the humanitarian disasters that have attracted international concern have some multinational component at their core. There is, unfortunately, no shortage either of human suffering or inequity in the world, and notably in multinational developing world states. During the Cold War, efforts to understand and create solutions for these kinds of problems proceeded in the shadow of more direct Cold War, geopolitical concerns, and so the effects were limited and, in some cases, decidedly half-hearted. The contest between Cold War geopolitics and developing world stabilization was really no contest at all: geopolitics ruled, and the developing world got the leftover crumbs. As a result, when the Cold War ended, the international existence of developing world instabilities remained unattended in large measure. There were, indeed, more of these problems than could easily or even plausibly be addressed by an international system breathing a decade-long sigh of relief that nuclear Armageddon had been avoided. As the new millennium arrived, that sigh of relief was supplanted by a new geopolitical crisis in the form of terrorism. Developing world instabilities did not cease, and many of them, especially in the Near East and adjacent areas, even adopted some of the patina of terrorism-driven geopolitics (e.g., Somalia). Civil disorders with international consequences have endured; a consensual determination about what to do about them has remained elusive.

The dynamics that create international—and specifically American—interest in internal disorders is important and the third layer of the onion, because the nature and intensity of that interest is a primary determiner of whether the United States may develop a sufficient interest in a particular place to contemplate or actively involve itself through physical intervention. At the same time, the forms of motivation that capture the American interest help determine the nature and quality of actions the United States may contemplate and implement. In turn, those determinations are the core of the onion: what will the United States do, and can it succeed?

Siren's Call: Intervention and Delusion

The instinct to try to relieve great human suffering is certainly not ignoble. The natural reaction to events that place other humans in dire straits is to reach out and help, and it is not an urge held exclusively by Americans. When the cause of human deprivation and misery is the malevolent actions of other people and the visible impact is an obvious slaughter of the apparent innocents, the result can be a righteous rage that seeks both relief for the afflicted and even retribution against those who inflicted it. It would be somehow inhuman not to feel this way.

This instinct is certainly a strongly held impulse of Americans. In other works, I have referred to this as the "do something syndrome," a catchphrase intended to capture the unfocused reaction to try to rectify perceived wrongs. Wanting to help is an instinctual reaction; the problem comes from responding before one fully understands the nature of the tragedy one is encountering and thus what can and cannot, should and should not, be done. When one fully understands the situation, one can assess accurately pathways to relief. If one fully comprehends the nature and causes of a humanitarian tragedy, doing something may result in doing something good. If one does not understand this dynamic, doing some-thing may change things, but not necessarily make the situation any better, and perhaps even worse. In this latter case, some or all of the victims may resent rather than appreciate the effort, and the result may be disillusion both for those doing something and those for whom that something was done.

Manmade humanitarian disasters often make solutions appear easier than they are in fact. Situations of extreme suffering and political disorder are by their very natures fluid and confusing. The images that one has are those that can be captured by observers and participants whose perspective may be limited or impure: journalists recording horrific events, the genesis of which they do not understand, or participants who want to publicize a particular side to the violence. What is visible and activates the urge to do something is the horror and violence; what is not so evident is what dynamics underlay the tragedy, who is doing what to whom and why, and what the consequences of various actions may be for both the target population and for those moved to intervene on their behalf. These calculations are rarely as easy and as clear cut as they may appear at first blush.

Careful analysis is not necessarily a characteristic of activating the do something syndrome. Internal violence is normally and inherently passionate and brings out extreme behavior on all sides. That passion is all too often manifested in gruesome injuries to people whose apparent sin is no more than being in the wrong place at the wrong time. If the violence is sustained, atrocities are likely to accumulate as both (or all) sides seek to consolidate what they have won or recoup what they have lost. It is the public manifestations that are reported, increasingly visually in a world where anyone with a telephone can also be a cinematographer and effectively an international affairs reporter. It is the images of horror that activate the emotional resolve to try to alleviate the suffering—to do something.

The underlying emotions and dynamics of the do something syndrome are understandable and even noble, but they also are likely to be the result of over-simplifying caricatures of a situation and what effect any outsider actions will have. There are at least two broad ways in which the do something syndrome can distort truly tragic realities and mislead the most well-intentioned efforts. The 2012 crisis in Syria and 2011 efforts in Libya and outside reactions to them offer examples of these dynamics.

The first distortion arises from an oversimplification of the physical and political struggle that has produced the violence to which one is reacting. In almost all the developing world situations that degenerate to the point that outside interference may seem warranted, bloody excesses are the symptom of the problem, not the cause. The initial instinct that may activate an outside response is somehow to stop the killing and, in cases like Syria, to punish the government that has apparently been responsible for the suffering. Once again, this reaction is entirely understandable and may be reinforced by actions of the offending government or movement; Bashar al-Assad, after all, responded to criticism of his actions and calls for his removal by upping the ante of violence. This kind of reaction, in turn, only reinforces the initial feeling of and righteousness about doing something to relieve the situation.

The problem is that the reaction may only serve as a Band-Aid to cover and staunch the immediate flow of blood, while not addressing the deeper, underlying causes that must somehow be fixed or "cured" before the pathology is truly cured. Alleviating symptoms may be paramount to the innocents under siege, but if the underlying causes of the violence are not addressed and solved, those efforts may prove to have been only transitory and temporary and leave the long-term situation even murkier and worse than it was before. It is a foreboding of these possibilities that should act as an inhibitor in activating the do something syndrome.

The contrasting international reactions to Libya and Syria illustrate this part of the dynamic. In both cases, international interest, attention, and calls for intervention occurred because of violent repressions of uprisings by the governments of the two countries that included brutal, bloody, and reprehensible acts against the civilian populations. In both cases, factions in the United States counseled active American intervention, although stopping short of calls for inserting land forces. In Libya, the military situation was such that intervention from the air could prove critically helpful in bringing down the Gaddafi regime, whereas the military prospects were much murkier and less predictable in coming to the assistance of Syrian rebels. Intervention by air against Libyan forces by NATO almost certainly hastened the overthrow of Gaddafi; the reluctance to take direct military action probably prolonged the campaign against the Assad regime.

In both cases, action was counseled with no real certainty of its impact beyond the removal of the old regime. The Libyan resistance came to power, but whether they represented a major change for the good of the whole country remains uncertain. That is not surprising, since authoritarian governments repress, rather than nurture, political opponents whose views on governance can be influenced and learned. The same was even truer of the Free Syrian forces, and uncertainty was made even more opaque by the existence of deep religious and ethnic cleavages within the population. Overt, physical support from regional countries has had mixed impacts, and this ambiguity was recognized in Western capitals. The results were differential: exhortations to staunch the bleeding in Syria and limited intervention in Libya. How either situation will eventually come out is not certain, but a major intervention was avoided in both. That is not always the case, and much of the reason arises from the second source of distortion.

That source, arising from the first, surrounds the extent to which outside intervention can actually assist in the resolution and amelioration of the violence that is the symptom of deeper causes of that violence. In a general sense, there is a tendency of countries contemplating intervention in domestic instability to overestimate the degree to which they can affect outcomes. At least implicitly, this tendency reflects a virtually narcissistic assumption that the intervener has such overwhelming power, especially as measured in traditional military terms, that his mere presence will be decisive. In turn, given the tragedy that the intervener confronts and seeks to ameliorate, he is likely to believe that he is so obviously a force for good that the participants will not only be awed by his power but also the righteousness and wisdom of his actions.

Real world situations are rarely so simple and their solution as obvious as a concentration entirely on the violence would suggest. More typically, situations where intervention may be considered are the outgrowth of deep and fundamental disagreements among portions of the population that the internal factions have been unable to solve by non-violent means and which continue as violent clashes the outcomes of which are indeterminate. There is, in other words, a balance of power between the contending sides, and outside intervention upsets that balance. That interference will be applauded, at least initially, by those on whose side the intervention occurs and condemned by those it disadvantages. Particularly when outside force attacks opposition centers of gravity (vital places and qualities of the side at which they are directed), that interference may decisively tip the balance from one side to the other.

The problem, however, is that the intervener creates a new dimension to the internal conflict that changes the dynamic in ways the intervener is unlikely to anticipate in advance. Outsiders entering a country with military force may be welcomed in the short run if they bring relief to obvious deprivations and suffering (such as the slaughter of civilians), but they quickly overstay their welcome. The longer those outsiders remain, the more internal resentment is likely to build toward the intervening force. Adulation over liberation is fairly quickly followed by questioning of why the intervener insists on staying: appreciation then turns to resentment when the intervener overstays its welcome. Regardless of the purity and impartiality of its initial motives, the intervener inevitably favors some factions and opposes others. Those who suffer from the intervener's continued presence will try to exploit misgivings, charging, among other things, that those the intervener supports are nothing more than "lackeys" or "running dogs" (a Cold War aphorism) of the intervener, who is likely to be depicted as a "neocolonialist."

In this circumstance, the intervener is likely to conclude that its best approach is to prepare the side it supports as well as possible for self-governance and continued resistance and to prepare to leave. The intervener feels stung by criticism over its continued presence, which it believes is necessary to stabilize the situation and to permit a satisfactory outcome after departure. One must remember that intervention, beyond its initial humanitarian intentions, is also governed by some set of objectives for the state in which intervention has occurred. In Afghanistan, for instance, the United States wants a post-war Afghanistan where the Taliban cannot conduct their terror against the population, but it also wants a government that will resist the return of Al Qaeda. Sometimes the interests of the intervener and its indigenous ally will not be the same. In these cases, whose interests prevail?

The calculation of intervening, setting things right, and departing is further complicated by other perplexing realities that affect the relationship between the intervener and those it seeks to support. If, for instance, the United States determines it must come to the aid of a beleaguered government, what does that say about support for that government within the population? It probably says that the government cannot prevail without the assistance of the outsider, making the government dependent on the outsider, a point the opposition will undoubtedly and obviously use to its advantage in the battle for the hearts and minds of the population (popular loyalty) that is the critical objective in any internal conflict.

Even if the intervener comes to realize that its presence has become part of the problem (a difficult self-realization to reach), what can be done? If it stays, the resentment its presence creates will increase and be exploited by the opposition. If it leaves, there is the very real possibility that the side it has supported will fall. How can the intervener win in this circumstance? The intervener cannot.

Making the situation even more maddening, the relationship between the length and effort expended on an intervention and the amount of leverage the intervener has over the side it supports is inverse. In internal conflicts, the longer and greater an outsider's intervention is, the less influence the outsider has on the client. President Ngo Dinh Diem of South Vietnam first figured out and exploited this anomaly. He reasoned (quite correctly in the circumstance) that the Americans had invested too much in his cause simply to abandon it and walk away for domestic political reasons in the United States: abandoning the South Vietnamese would be an admission that the investment had been a bad and, as it accumulated, an increasingly expensive proposition. As a result, when the Americans offered Diem "advice" on how to improve his side's position in the war with the North Vietnamese and their National Liberation Front allies, he could simply ignore that advice if he disagreed. It did not matter how sound the advice might be (certainly from an American viewpoint) if it differed from what Diem wanted to do. The frustrated Americans could (and did) threaten to cut Diem off for non-compliance with suggestions Americans thought would strengthen the South Vietnamese cause, but the threats were hollow and Diem knew it. The American demands centered on land reform and redistribution, since most land was controlled by a relatively few large landowners who also happened to form much of Diem's political support base. The communists, of course, called for massive land reform, giving land to the peasantry who formed their support base and the majority of the citizenry. The Americans reasoned, probably correctly, that the South Vietnamese government could never gain majority popular support as long as it resisted giving land to the peasants. Diem believed giving in to the American demands would alienate his support base and resisted. It was a classic standoff wherein Diem won in the short run and the Americans and their South Vietnamese allies lost in the longer run.

The parallels between this situation and the relationship between the United States and the current Afghan administration are striking. In the current case, the problem is not land but governmental reform. Afghanistan has one of the most corrupt governments of any country in the world as ranked by independent international agencies. The American goal is for the Afghan regime to emerge from the war as a strong enough central force to be capable of suppressing and preventing any terrorist return to Afghan soil. While a strong central government runs counter to Afghan tradition and may be impossible under any circumstances, it is doubly so given the corruption of the central government. Time and again, hostile areas of Afghanistan have resisted "liberation" by the government on the grounds that if the Afghan government moves in, its corruption and brutality will be worse than having the Taliban in control. No one much likes the Taliban, but many dislike the government more. The United States thus argues that the regime in Kabul must clean up its act and threatens to withhold assistance if it does not. President Karzai understood these demands and vowed to clear up corruption, but it never seemed to happen. One reason may be that Karzai's own supporters are so much of a part of the problem that to clamp down would alienate them. Another part may be that the Afghan president realized there was not much the Americans can do if he ignored them given the huge American investment in the country.

These sorts of dynamics are virtually inevitable when one contemplates interfering in the internal politics of developing world countries. This dynamic is exacerbated when one intrudes in places where one does not clearly understand the subtleties of those internal politics and thus upsets those internal politics in ways it has not anticipated because it could not. In Libya and Syria, a major restraint was that the United States recognized that it did not know enough about the anti-government forces in either country to be able to predict the effect of a major tilt and restrained itself for fear either of being ineffective or promoting groups who would be different but not much better than what existed (essentially the problem in Iraq). The siren's call of intervention was resisted, but with a cost in terms of continued suffering, some of which might have been alleviated if more decisive action with positive outcomes could have been predicted. The alternative of diving into situations with ambiguous knowledge has often been frustration and eventual disillusion when the outcomes one hoped for did not occur. Despite this likelihood, the propensity toward intervention remains a "tender trap" that leads to involvements in impossible situations.

The Tender Trap: Why Intervention Does Not (and Cannot) Work

Shorn of Cold War ideologies, unstable conditions that have led or could lead to violence and suffering in developing countries are almost always primarily internal conflicts. This characteristic makes them fundamentally different from violent situations between states—the kinds of wars for which the Western, European military tradition is developed and at which it is most applicable—in critical political and military ways. Politically, interstate wars are about governments influencing one another, wherein the interplay of military forces is intended to compel one side or another to accept the political objectives each espouses. Any attempts to reconcile the population of the defeated side is generally a concern of the post-war peace period in the form of a reconciliatory rather than a punitive peace, and one assumes a basic antipathy between the personnel on each side that is institutional rather than strictly personal. Militarily, such wars are clashes between similarly oriented armed forces where each has the goal of overcoming the hostile will of the other by subduing the other's armed forces or convincing the enemy government that continued opposition is futile.

Internal wars have fundamentally different dynamics that make the application of principles designed for conventional interstate war dangerous. The political goal in internal wars, control of government, is a much more personal matter to participants than that of interstate war. The critical political element in such wars is popular support, and the winner is normally the side that succeeds in the battle for what Lyndon Johnson called "the hearts and minds of men" in Vietnam. Military action may contribute to that political battle—creating the images of one side or the other as a "winner" or as a "loser," for instance—but it is the political outcome that is decisive. At the military level, internal conflicts tend to be unconventional or, in more contemporary language, asymmetrical. Such warfare is specifically designed to frustrate the practice of European-style war machines, since typically the government side has been organized and equipped by the West.

Outside intervention in these kinds of conflicts is *never* decisive. In 1993, I published a book (the first edition of *Distant Thunder*) in which I made the following assertion: "Since 1945, there has not been a single instance of a successful intervention in an insurgency with substantial support by a racially distinct outside intervening nation." No one challenged that assertion at the time, and its truth holds for the two decades since I first stated it.

The assertion contains three important qualifiers that establish its universality. First, it applies to situations where a challenging insurgent group has "substantial support" in the population, a qualification that exempts the case of Bolivia, when Ernesto ("Che") Guevara unsuccessfully led a band of Argentine revolutionaries trying to foment rebellion among Bolivian miners in 1967 (Guevara was captured and killed in the attempt). The other exception that is sometimes suggested is to the successful British intervention in Malaya in 1948 against insurgents fighting the new government there. That insurgent movement was made up almost exclusively of ethnic Chinese who did not have the support of the native Malays; thus the insurgents lacked critical indigenous support. Second, the statement was made in the specific context of movements during the Cold War which adopted some form of the Maoist guerrilla strategy of wars of national liberation. Modern asymmetrical wars often have some of the military characteristics of Maoist warfare, but usually in a modified, adaptive way. The generalization still holds. Third, the observation specifies the lack of success of racially distinct interveners: there have been some minor intervention successes in places like Africa since, but they have almost all been conducted by other Africans who, although tribally distinct from the people in whose countries they intervene, do not stand out as obviously as Western troops (e.g., American and other NATO members), who regularly fail. Westerners can prevail when they become involved with other Europeans, as in NATO (including the United States) intervention in Bosnia and Kosovo.

Why does intervention seem doomed to fail? The answer, broadly speaking, is that it involves sending the wrong people into the wrong situation doing the wrong things. That sweeping statement, of course, needs to be specified. One way to do that is to divide the problem into its two major components, the political and military dimensions.

The Political Dimension: Centers of Gravity and Hearts and Minds

Internal conflicts are about who governs and in what manner they govern. These qualities make the conflicts very intense and personal for the people who live where they are conducted, since the outcome affects directly and intimately their lives. These conflicts occur almost exclusively in developing world countries where there are generally differences in the quality of life that some see as inequities remediable only through violent action and where methods of peaceful conflict resolution are not so well established as to rule out the recourse to force either by the government or its opponents. Perceptions of inequality and inequity are not, of course, unique to the developing world; what distinguished these situations from similar perceptions in so-called developed countries is that in the latter, there are generally better defined and institutionalized prohibitions on the use of force to decide political differences.

When situations approach or reach the point of combustion, it means that whatever bargain the governors have with the governed over how they reign has been broken or strained to the point that inhibitions on the recourse to violence have dissolved. Put more simply, *something is wrong* (or perceived as wrong) or instability does not turn violent. The degree to which the parties involved and outsiders perceive these problems as important or just will vary considerably: if one supports the existing regime's values, for instance, one is likely to view grievances as a lot less important and valid than if one agrees with the dissenters. In either case, the result can be to distort the nature and gravity of the situation, and this is especially true for outsiders contemplating involvement. Any analysis must begin from the realization that there must have been something awry, or there would not be violent opposition. In turn, how the sources of discontent are resolved is almost always more vital to the outcome of violence than is a strict accounting of the battlefield.

In civil conflict, the *center of gravity* for both sides is the same: the political support of the population. The concept of *center of gravity* refers to whatever quality or condition is necessary for a combatant to continue the struggle and to succeed. In conventional war, the two sides (normally states) have separate centers of gravity: particular characteristics of their societies or their war-making capacity that are absolutely essential for the states to continue the war effort. World War II, for instance, was largely a battle of total state capacities in which the physical ability to produce the wherewithal of continued war was considered the critical center of gravity. This translated into such things as the industrial capacity (e.g., steel industry, weapons manufacturing facilities) of the state and, especially in the case of the Axis, their ability to produce the petroleum-based products (oil, gasoline) on which a mechanized war machine absolutely depends. As a result, much of the Allied air campaign was directed at destroying German and Japanese factories and petroleum-refining facilities. In more contemporary terms, the critical center of gravity for the United States is arguably the will of the American people to continue to support overseas wars in cases where the efforts are not unambiguously involvements of necessity. Inflicting casualties on American troops to accentuate American angst over such involvements has been a method for assaulting American cost-tolerance and thus indirectly attacking the American center of gravity.

Internal war is, in important ways, conventional war inverted, and the concept of center of gravity is a particularly good illustration. The critical element in internal wars is popular support, and generally speaking, the side that has the most support (or which denies its opponent that support) is likely to prevail. The critical center of gravity *for both sides* is the same; it is the hearts and minds (loyalty) of the country's people. That fact changes fundamentally the nature of internal war and has enormous—and mostly underappreciated—consequences for the calculation of outside intervention in internal conflicts.

The mutuality of centers of gravity creates a unique perspective and problem in internal war: how does one maximize one's own appeal to the hearts and minds of men of the population while simultaneously denying the center of gravity to the opponent? Put a slightly different way, how does one attack the other side's center of gravity without destroying one's own? If one indiscriminately attacks a town or village that is a redoubt of the opponent, for instance, one may kill many of the enemy, but it is also likely that the town contains people who support the attacking side and others who have been neutral but who may also become casualties. How will they respond to such attacks? In conventional war, this is not a problem, since everyone is either friend or foe and the impact of action on the political views of the target population is not an issue. In internal war, *essentially all military actions have political consequences in terms of the contest over the common center of gravity*; any side that ignores this reality is likely to do so at their considerable peril. It is not a concern for the traditional interstate warrior.

The differences and their consequent frustrations become particularly important in the contemplation or actuality of outside intervention. The first reality that a country contemplating intervention must confront (but which it rarely does in these terms) is that internal wars are exactly that, internal. As such, they are feuds, the underlying success of which requires winning the crucial battle for the hearts and minds of the people, and this is not a struggle that surrogates can win for them. One side or another may call for outside assistance because their situation is dire and they fear collapse and defeat without some outside help, but the potential intervener has to realize the limit of its effective contribution. In turn, the intervener must include in its assessment of prospective intervention how and why the situation has become so desperate that only outside help can save the day, and it must ask if its help can really be critical in the long run. Unless something is truly amiss—which means there is considerable opposition to the side asking for assistance—outside intervention will not be requested. If outside assistance is needed, moreover, the situation may be beyond recovery under any circumstances. The conclusion, which I have elsewhere referred to as the *outsider's frustration*, is that if assistance is necessary, the situation may be too dire for it to do any good in the long run. If the situation is not so dire as to need outside assistance, then that assistance might be helpful in reaching a positive outcome. In the latter case, however, the question then arises whether the American public will support an effort in which they are not absolutely needed. This part of the problem, which Todd Greentree called the *democratic contradiction* (see, for instance, *Crossroads of Intervention*), is a difficult dilemma to confront and overcome.

None of this kind of calculation matters if one is contemplating intervention in a traditional war between states. Intervention always provides additional force for the side which receives it, and if that increment can change the balance of power toward the side to which it is extended, it is valuable. The fact that the side against which that force will be used is alienated politically is beside the point, since the military conduct of the war does not contain the battle for hearts and minds as a part of the objective. However, since that battle is central to the outcome of internal war, the impact of outside intervention is critical, in at least five interconnected ways.

First, outsiders (especially if they are ethnically or physically different from the indigenous population, as they usually are) immediately become part of the problem as well as the solution. The reason is simple and direct: outsiders are intruders, and some in the population will reject their presence on that basis. A negative reaction to an American presence as a foreign occupier is both natural and predictable. This point has been made before, but to judge from the reactions of American officials when this happens, it is unanticipated and surprising when it should not be.

There are undoubtedly multiple reasons why American officials fail to recognize these obvious dynamics. One is that the Americans usually intervene with some kind of missionary zeal, the beneficence of which seems so self-obvious it is impossible to see our assessment is not shared by the recipients. Another is that the initial, short-term effect of American intervention may be positive and met with enthusiasm by the indigenous population: the overthrow of Saddam Hussein and the removal of the symbols of his authority (e.g., the famous toppling of a statue of the dictator in Baghdad) may well be met with enthusiasm, and this may create the false belief an American continued presence is much more welcome than it is in fact. The problem is that when interveners enter and set up what appears to be an open-ended stay, their differences with the population become clearer and more amplified. Nobody likes the presence of imposed, ruling foreigners in their country, and the longer those outsiders stay, the more their presence will be resented. Is that such a difficult concept to comprehend?

Intervention, in other words, breeds resentment and contempt, no matter how pure the intentions of the intervener are, and this resentment builds the longer an intervening party stays. There is no public evidence that the inevitability of a negative host reaction to American continued presence has been a factor included in planning for past interventions, and it clearly should be. If the United States could sweep into a country, excise some terrible wrong (e.g., removing the tyranny of Saddam Hussein, capturing Al Qaeda) and then leave, this reaction may be avoided. If the American mission had ended in Afghanistan by the end of 2001 or if the United States had withdrawn from Iraq before Labor Day 2003 as Rumsfeld predicted, resentment might not have needed to be a planning factor. However, rapid insertion and equally rapid withdrawal of force simply tends not to happen.

Second, the more assistance that outsiders provide, the more visible they become and the less good their assistance does—a dynamic that increases over time. Part of the reason arises from misdiagnosis of the problems that have prompted intervention. When the United States anticipates involvement, our attention has normally been focused on whoever has created the instability and to assume that if they can be defeated, the problem will be solved. The problem, of course, is rarely so simple. To repeat, the emergence of violent instability usually occurs because the existing government has performed unacceptably, normally because it is incompetent or venal. U.S. intervention may physically weaken the armed resistance to that government, but unless it is combined with a strong, effective program of reform and performance enhancement by the government, that victory will be ephemeral. Intervening and propping up a bad government can relieve that government of the feeling it must change, since it has the Americans to protect it from its opponents. The longer the intervention, the more the perception is likely to grow that the Americans are simply protecting, even promoting, government the people do not support. Because the American ability to influence the government is inversely proportional to its accumulated investment, the more a continued American presence may contribute to alienation of the target population and thus the loss of the battle for peoples' loyalties. This dynamic also may reflect very real differences in the perspectives and objectives of the host and intervening governments.

Third, there will be operational differences in the perspectives of the interveners and their hosts, especially in terms of the impact that outsider's actions have on the critical battle for hearts and minds. The objectives of the United States and the host country, in other words, are rarely identical. For the government or other entity on whose side the United States intervenes, the basic motivation is likely to be simply to attain or to retain power. Depending on whether that entity is democratic or not, it may or may not be especially interested in the battle for hearts and minds, but may instead be more concerned about what is necessary to beat down the opposition sufficiently to retain power. The intervening party, on the other hand, may have broader geopolitical aims in mind that support of the side is supposed to serve. Operationally, these objectives may come into conflict. In Iraq, for instance, the Americans (at least the neo-cons) argued the virtue of a democratic Iraqi state as a geopolitical magnet in the region to promote regional stability. To the Iraqi Shiites whose majority in the population makes them the beneficiaries of democratization, the motive is much more elemental: democracy allows them the ability to rule over (and seek retribution against) the Sunnis who had previously ruled the country. The Shiite goal virtually guarantees the absence of reconciliation among the various elements within Iraq, a requisite for achieving the American goal. In this clash of objectives, which side will (or should) prevail? It is their country, after all, but it is our blood that has contributed to establishing it.

Fourth, the host government and the intervener may come into conflict over the physical conduct of the intervention. This may reflect the difference in the approach and emphasis each partner has. The host, who views the intervention as a way to bolster its internal status in the battle over the common center of gravity, may see the matter one way. A Western-oriented intervener like the United States, on the other hand, may see the mission more in terms of the traditional defeat of an armed opponent, either to buttress the host's hold on power or to achieve its own geopolitical goals. The result of this disagreement can be a sometimes very public difference in objectives between the intervening state and the government on whose behalf the intervention occurs.

The use of American drone attacks in Afghanistan illustrates this dichotomy. The use of pilotless aircraft to attack concentrations of enemy troops and leaders located in places that are inaccessible or difficult to access in other ways (such as by ground forces) is an innovation of the campaigns in both Afghanistan and Pakistan made possible by advances in aerospace technology and made attractive by the forbidding terrain of the region. These attacks have been quite effective in locating and killing leaders of both the Taliban and Al Qaeda, both of which are major American goals. They have also, however, been controversial and have aroused the ire of leaderships in both countries where they have occurred. In Afghanistan in particular, President Hamid Karzai has been a particularly vociferous opponent and has called repeatedly for the United States to desist in these attacks. Why?

The drone attacks highlight differences in American and Afghan perspectives on the war. For the United States, they are principally a way to attrite more effectively the enemy by effectively taking away its sanctuaries. Increasingly, there is nowhere that Al Qaeda and Taliban fighters and leaders are safe. The problem arises because, despite efforts to make attacks by drones precise and thus to reduce collateral damage, there are often unintended civilian casualties in the wake of drone sorties. These casualties can have a negative impact on the battle for the hearts and minds of portions of the Afghan population, principally different Pashtun tribes that suffer them. Since the Pashtuns are the principal source of Taliban fighters and revenge is an integral part of the Pashtun code of honor Pashtunwali, the net effect can be negative. There is, for instance, the old Pashtun saying "Kill one enemy, make ten more," an effect that may be especially important when adding up the negative and positive impact of drone attacks. Karzai, who is himself a Pashtun, understands this Pashtun entreaty, has done the math about the impact, and thus calls incessantly for a cessation of the attacks. Since the Americans see the drones as one of their clear sources of military advantage, the result is an impasse between the allies.

Fifth, the democratic contradiction will almost certainly arise if intervention is protracted (as it almost always is), indeterminate, and controversial. As the first four points suggest, all three of these criteria are likely to be present in developing world interventions. It is, for instance, not clear that the calculation of intervention includes the virtual certainty that the intervention will become a recruitment device for whoever opposes those on whose side it occurs. Yet that is what happens, as opponents can argue that the side the interveners support is nothing but lackeys of the foreign invaders and that supporting them helps bolster the movement to expel the unwelcome outsiders.

The result is a more complex and likely more protracted mission than interveners originally envisage. That longer involvement is also likely to become increasingly indeterminate in light both of unanticipated aspects of the mission and increased obstinacy by the opposition. As involvement drags on with no apparent "light at the end of the tunnel" (to borrow General William Westmoreland's 1967 assessment of the mission in Vietnam—which lasted until 1973), the result is likely to be increased popular opposition to the intervention within the American public, which increasingly questions both the worth of the enterprise and its attainability (the criteria of importance and winnability). If it appears that the side being supported is of dubious virtue—as it often is—the democratic contradiction is simply multiplied.

These factors accumulate to produce some harsh and unappealing realities that confront the potential intervener as it contemplates future excursions into developing world conflicts. These realities arise from two major observations that can be distilled from the general discussion of political dimensions of DWICs.

The first is that the critical element of these conflicts is the battle over the singular center of gravity in any domestic dispute—the basic loyalty or support of the population. Whoever wins that battle almost certainly wins the contest. This statement may seem too simple, and in a way it is. The battle for hearts and minds is not always a high-political-road contest between noble aspirants or between one noble and one ignoble contestant. Particularly if measured by Western ideals (as opposed necessarily to practice), movements (governments or insurgents) are likely to come up wanting to some degree. The government must not be entirely faultless and noble, or it would not engender so much opposition as to constitute a violent conflict that can endanger it. Those who oppose the government will also act ignobly, in all likelihood.

The sources of these shortcomings are numerous and include venality, corruption, bloodlust, even cruelty and savagery, or they may reflect nonviable, multinational political units which are bound to come into conflict and where good and bad are very difficult to assess. In these situations, the attempt to depict the side one chooses to support as virtuous—the wearers of the "white hats"—and the other side as contrastingly evil—the "black hats"—involves a distortion of the situation.

Such a depiction may make good public relations in building support for the chosen side, but if those making the decisions take their own propaganda too seriously, it is likely to result in bad policy born of a misapprehension of the ability to appeal to the hearts and minds of the population. It is therefore incumbent on the United States to ask, in the most critical way possible, of those it proposes to support, "What is wrong that has gotten these guys into the trouble they are in?" If the answer is clear cut, a study in black and white, it is probably wrong.

This observation seems so obvious that one is tempted to dismiss it. As a colleague of mine who is a retired admiral with experience on the National Security Council staff never tires of saying in response to this kind of objection, "Come on. There are very bright people who make these decisions. You can't honestly believe they wouldn't figure these things out." Unfortunately, they do occasionally make those kinds of mistakes. One must remember that during the Cuban Revolution of 1959, for instance, the United States considered Fidel Castro the liberating hero of Cuba and did not realize until he had consolidated power that he was not exactly the answer to our western hemisphere prayers. The United States championed Ngo Dinh Diem as the president of South Vietnam until his venality finally caused us to turn on him in 1963. The frustrating Hamid Karzai, who speaks very good American English (he has a number of family members who live in the United States) was once viewed as a fine fellow, and *any* Iraqi seemed a better alternative than Saddam Hussein.

Picking the right horse in developing world conflicts is extremely difficult, perilous work, but it is absolutely necessary, because the outcome of the battle for the hearts and minds of the population in these contests is one that must be won by the natives themselves. The other entirely clear reality surrounding outside intervention in these conflicts is that outside intervention is rarely if ever the critical element in these affairs. Extreme brutality of the kind practiced by Genghis Khan or, in somewhat dilute fashion, the Soviet Union may produce interim results that appear decisive, but they are likely to be transitory (e.g., the Soviet Union in Afghanistan in the 1980s) or impossible to sustain in the modern world, where brutality and atrocity can rarely be hidden from citizens with smartphones. The belief that outside interference may be decisive enough to warrant its consideration arises primarily not from a political analysis—certainly not like the one just presented—but from a conventional military view of situations. Positive military assessments are also subject to critical examination.

The Military Dimension: Shooting Symptoms and the Brushfire Corollary

The inversion of political and military factors in DWICs is not the only unfamiliar, uncomfortable aspect of these conflicts for an outsider like the United States. The intimate relationship between military actions and their immediate and long-term consequences on the battle for hearts and minds is one way in which these wars are different, and the United States military has, with mixed results, attempted to alter its own doctrines to deal with this aspect of the problem (see the Marine guide on conduct for its troops in Afghanistan as a prime example). The deeper problem is that these kinds of wars tend to be *asymmetrical,* in the language currently in vogue to describe non-European-style warfare, and this has posed particular difficulty for Western-oriented interveners like the United States.

The term *asymmetrical warfare* is much newer than the phenomenon it seeks to describe. Although it has been discussed in passing at various places in this book, it is worth reviewing in somewhat greater detail as a source of problems for the United States that weighs heavily in the attractiveness of enmeshing ourselves in this kind of fight. More specifically, the United States has not evolved a successful way to "win" asymmetrical wars and, given the dynamics of these kinds of situations, the failure to prevail is tantamount to failure. The problem of asymmetrical warfare is a problem of the winnability of these wars.

Asymmetrical warfare refers generically to the situation where one party to war fights in one manner, while the other side does not fight in that same manner, adopting different methods and usually ignoring whatever rules of engagement (ROEs) the other prefers. Asymmetrical warfare is not, however, so much a method of warfare as it is a methodology for conducting war. What this means is that the asymmetrical warrior is not equipped or burdened with a set of doctrinal beliefs about how to engage and defeat an opponent, so much as a problem-solving attitude about what ways that he can overcome the inherent strengths and advantages of the opponent and in effect "level the playing field" to give himself some prospect of prevailing. Implicit in this approach is the assumption by the asymmetrical warrior that he cannot prevail unless he somehow changes the terms of engagement and that he will almost certainly lose if he plays by the opponent's ROEs.

This physical assessment describes the situation confronting most developing world movements when they face an outside intervener like the United States. With the most lethal conventional force in the world by standard measures, it is suicidal for any developing world movement to contemplate fighting the Americans on Western, European-style terms. Generally speaking, such movements are comparatively poor and are certainly technology and equipment poor: they lack the counterpart weapons and "mass" to compete on the traditional battlefield, and if the contest is settled by fighting the way the intervening party prefers, the developing world natives know they will lose. The last developing world force that tried to do so in a concerted, sustained way was Iraq in the Kuwaiti desert (its 2003 resistance was much less complete), and its own Western-style military did not stand a chance against the more lethal, technologically advanced Americans. The lesson was observed and learned by others in the developing world: fighting the Americans on their own terms amounts to committing suicide. The only way to defeat the Americans is to change the ROEs in such a way as to reduce or, hopefully, negate American advantages. Turning the methodology of adaptation to a successful doctrinal formula is a matter of finding the right circumstances and methods to frustrate the superior force. The intellectual logistics of the clash is about which side adapts most successfully to the situation: the asymmetrical warriors in their quest to negate their disadvantages, or the Westerner's adaptations to counter those adaptations. To this point, it is not a competition at which the United States has been terribly successful. The question is why that is the case. Possible answers include an intellectual sclerosis that makes Westerners aversive to change, a lack of dedication to that change, and the impossibility of prevailing.

Trying to counter asymmetrical warfare introduces several bedeviling problems that give advantages to the asymmetrical warriors despite their conventional inferiority. For one thing, interventions are expeditionary wars, whereas they are defensive contests on the home ground of the asymmetrical warriors being confronted. That means the asymmetrical warriors fight in familiar territory, which gives tactical advantages of knowing the terrain better than their intervening opponents. They are fighting for "hearth and home," which increases their motivation and appeal within the population (they can and do depict themselves as defenders against foreign invaders, after all). Moreover, the Western-style military machines exemplified by American forces are designed for primary combat in relatively well-developed areas—places where there are adequate roads along which its instruments of war can travel. These infrastructure characteristics are often not present in developing countries and help negate some of the advantages of the superior conventional force. In Afghanistan, for instance, the Soviets attempted to compensate for the lack of a transportation network by importing helicopters, but the Afghans (with the help of American-supplied Stinger missiles) shot them down. One reason that Al Qaeda escaped Afghanistan was that their route to safety was over foot paths through the mountains at night, obviating American surveillance and attack technologies.

Environmental factors cause and facilitate the asymmetrical warrior adopting methods of fighting that may be quite alien to the intervening side. The lush jungle vegetation of parts of Vietnam, for instance, provided cover for roadside ambushes of American convoys that the Americans responded to with defoliation. Facing firepower deficiencies that become particularly obvious when the opponents meet face to face in traditional battle, the asymmetrical warrior takes advantage of his superior knowledge of things like terrain to substitute ambushes for traditional firefights. Some of the tactics that are adapted are old and are simply extensions of existing practices such as Maoist mobile-guerrilla warfare; some are unique adaptations to technology and circumstance, like the use of improvised explosive devices (IEDs) that became common in Iraq and have moved to Afghanistan as well. The use of *kamikaze* style suicidal bombers, which the United States encountered in Pacific theaters like Okinawa in World War II, have popped up in the popular uprising against the Syrians, as well as in Afghanistan. The point is that the asymmetrical warrior is not limited to a set method of conducting war against an opponent; rather, his methodology tells him to adapt and to try various methods until he hits on one or more that work. Anticipating which method will appear in particular circumstances is a very difficult and inexact form of the military "art."

Interveners also upset the centers-of-gravity equation in ways that may be detrimental to them. The heart of the problem remains the same: the competition for citizen loyalty between the government and its opponents. Outside interveners complicate that equation in complex but basically negative ways. If the asymmetrical warrior is foolish enough to expose itself to the firepower of the intervener, then the intervener may be able to decimate the asymmetrical warrior and to swing the balance of power decisively to the side it supports and positively affect the political competition by branding the asymmetrical opponent as a loser. Since the asymmetrical warrior's methodology begins from the premise of maintaining survival as his base value, he is unlikely to cooperate in his own destruction, and will instead use the foreign intrusion as propaganda to build support for his own cause. Thus, outsiders can effectively become recruiting posters for the opposition.

There is a further source of center-of-gravity complication for the intervener. If the intervener is to succeed, it must be cognizant of how its presence and actions affect the internal battle for hearts and minds. The intervener, however, has a second center of gravity which the asymmetrical warrior is likely to try to exploit. That second center of gravity is public support within the intervener's population, in this case American popular support. As amply noted, developing world interventions, if they become protracted, breed opposition based in questions of worth and winnability. The question of how much sacrifice the American people will endure in a war of dubious importance and ambiguous outcome is a question of cost-tolerance. The asymmetrical warrior may conclude, using the American performance in places like Vietnam as a precedent that if he can drag the war out long enough, the American public will tire of the effort and demand withdrawal. The objective becomes not so much to "defeat" the Americans in any traditional sense, which is patently impossible, but to bleed them in terms of human and material loss to the point they say "enough" and quit. It is a strategy that has worked before (Vietnam), arguably has worked more recently (Iraq), and appears to be working again (Afghanistan). The antidote, of course, is swift and decisive campaigns in which cost-tolerance does not become a factor, which of course is exactly the kind of outcomes asymmetrical approaches are specifically designed to avoid.

This conundrum is further complicated and the danger of exceeding cost-tolerance increased by different definitions of success for interveners and their asymmetrical opponents that are also to the asymmetrical warriors' advantage. For the intervener (and the government or force it assists), the standard for success is absolute and exacting: it must destroy the insurgents and thus end their contest for the hearts and minds of the indigenous population. It can, to put it slightly differently, only win by winning, since as long as the opponent exists, so does the problem he poses. For the asymmetrical opponent to succeed, the calculus is reversed. Since the asymmetrical warrior is a player (and thus a problem) as long as he is in business, he succeeds (or does not fail) as long as he continues to exist. Put in parallel terms, the challenger wins by not losing. The reason for this dynamic is that the longer that the conflict can be protracted, the more likely that the intervener's cost-tolerance will be exceeded. The intervener's presence is probably critical to the success, even survival, of the side it supports or it would not stay. Thus, if the asymmetrical challenger can outlast the intervener by exceeding his cost-tolerance and causing him to quit the contest, then all that is left between the challenger and positive success is the exposed patrons of the intervener, who cannot stand up to the challenger on their own (if they could have, they would not have invited intervention in the first place). Thus, the challenger's calculation of success in the face of outside intervention has two sequential steps: avoid annihilation by the intervener (win by not losing) and, once the intervener has given up, defeat the indigenous opponent (win by winning).

This strategic calculation and vision is likely to be successful against an outside intervener because of the relative importance of the outcome to the asymmetrical warrior and the intervener. Internal wars, as noted, are desperate and usually total wars of necessity to the parties involved. The consequences of winning or losing are sufficiently dire that they will be pursued with full vigor: they are unquestionably of vital importance to the indigenous combatants. These conflicts are rarely that important to the intervener. Rather than being matters of survival, they are generally justified on some geopolitical basis that is both open to question and of a clearly less vital level of interest than for the indigenous forces. Interventions are, or border upon, being wars of choice, and choice is a much more changeable condition than is necessity.

The cost-tolerance of internal combatants is rarely at issue because of the clear importance of the struggle; that same cost-tolerance is almost always a potential issue if one can raise continued intervention in debatable necessity/choice terms. America's opponents recognize this asymmetry and seek to exploit it. In the American debates over places like Vietnam, Iraq, and Afghanistan, an ironclad case of the necessity of involvement is rarely hashed out in advance through thorough analysis and convincing advocacy (probably out of a fear of the outcome of such a debate). Instead, when public determination to continue inevitably emerges as an issue, there is an ex post facto campaign by supporters of the war to convince the public of the necessity of vigilance and a patriotically draped derogation of those questioning that necessity. The dynamics of potential challenges to cost-tolerance, in other words, are not raised until public support becomes a problem, at which time it is usually too late to change the American public's mind.

The result of the military conundrum stated in this manner should be more cautionary than it has always been. The dynamics of asymmetry, cost-tolerance, and the like are not military calculations in the traditional sense, and they are thus not factors that military professionals have been trained or educated to assess or include in their planning. These are not, to repeat, the kinds of problems one faces in conventional warfare, where the political consequences of all actions are not as immediate nor as intimate as they are in modern DWICs. There have been sporadic and often insightful analyses of these problems, but they have not thoroughly or certainly completely permeated the way that the military views these kinds of wars. Before fundamental progress in assessment can be made, two difficulties that certainly plagued thinking about the Vietnam War and which arguably linger to the present must be overcome. One of these is how basically to think about these wars as problems, and the solution is in overcoming something called the *brushfire corollary* (a term coined by Greentree) in the post-mortem of Vietnam. The other is in how to measure the actuality as opposed to the illusion of progress, and it is captured in the concept of *shooting symptoms*.

Although the analogies may be somewhat contrived, the dynamic they portray is not. The term *brushfire war* was devised in the 1950s to describe developing world conflicts as essentially analogous to the outbreak of brushfires in the California hills. In these arid places, underbrush would sometimes ignite for natural (e.g., lightning strikes) or manmade reasons (e.g., the failure to extinguish campfires), and the result would be to catch the undergrowth on fire. These fires could be extinguished by rushing supplies of water or retardant to drown out the flames, which was the general approach of the time in California (it is not a coincidence that the analogy was devised in southern California by the RAND Corporation, whose headquarters were in Santa Monica). The analogy oversimplified the problem in two ways. First, it implied that developing world wars were more or less random in their origins, which American experience with similar conflicts in Latin America should have taught to be false. Second, it assumed that combating these outbreaks was fairly simple and straightforward, which it was not. Having conveniently forgotten its experience in the western hemisphere, however, the analogy gave policy makers and commentators a conceptual way to describe this "new" phenomenon.

Conceptualizing how to think about why these wars occurred and what to do about them was not the only problem. Another of the bedeviling ways in which contemporary developing world conflicts are different than traditional wars is in determining if, or to what extent, one is succeeding or failing. In traditional war, one can gauge progress by measures such as battles won (measured in a variety of ways, including how many of the enemy are killed, wounded, or captured) and by measurement of territory won and controlled. None of these measures entirely captures the dynamics of DWICs. How does one know and convince one's own public that one is winning these conflicts? Since territorial possession is often not the critical metric, the direct application of firefighting principles like 'percentage of the fire contained' does not readily describe the situation. The one concrete measure you have is how many of the enemy one has killed, and particularly how favorably that number compares to one's own losses. This solution was applied in Vietnam, and it proved illusory.

The United States needed to convince an increasingly skeptical American public that progress was being made toward putting down the North Vietnamese attempt to take over the whole country, but traditional depictions like territory won or lost were not compelling. The enemy, forced to confront a much more powerful American military machine, incurred much greater casualty rate than did the Americans, and from this comparison was born the famous daily "body count" of American and South Vietnamese versus North Vietnamese and Viet Cong casualties for the preceding 24 hours with which nightly news programs almost always began. The comparison showed much higher attrition rates for the enemy and suggested that the war was thus being won—even projecting that the opponent, at the rates being reported, would literally run out of soldiers. These projections, of course, turned out to be wrong, because they missed the point: the soldiers we killed were symptoms, not the cause, of the conflict. Shooting these symptoms and calling that decisive progress was a delusion.

The delusion was the result of not seeing the reasons there were enemy soldiers willing to die and the effect killing them had. The enemy incurred much larger casualties than we did and more than *we would have tolerated*. The analogy was drawn that at some point, the enemy would either be bled dry or or would conclude his continued resistance to American pressure was not worth it. This calculation involved an explicit extension of our own sense of values and our own cost-tolerance threshold onto an opponent whose sense of values was quite different. For the United States, Vietnam was a limited war, and that meant there were, among other things, limits to how much suffering we would endure to achieve our goals. To the opponent, the war was total and vital, and thus his cost-tolerance was much higher. The North Vietnamese would accept much higher losses than we would, and they knew that eventually the calculus of acceptable attrition would be on their side.

Some of these lessons have been learned in the interim since the Vietnam War, but not all of them. There is a greater appreciation that these situations are complex and subtle. Military doctrine in places like the joint Army-Marine Corps manual on counterinsurgency (the so-called Petraeus manual) acknowledges that simply killing enemy combatants is not a prime goal and even that physically eradicating the enemy is not only irrelevant but occasionally counterproductive, an acknowledgement that the shooting-symptoms analogy may have some validity. At the same time, there is a greater appreciation of the complexity of these wars and the greater domination of political dynamics that make prevailing more difficult, even unlikely. And yet, we continue to become involved in these situations.

Bibliography

Bacevich, Andrew C. *American Military Policy in Small Wars: The Case of El Salvador.* Cambridge, MA: Institute for Foreign Policy Analysis, 1989.

Baritz, Leon. *Backfire: A History of How American Culture Led Us Into Vietnam and Made Us Fight the Way We Did.* New York: William Morrow, 1985.

Beinart, Peter. "The War We Abandoned: The U.S. Started the Bloodshed in Iraq. Time to Own It." *Newsweek*, August 6, 2012, 17.

Blaufarb, Douglas S., and George K. Tankam. *Who Will Win? A Key to the Puzzle of Revolutionary War.* New York: Crane Russak, 1989.

Cable, Larry E. *Conflict of Myths: The Development of American Counterinsurgency Doctrine and the Vietnam War.* New York: New York University Press, 1986.

Drew, Dennis M., and Donald M. Snow. *Making Strategy for the Twenty-First Century: An Introduction to National Security Processes and Problems.* Montgomery, AL: Air University Press, 2006.

Gallagher, James J. *Low-Intensity Conflict: A Guide to Tactics, Techniques, and Procedures.* Machanicsburg, PA: Stackpole Books, 1992.

Giap, Vo Nguyen. *People's War, People's Army.* New York: Praeger, 1992.

Greentree, Todd R. *Crossroads of Intervention: Insurgency and Counterinsurgency in Central America.* Annapolis, MD: Naval Institute Press, 2009.

——*The United States and the Politics of Conflict in the Developing World.* Washington, DC: U.S. Department of State Center for the Study of Foreign Affairs, 1990.

Guevara, Ernesto ("Che"). *Guerrilla Warfare.* New York: Monthly Review Press, 1961.

Haass, Richard N. *Intervention: The Use of American Force in the Post-Cold War World.* Washington, DC: Carnegie Endowment for International Peace, 1994.

Hailand, Gerard. *Guerrilla Strategies: An Historical from the Long March to Afghanistan.* Berkeley, CA: University of California Press, 1982.

Hanson, Victor Dadis. *Between War and Peace: Lessons from Afghanistan and Iraq.* New York: Random House, 2004.

Hentz, James J. (ed.). *The Obligation of Empire: United States Strategy for a New Century.* Lexington: University of Kentucky Press, 2004.

Kilcullen, David. *The Accidental Guerrilla: Fighting Small Wars in the Midst of a Big One.* Oxford, UK: Oxford University Press, 2009.

Manwaring, Max G. (ed.). *Uncomfortable Wars: Toward a New Paradigm of Low-Intensity Conflict.* Boulder, CO: Westview Press, 1991.

Mao Zedung. *The Collected Works of Mao Zedung*, Vols. 1–4. Beijing, China: Foreign Languages Press, 1962.

Metz, Steven. *America in the Third World: The Future of Counterinsurgency.* Carlisle Barracks, PA: Strategic Studies Institute, 1995.

O'Hanlon, Michael E. *Defense Strategy for the Post-Saddam Era.* Washington, DC: Brookings Institution Press, 2003.

Paschall, Rod. *LIC 2010: Special Operations and Unconventional Warfare in the Next Century.* Washington, DC: Brassey's, 1990.

Rice, Edward E. *Wars of the Third Kind: Conflict in the Underdeveloped Countries.* Berkeley, CA: University of California Press, 1988.

Shafer, D. Michael. *Deadly Paradigms: The Failure of U.S. Counterinsurgent Policy.* Princeton, NJ: Princeton University Press, 1988.

Snow, Donald M. *September 11, 2001: A New Kind of War?* New York: Longman, 2002.

——*Third World Conflict and American Response in the Post-Cold War World.* Carlisle, PA: Strategic Studies Institute, 1991.

Thompson, Sir Robert. *Make for the Hills: Memories of Far Eastern Wars.* London: Lee Cooper, 1989.

United States Army and U.S. Marine Corps. *Counterinsurgency Field Manual (U.S. Army Field Manual 3-24, Marine Corps Warfighting Publication 3-33.5).* Chicago, IL: University of Chicago Press, 2007 (referred to as "Petraeus manual" in text).

U.S. Marine Corps. *Afghanistan: Operational Culture for Deploying Personnel.* Quantico, VA: Center for Advanced Operational Cultural Learning, 2009.

6

DEFYING EINSTEIN

Repetition and Results

Albert Einstein would probably shake his head in sad bemusement at the way the United States has reacted to internal instability in developing world countries since the middle of the twentieth century. The German-born physicist, who died in 1955, was famous for his definition of *insanity*, and had he been able to apply it to the U.S. adventures in Vietnam, Iraq, and Afghanistan, he would likely have been appalled. The United States seems to keep doing the same thing in similar situations, apparently expecting different results. Is that insane?

To this point, much of the argument has been based on the similarities between internal developing world wars and the predictably negative effects of outside (American) intervention in those conflicts. The gist of the argument is that these negative outcomes are knowable in advance, and that in each case where the United States dispatched armed forces, there were prescient warnings of what eventually happened. In each case, that advice was ignored, and the predictable result occurred. What causes these tragic repetitions?

The short answer is that real world situations are seldom as simple as this construction suggests: any reader who maintains this formulation is a "straw man" is not entirely wrong. Real decisions are influenced by a wide variety of factors that may distort the decision process and policy outcomes. This chapter will examine some of these factors.

There is no shortage of explanations of decision making and what influences it. Any formal examination of the considerable literature on that subject goes well beyond present purposes. Rather, what is important is what has caused people to repeat mistaken decisions about entangling the country in DWICs where it cannot succeed.

Some of the reasons (or at least partial reasons) are institutional. The Department of Defense is dedicated to protecting the country against threats to its security, and will place great emphasis on finding anything that might be threatening.

Some explanations view the pressures within institutions to develop common views on problems: someone who believes there is little threat will not thrive in the national security decision-making environment. Others are more indirect and even skeptical: does the fact that some people profit from threats to security predispose them to see threats where others might not see them? The list of perspectives and explanations goes on and on.

Our modest journey begins with the simple question of why decision makers seem to keep making the same wrong decisions about the kinds of internal wars we have been examining. All those involved would deny rigorously that they are insane under Einstein's criteria. Looking briefly at the bare bones of why they would deny the charge may help point the direction for a more in-depth look.

The most obvious point that defenders of these decisions would make is that their depiction as repetitions of the same dynamic is wrong. It is a familiar argument that has been raised before in these pages and is based in the idea that DWIC situations where the United States has used force are sufficiently different that one is not repeating the response from a similar debacle. Moreover, the charge of repetition suggests that the *same person or people* are repeating these mistakes, which is generally not the case. The exception, of course, would be Iraq and Afghanistan, the decisions regarding which were made basically by the same team of George W. Bush administrators, prominently the neo-cons. This rejoinder, of course, denies that education serves as a vicarious form of experience: that people can learn from the mistakes of others.

If the country is to avoid making those same mistakes again in the future (and the past suggests we may well do so), it is necessary at least to try to glean what influences have led to a repetition of similar mistakes in the past. There is no pretense that this discussion will be definitive and lead to an infallible road map to allow avoidance of mistakes in the future. Rather, the remaining pages of the chapter will look at some partial influences, how they may affect critical decisions, and how they may individually and collectively contribute to a decision process that sometimes gets it wrong in critical situations. It is a pastiche of some of the reasons people may have made wrong decisions, not a systematic, scientific explanation.

The discussion will begin with some of the more conventional, institutional para-meters on decision making, then move to the American obsession with technological "fixes" to military problems, the influence of the military culture of American armed forces, and the possibility that narrower-than-national self-interest may influence policy. The chapter will conclude with a discussion of how such activism affects the broader question of American security in a resource-constrained world.

The Insanity of Doing the Same Thing and Hoping for Different Results: Institutional Factors

All organizations make decisions within an institutional framework that defines how those decisions will be made and by whom. This framework includes the roles that different individuals and groups play in the decision process at different levels within the organization, and the different actors generally have or develop their own particular vantage points on both the process and the substantive concerns with which it deals. From the experience that the organization accumulates, a pattern emerges, and this pattern will include unique attributes associated with different actors and their perspectives on the problems that confront them. Cumulatively, this area is known as *organizational behavior*, and different academic disciplines study it within their own disciplinary contexts.

Regularizing the decision process is necessary to add some structure and predictability to reaching decisions which, in the absence of some organization, would have to be made on an *ad hoc* basis with unspecified actors influencing each decision. The result of an unsystematic approach would be institutional chaos and probably mostly random, and often very bad, decisions. At the other extreme, a decision process that becomes entirely confined to predictable methods and outcomes may turn sclerotic, and if the decisions it reaches turn out to be incorrect, the result can be the repetition of mistakes that fly in the face of Einstein's entreaty. Chaos and sclerosis are equal enemies of good decisions, and these extremes may be particularly acute in the area of national security decision making.

The nature of the national security problem predisposes it more toward sclerosis than chaos. National security is naturally conservative because of the potential for disaster not as present in other private and public areas of decision making. The decision by an automobile maker to manufacture gas-guzzling cars at a time when consumers are looking for fuel economy can cost the automaker sales, but it can be rectified by switching to more economical models. A local government deciding to allocate less money to road maintenance may create public uproar, but it can be rectified in the next budget cycle. A decision not to prepare for a military contingency can lead an opponent to seize on the omission and attack, with grievous consequences that may not be redeemable. Knowing mistakes can be ultimately costly naturally predisposes the decision process to act in conservative ways, such as clinging to tried-and-true remedies and erring on the side of overpreparation, to cite two examples.

This conservative loading can be seen throughout the defense-decision process. For illustrative purposes and because each is important in its own right, four influences stand out as possible reasons that Einstein is inadvertently defied.

The first area is *doctrine*. Doctrine is, in the summation of Dennis M. Drew and Donald M. Snow, "what is believed about the best way to conduct military affairs." There are multiple sources from which judgments about what is "best" are arrived at, and they boil down to "a compilation and interpretation of concepts, actions, and experiences that have generally been successful in the past." Put another way, doctrine is the accumulated wisdom of the military about the best way to conduct operations to achieve objectives. As such, it contains both positive and negative elements: what works and what fails. Because military organizations are highly success oriented, their emphasis tends to be on ways of doing things that succeed rather than those that fail.

Doctrine is essentially a way to educate future forces based on past experiences: it vicariously instructs those without previous experience in particular situations on how to do those things in the present. As an educational tool, it is an important aspect of the military worldview, but it can also be a source of limitation and distortion in the decision process as well.

Doctrine is, at heart, an interpretation of history, and this has its own limits. For one thing, there is almost always disagreement about what happened in the past and why, and this is particularly true in situations where things did not go exactly as hoped. Interpreting the military lessons of the Vietnam experience became a military intellectual cottage industry as different analysts tried, from a variety of perspectives, to interpret what went wrong. People who opposed the war, for instance, tended to lay blame in different areas and directions than combat veterans, and especially veterans who were in command positions who issued orders (based in the doctrines of the time) that did not produce the expected results. The result has been conflicting interpretations that have muddied the doctrinal "takeaways" from the war. At the same time, equation of events creates controversy. Since the past is so rich in experiences, there are always multiple lessons from which one can choose, and there is always the danger of choosing the wrong one. Doctrine provides more choices than its strongest adherents would always readily admit.

Military organizations tend to be institutionally rigid in the sense of clinging to organizational and behavioral artifacts from the past. One way this is manifested within the military is the "school solution," the idea that there is a "right" answer to problems, and that the essence of military training is to learn the correct ways of going about things. Beyond strictly organizational imperatives (rigid rank order designations, conventions about how people of varying ranks interact with one another and the like), doctrine plays an important role in determining what those correct forms of behavior are. The foot soldier is taught what to do in particular situations he might encounter, not *how to think about* what to do in those situations. The reason is clear and justifiable, since less than an instantaneous, automatic doctrinal response may result in the soldier's death.

The problem of having, searching for, and institutionalizing correct answers is that it directs the organization to orthodoxy and, in turn, can lead to intellectual stagnation and sclerosis. Once a mode of behavior becomes established in a hierarchical, conservative organization like the military, it tends to be carved increasingly in granite and difficult to change, since change can affect the entire structure. In military organizations, doctrinal imperatives, moreover, tend to get implemented not only in instructions about the most efficacious behavior, but also in elaborate, expensive, and extensive support structures. The American Army, for instance, has doctrinally influenced investments in things like large stores of tanks and heavy artillery, which experience in the conventional European-style warfare of the twentieth century translated into doctrinal preference and force preparation. It is a difficult, wrenching, and thus partially resisted process to adjust established, even comfortable ways of doing things to dissimilar situations.

All of this suggests that doctrine can act as a source of dissonance when changing situations and assumptions are presented that challenge the doctrinal nexus from which a military organization proceeds. The United States, especially in the early going, treated the Vietnam War as largely a conventional war because it had a doctrine that covered preparing for and fighting such a conflict, and had only the most cursory understanding of the new challenges that the asymmetrical warriors of North Vietnam posed for it. Since doctrine is based on prior lessons, it is by definition backward looking; asymmetrical warfare, which is the major problem the United States confronts in DWICs, seeks to negate doctrine by presenting the opponent with dilemmas for which its doctrine offers incomplete or incorrect guidance. To bedevil the situation further, the asymmetrical warrior's methodology has as a basic tenet continual change and adaptation to confuse and complicate the actions of its opponents. That view of the conflict—frustrating the other side's doctrine—is an important aspect of how the asymmetrical warrior seeks to level the playing field with an opponent who believes that one of his advantages is a superior doctrine.

The danger in all this is that doctrine, rather than representing the "best" way to do things in war may instead simply become the "most comfortable" way to approach problems. The doctrinal solution to the kinds of conflicts in which the United States may become involved in the future requires doctrinal flexibility, and the very nature of doctrine and its development makes such a process particularly difficult. The effort to develop and inculcate in Army procedures a comprehensive doctrine for counterinsurgency, most publicly visible in the Petraeus manual, is really designed to teach a new war-fighting doctrine to the military, and it has been met with considerable resistance, much of it passive, from a military hierarchy more clearly steeped in a doctrinal understanding of war based on twentieth-century conventional lessons. Special Forces have unsurprisingly played a large and increasing role in dealing with the developing world warrior, because Special Forces are less burdened with conventional doctrine than other kinds of American warriors. Indeed, the methodology of the Special Force warrior inverts the training precepts of the conventional soldier, emphasizing ways to think through particular situations rather than fixed, established solutions to problems.

The second area is *conventional wisdom*. The concept refers to a generally accepted body of knowledge and interpretation of what is known about different aspects of the policy environment. As such, it is akin to military doctrine but is generally broader in scope, with an emphasis more on the policy and grand strategic levels than the more tactical level at which doctrine tends to be concentrated. Conventional wisdom suggests general approaches that have proven fruitful in dealing with different kinds of situations; doctrine tells one how to conduct military operations if conventional wisdom suggests that military power may be the appropriate tool for solving a particular national security problem.

Conventional wisdom also tends to be backward-looking. It tries to see how past experiences can be applied to the present rather than looking for innovative, different approaches to problems. Conventional wisdom tends to be the bailiwick of the most seasoned, veteran individuals within a decision-making unit, the elders as it were. These people are likely to be the most conservative members of a decision-making group, and the nature of national security situations reinforces and elevates the centrality of their conservativism.

Conventional wisdom has arguably been the enemy of viewing DWICs as a different kind of problem than conventional wars. The conventional wisdom about American military force, including its utility as a tool of foreign policy and its efficacy in different situations, is an artifact of the American experience at conventional war in the twentieth century. Conventional wisdom was reinforced by the American military approach to and success in the Kuwaiti desert and again during the initial invasion of Iraq, where a traditional approach did produce an initial "shock and awe" effect that masked as a solution to the Iraqi problem.

Conventional wisdom tends to reside in the upper levels of the national security establishment, among flag-rank uniformed officers and senior civilian policy makers and administrators, all of whom share long and common backgrounds and tend to view problems and solutions in similar manners. Uniformity of conviction and worldview is, indeed, one of the major criteria by which senior leaders move from junior to senior positions. The reason is captured in a traditional public administration concept, the *principle of agency*. This concept, briefly put, is that those in more senior positions within organizations tend to view those who basically agree with them as more reliable and brighter than those who do not, since they accept the wisdom of the position that the senior leaders take. Dissenters, on the other hand, are seen as somehow misguided, less informed, and thus less reliable than those who conform to the prevailing orthodoxy. The tendency to reward adherence to the common wisdom and not to unconventional, maverick behavior is not always openly admitted or, in some cases, even realized by those who practice it, but it is nonetheless present to some extent in all organizations. One of its pernicious effects is to weed out the more innovative, unconventional thinkers in any organization, those who are most likely to retain the intellectual flexibility to deal with unforeseen, new problems.

The extent to which the conventional wisdom dominates and strictures organizations and their responses to problems is also partly the result of the extent to which the third influence, *groupthink,* is embedded in organizational behavior. This concept, introduced by Irving Janis in a book with that title in 1982, dealt with "the psychological tendency for individuals within organizations to alter their views or perceptions in ways that allow them to conform to other members of a group with which they all identify." Janis' major interest was in how this conformance-producing dynamic fostered the ability of groups composed of the "best and the brightest" to ignore contrary evidence and to base decisions on incomplete or incorrect assessments of situations. Significantly, the two national security case examples on which he drew in particular were the Bay of Pigs fiasco of 1961 and American decision making during the Vietnam War.

The extent to which groupthink exists and how much of an influence it has varies from organization to organization and is to a large degree a matter of the amount of unanimity and intolerance of contrasting ideas that any organization tolerates or encourages. The principle of agency has as one of its major elements peer pressure to conform, and this tendency is reinforced in hierarchical organizations, of which the military is a primary example. Given our subject matter, the dynamic as it occurs within the military is especially salient. The military is the ultimate hierarchical organization, much of the operation of which is based on unquestioning acceptance and implementation of orders issued from higher to lower levels of the organization. For much of what the military does operationally, this characteristic is infinitely sensible and functional. One would not, for instance, want individual units pondering and deciding about whether or how to carry out orders in the middle of a battle in which their perspective is much more circumscribed than at command levels.

Hierarchical organizations are particularly prone to conventional-wisdom-based groupthink, however, and that can be a limitation when they are confronted with problems for which that conventional wisdom is questionable and where real innovation and dissenting debate may be more functional. What the group thinks in military organization is often what its flag-rank officers think (or what those beneath them believe they think). Commanders, in turn, are likely to be highly conventional in how and what they think, because the principle of agency suggests that conventional thinking got them promoted to leadership positions. In turn, acceptable, "responsible" thinking is likely to reflect what those making promotion decisions view as appropriate, and that is likely to reflect heavily the conventional wisdom on military subjects. The result is organizations led by those who have survived a promotion process that does not reward, and can even penalize, innovative, original thinking.

Military officers are, of course, well aware of these problems, particularly at the intermediate and senior levels below general or admiral rank. There has, for instance, been some very innovative, original work done within the military on questions and problems of developing world violence, but it has mostly been done by majors and colonels and not embraced wholeheartedly by the generals, who are part of a basic groupthink fraternity that defends the traditional ways of doing business for the military. Occasionally a "shooting star" arises from the ranks such as Generals David Petraeus and H. R. McMaster, but such an individual is certainly the exception to the rule and, in the case of Petraeus, has been much more highly regarded outside than inside the Army itself. A major consequence is that military institutions tend not to lead innovation in areas such as adaptation to involvement in DWICs.

There is a fourth, and somewhat unrelated, characteristic that should be mentioned—the idea of *noise*. As noted several times previously, there have been what proved to be accurate assessments of the negative consequences of American involvement in places like Vietnam, Iraq, and Afghanistan that were not acted upon positively at the time decisions were made. Part of the reason they were rejected was because they were at variance with conventional wisdom and thus were discounted as heretical and less-informed interpretations of reality than was available to the right-thinking veterans in positions of decision-making authority. Part of the reason may also be that negative suggestions came from people outside the decision process—academics or government officials in positions several layers removed from the actual decision makers, in which case those who made decisions may have been unaware of the recommendations. Another part of the reason may be that the accurate recommendations were buried in a sea of competing recommendations, such that those in decision-making authority had such a wide range of contradictory advice that they did not know what to accept and what to reject.

The problem thus can be and often is overabundance of advice (or information overload), and this is the heart of "noise." While there were a number of analysts who advised against intervening in Vietnam, there were also a lot of others imploring the United States to jump into that fray. In the Vietnam context, most of those calling for activism based their arguments in Cold War geopolitics, and the geopolitical argument drowned out the objections. In Iraq and Afghanistan, the chorus of impassioned advocacy of "doing something" in the war on terror similarly drowned out voices urging restraint. There was simply too much noise, the components of which could not be distinguished from one another to allow all sides of the argument to be adequately evaluated. Information overload favored the most numerous and vocal, who happened also to be incorrect. The information overload that is a prominent component of noise is a ubiquitous characteristic of the modern, electronic world, meaning that on any matter of policy choice, cyberspace will be awash in alternatives, some of which will in retrospect prove to be correct and some of which will not.

Technological Fixes: An American Fascination

Reflecting the historical advantage and defining characteristic of the United States as the leader in the discovery and application of science, the United States military has a virtual addiction to how science can be used to buttress the American superiority at war. Possessing weapons that are more sophisticated and capable than those possessed by adversaries gives the United States a critical edge against many opponents and potential adversaries who realize they must face a technologically superior American force. Such superiority also reinforces the predilection toward a more activist national security policy than a more modest capability might encourage.

In some important ways, a superior technological base and capability is an outgrowth of and substitute for the overwhelmingly superior American industrial base that was critical to success in World War II. During the two world conflicts of the first half of the twentieth century, the United States provided the critical additional manpower in one to push the enemy over the edge to defeat (World War I), and its industrial machine literally drowned the enemy in a tsunami-like mass of weapons and matériel in the other (World War II). The American role in the second war was particularly important, because the United States, acting as the "arsenal for democracy," established itself as the quantitative and qualitative standard of military production and armed might, a distinction formerly held by Germany.

The Cold War moved that advantage to the qualitative side of the ledger in three related ways. First, the Soviet opponent was a quantitative match for the United States, apparently obviating that source of superiority. The major basis of quantitative equivalence was an enormous Soviet force the fighting characteristics of which were unknown and a vast arsenal of equipment that was aging and dubiously capable, but all "bean counting" exercises pointed to Soviet equivalence or, in some cases, numerical superiority. The United States' edge had to be qualitative.

World War II spawned the other changes. The most dramatic was the unique contribution of breakthroughs in physics during the 1930s and 1940s, atomic weapons. The destructive capabilities of these nuclear weapons represented a qualitative escalation of military power for its possessors. As arsenals grew to enormous sizes (a process that began in the 1950s), it is not at all coincidental that the countries with the largest store of thermonuclear bombs (the United States and the Soviet Union) became known as superpowers, and everyone with no or only a few of these weapons occupied a lower military and geopolitical status. Nuclear technology became a defining dynamic of the Cold War order.

Airpower was the other technological force in the qualitative military equation. Heavier than air flight had, of course, been around since the earliest part of the twentieth century (the Wright Brothers' seminal flight was in 1903), and aircraft had played a minor role, limited mostly to reconnaissance of things happening on the ground, in World War I. Buttressed by doctrine developed between the wars that predicted the crucial importance of aerial bombardment on modern wars and advances in aircraft design, airpower made its strategic debut in World War II. It remains a major technological fix for fighting wars.

As long as military problems and solutions remain broadly conventional, technological fixing is attractive as a way to buttress American superiority. Historically, the United States scientific base has been unsurpassed, providing the knowledge base that could be militarily exploited through technological innovations. American wealth allowed those applications without cost being a limiting consideration. Moreover, technologically based outcomes can produce, in the appropriate forums, spectacular evidence of American superiority and convincing reasons why one should not confront the Americans militarily—at least not on American terms. Iraq tried to stand toe-to-toe with the Americans in conventional combat in the Kuwaiti desert in 1990–91 with disastrous results, and American technologically derived firepower did produce the "shock and awe" that convinced the Iraqis not to resist the American invasion in 2003 directly.

Applied in appropriate manners and in applicable circumstances, technology does serve as a "force multiplier" that can increase the military efficiency and effectiveness of the possessor. In addition to making McInerny's "kill chain" more efficient at eliminating enemy forces, satellite imagery of battlefields displayed on distant high-definition monitors can provide the possessor with critical information like deployment locations unavailable to non-possessors, a distinct tactical assist. Individually and collectively, the aim of technological innovations is to make American forces more effective against technologically inferior enemies. The critical importance of this technological impact has become an unquestioned assumption of much American thinking about war, and technological fixes are one of the first resorts to which military planners turn in assessing current and future barriers.

Fixation with technology, however, has led many American planners to ignore the limits of technological advantage. In a conflict in which both sides agree that the technologically superior side will be the winner and the determining factor in fighting is the clash of technologies, technology is indeed critical. Conventional European-style warfare at least implicitly accepts this premise, but the truth of the assertion of technological criticality is not necessarily universal. Working from the premise that technology is a cure-all can have pernicious effects. Three of these are worth brief exploration.

The first problem is that there will inevitably be an attempt by a technologically inferior opponent to lessen or obviate technologically based disadvantages. It is, after all, a basic tenet of asymmetrical warfare to employ ROEs that negate the advantages of the opponent to level the playing field. If the opponent happens to be the United States, many of these disadvantages will be based in technology, and the Americans, secure in their superiority, may not bother to devise ways to overcome attempts to negate their advantages. For example, one of the major technological advantages the United States has is in identifying enemy leadership and troop locations via satellite imagery and in being able to attack these targets with precision munitions. Beyond finding better ways and places to hide, a major response to that American advantage has been to embed those targets in civilian areas. No matter how precise the American attack may be, there will be some civilian casualties (collateral damage) for which the Americans will be blamed. In internal wars where the contest for hearts and minds is the central competition, the enmity created can cancel out the beneficial effects. The side effects of drone use in Afghanistan and Pakistan (killing innocent people—collateral damage—and in the process making more enemies than it eliminates) is an example.

The failure to recognize technological limits can also have a second effect on planning, which is overreach. This is a particular problem for the evangelical Americans who, as Andrew C. Bacevich and others have pointed out, suffer from a missionary zeal that implores us to spread our system and values everywhere, including into places and among people who do not clearly want to be so blessed. In the words of folk singer and writer Tom Paxton in an indictment of the war in Southeast Asia, we set out "to help save Vietnam from the Vietnamese," whether they want to be saved or not.

Quite aside from the ability of outsiders successfully to impose their own values on reluctant others, the fixation feeds a misplaced sense of omnipotence: we not only need to save the world from itself, but we can succeed. Both the desire and belief depend on the correctness of the assertion that the United States is so technologically superior and resource abundant that it can achieve whatever it wants, with little sense of the need to create priorities or to measure potential actions against limiting criteria like the importance of outcome to American interests. The string of unsuccessful forays in Asia should dampen the conviction that all barriers can be surmounted and all goals accomplished.

The third, and less discussed, possible pernicious effect of technological fixation may be to dehumanize war and, in effect, to make it easier to wage. Generally, those who promote newer technologies justify them on one or both of two bases: that they make military action against an opponent both more effective and efficient, and that they provide additional protection for American combatants and thus lower U.S. casualties. The intent, in other words, is to endow American forces with advantages others do not enjoy, giving those opponents additional pause before taking on the Americans and aiding in the defeat of those opponents if they are not dissuaded. These advantages may seem "unfair" to opponents or neutral outside observers, but then, the purpose of war is victory, not fairness.

The advantages measured in terms of lowering expected American combat losses are potentially the more morally ambiguous and may make the recourse to war easier. One of the conditioning factors in any military action is the self-sacrifice that such action may entail, a concern from the lowest tactical level to the grand strategic consideration of going to war at all. This concern is a potential inhibition on any given actions, and is especially a constraint in political democracies, where those who may become casualties are constituents and their families. Part of this inhibition has been removed by moving toward the professional, all-volunteer concept of military manpower (discussed below). The impact of technology can be an offsetting effect.

To the extent that technological advances insulate American forces from taking casualties or reducing the number that must be endured, does this make it easier to reach the decision to go to war in situations where the expectation of higher physical losses might make the cost-risk benefit of fighting less appealing? In other words, does knowing that one will not face the electoral or other wrath of voters because of the slaughter of Americans allow justification of wars of lesser importance (wars of choice, for instance) than is the case when a spirited and convincing defense of actions might be made necessary to an electorate that will be personally bloodied by war?

The Military Malady: Can or Can't Do?

Historically, the United States has been a very confident, successful, optimistic country. History has been a positive factor for most of the American experience, from independence from British rule to sweeping across the North American continent (despite the occasional objections of people who were already there) to saving European democracies from defeat in the world wars. The United States has, at least until relatively recently, been remarkably successful by almost any measure. This success has had a distinctly interactive relationship to the American experience at arms, and the resulting synergism has in turn reinforced the virtually missionary zeal many Americans have about the American role in the world.

Much of the basic attitude was formed in the period leading up to and including World War II, and the last great American war has been a watershed for the development of American optimism since World War II. Recent experience has not been as positive as the earlier period, but the American self-image has not adjusted to a different image than the "can do" myth by which it operates. Expressed by Bacevich as the "credo" of the Washington rules, the cumulative lesson is that the American mission in the world is to uplift the rest of humankind—which operationally means make it approximate the American system and values—and that American armed forces can accomplish that task. Our evangelism tells us we "must do," and the military tradition says we "can do." This tradition persists despite recent experiences that seem to contradict both propositions.

The derivation of the catchphrase "can do" comes from the American military experience, and it is part of what I have called in the various editions of my national security texts the "myth of invincibility." As described in the fifth edition of *National Security for a New Era*, its "core is the idea that regardless of the circumstances, when the United States is forced to fight, it prevails." The myth is exactly that, a belief based partly in an accurate assessment and partly in a romantic and not altogether true recollection of the past. Its military translation, however, is in the idea of "can do," the response of the American military to any challenge issued to it by political authorities.

The idea that the United States has a unique saving mission has long historical roots in the American self-perception as a special place, a "house on the hill" whose glow serves as a beacon for others. For the first century or more of American history, that sense of "specialiness" translated into the desire to remain an aloof, distant light providing an example for others to emulate. This sense is captured in entreaties like those of Washington's Farewell Address and Jefferson's First Inaugural Address, and was, until the twentieth century, an article of faith-guided American interaction with the world.

The experience of the world wars and the ensuing Cold War added an evangelical sense of activism to the American self-image. The United States felt it averted a European self-made disaster in World War I, and while retreating to its historic policy of aloofness between the wars, had developed a sense of missionary zeal in its effort "to make the world safe for democracy." A portent of attitudes to come is found in President Woodrow Wilson's call to Congress for a declaration of war in 1917: "The day has come when America is privileged to spend her blood and her might for the principles that gave her birth and happiness. God helping her, she can do no other." In World War II, the United States expended both blood and treasure for similar ends and emerged as one of the world's two remaining powers, facing yet another evil in the form of Soviet communism. The mission to spare the world of this scourge became the basis for American activism; much of the burden fell upon an American military willing to bear the load. The dynamics have been extended to the scourge of terrorism.

The can–do attitude has both positive and negative effects. Positively, it creates an attitude and élan among military members that is a clear source of fighting morale and an important source of tenacity and innovation in approaching military problems. "Can do" is an antidote to any sense of defeatism, and it endows the American military with a sense of swagger and self-confidence that adds to its formidability as a fighting force. "Can do" has a negative side, however, because it can preclude, or at least lessen, the likelihood of recognizing there are situations where the American military "can't do."

This positive, if inflated, assessment interacts with the missionary zeal that the United States has toward an imperfect world: the world not only needs saving (if from itself), the United States is capable of providing that redemption. Both presumptions are suspicious, and especially when applied to DWICs. Regardless of the purity of American motives (a matter not to be taken for granted), it is not at all clear that indigenous populations always welcome the kind of transformations that the United States offers when it interferes in their affairs. When the Americans intervene and are welcome, it is normally because they may prove helpful in ridding the country of some unwanted condition, such as a brutal dictator (Saddam Hussein) or a bizarre, offensive regime (the Afghan Taliban in 2001). If American action was limited to the "hit and run" tactic of tearing down an old edifice and leaving its reconstruction to the natives, the indigenous population might well be thankful for the help. The American vision to "do good" goes well beyond simple cleansing to leaving behind its own distinctive "improvements." These improvements often involve a prolonged American stay that the indigenous population comes to resent, and the improvements the Americans want to make may be at various levels of odds with indigenous values and desires. The result is likely to be resistance that grows over time and makes the accomplishment of the mission even harder.

Resistance to the American self-proclaimed mission complicates the military mission as well and moves assessments from the category of "can do" to either "we're not sure we can do" or even "can't do." Admitting there are missions assigned to it that it cannot accomplish is a difficult, bitter pill for the American military to swallow, and one it has a difficult time bringing itself to admit. The unfortunate side of the "can do" tradition is that it is sometimes difficult for the military to recognize its own limitations, both to itself and to those who seek to employ it to accomplish things beyond its purview and abilities. The prevailing ethic has always been, in effect, that no mission is too hard for the American military; some may be more difficult and take longer than others, but no problem is insurmountable. This trait provides an admirable sense of tenacity and an inventive approach that can yield better results than a more modest self-assessment would suggest. At the same time, the attitude can be, in effect, irresponsible if it leads the military into missions for which it is inappropriate and at which it cannot possibly succeed. In these cases, "can't do" is the more honest and responsible response.

The precise advice that the United States military leadership presented to the George W. Bush administration regarding the feasibility of Operation Iraqi Freedom (the code name for the war against Iraq) is not publicly known. The autobiography of its commander, General "Tommy" Franks suggests that it was very much a "can do" response. If the advice was that the U.S. armed forces could defeat the Iraqi army and topple Saddam Hussein but no more, then it was sound, responsible advice. If, however, "can do" encompassed the absolutely predictable Iraqi resistance to a prolonged occupation (which, it will be remembered, was not part of the original plan) and the additional requirement of installing a stable, democratic post–Saddam regime, "can do" strained credulity.

This distinction gets toward the heart of the dilemma facing the military. The Army learned from Vietnam, at least for a time, that involvement in internal wars is a minefield where victory is difficult or impossible and where avoidance is the best response. At least parts of the American military learned this lesson the hard way in Southeast Asia. At the same time, the military faced in 2002 an American political leadership that was obsessed with making war on Iraq and eliminating Saddam Hussein. The military was in a bind. It could respond "can do" and march into a briar patch of likely failure, or it could reply "can't do" and risk the ire of the administration. It chose the first option—unfortunately.

The problem is that the country's interests are ultimately served poorly by failure. If, as has been argued here, saying "can do" leads to failure, than the effect of military self-confidence is to serve the national interest poorly. This is not a comfortable position for those within the military to confront: do they hew to the mantra of "can do" and march off into military and political swamps from which they cannot successfully extricate themselves? Or do they admit that there are occasions where they "can't do" and risk alienating the political base on which they rely for support as well as disappointing themselves and those who believe in the mythology of "can do"?

The Political Puzzle: National or Self-Interest

The discussion to this point has proceeded on the implied supposition that those who have made what turned out to be incorrect decisions about using military force have done so out of reasonably pure motives based in their assumptions about the national interest and what the United States can accomplish in the world. The argument here has been that these decisions were incorrect and that those who made them had little excuse not to see the negative consequences of the courses on which they launched the country. From that vantage point, one can only wonder why the decisions were reached, and the conclusion has to be that those who made the decisions must have been influenced by factors and considerations that led them to make decisions that were misguided and incorrect. The people who made these decisions would not, of course, embrace this depiction of what courses they chose for the country. National decisions, after all, are presumably made by highly qualified officials—one generation or another's "best and the brightest"—and one implication of a negative assessment is that they were neither all that good nor all that bright. Another is that there were environmental influences that caused decision makers to reach conclusions that were incorrect. Getting some handle on those processes can be helpful in creating a future setting in which the same mistakes are repeated.

There is an alternative way to think about the operational environment and set of perceptions and circumstances in which these decisions have been fashioned and made that is simultaneously more and less sympathetic to those who have made them. The explanation is complex and controversial, but it can be condensed around two basic concepts: the *subjectivity* of assessments and decisions and the notion of *self-interest* rather than national interest as the driver in making decisions. Each individually and the two in combination provide a different setting in which decisions quite unlike those suggested here might be and have been made. The combination is more sympathetic to those who have made what have been described here as predictably bad decisions because it suggests that the decision makers saw a different world situation than that described here and responded to that environment, making them less irrational in the decisions they reached. It is less sympathetic in that the alternative environment that was created was driven more by narrowly defined self-interest than the national interest and thus suggests an unflattering level of venality among those decision makers.

Subjectivity

The first concept is the subjectivity of national security and what serves that interest. The notion of subjectivity goes to the nature of national security itself and how there can be different concepts both about the parameters and details of that concept and thus disagreement about what actions should and should not be taken to realize different perceptions. The heart of subjectivity comes from the different meanings that different people attach to different events and situations and their impact on keeping America and Americans safe.

When applied specifically to national security, there are two primary dimensions of the safety that is the core of the country's security that derive from the basic definition of *security*: safety or a sense of safety. One aspect is *physical safety*, and it refers to objective, physical forces that can pose a direct, tangible threat to the survival of the country or its interests. In the historic American experience, physical threats to the American homeland, the most basic interest that must be secured, have been bounded and limited, thanks in large measure to American geography. Broad oceans on two of its flanks and reasonably weak or friendly neighbors on its other borders mean there has been little direct threat of another country invading and conquering or otherwise menacing American citizens. The development of an operational intercontinental ballistic missile capable of carrying Soviet nuclear bombs to American targets and against which there were (and arguably still are) no means of defense fundamentally changed that calculation and added to the horror and fatalism of the Cold War. The 9/11 attacks created a similar sense of threat from international terrorism.

The other dimension of security is psychological: what makes people *feel* safe. It is on this dimension that subjectivity truly becomes a prominent part of national security calculations. Part of the reason is that people differ in what makes them feel safe and unsafe. While, for instance, everyone will agree that nuclear-tipped weapons aimed at the heartland pose a threat to survival, there are a host of other conditions on which the sense of threat is not the same for all people. During the Cold War, for instance, there was the question of how much danger possible communist inroads into the western hemisphere posed to American safety. This debate centered on Cuba, which sits 90 miles from the American coastline, and the Central American countries south of Mexico. How much danger did their destabilization pose? To some Americans, the threat seemed very real and very dangerous, resulting in the very negative policy toward Cuba aimed at overthrowing the Castro regime and in American interventions in places like Nicaragua and Panama to overthrow governments or to suppress movements that might be pro-communist. To other Americans, the threat seemed exaggerated and actions taken in the name of suppressing these threats seemed unwise and even hysterical. The divide between opposing perceptions reached a crescendo in the 1980s over the Iran-Contra crisis, the Central American aspect of which was the support for opponents of the leftist Sandinista regime in Nicaragua by the Reagan administration and opposition to that support in the U.S. Congress.

The Cold War highlighted the subjective dimension of the security debate. The activist, evangelical nature of the American approach to the competition with communism meant extending American security guarantees to places and situations where traditional American interests did not exist and where there was little or no physical threat to the United States on which to ground security policy. The highly emotional nature of the Cold War allowed inclusion of considerable extension of what made Americans feel secure as part of the Cold War paradigm.

The very kind of conflicts that form the heart of this book can be seen in this light. American military intervention in places like Vietnam, Iraq, and Afghanistan are exceptionally difficult to justify as part of the physical sense of security, although attempts have been made to do so. The domino theory, carried to its logical conclusion (some would say absurdity) ultimately suggested that the fall of Vietnam could put the United States itself at danger. Both Iraq and Afghanistan have been justified on the grounds that the failure to defeat terrorism in those countries amplified the danger of direct terrorist assaults on American soil. These connections have never been entirely convincing to the American people because they all involve long and tenuous causal chains, but if the arguments that each posed a threat to physical security were true, support would have been more forthcoming and probably more durable. The problem has been that each of these adventures flowed from an expanded sense of the psychological dimension of security. Since opinions about what makes people feel safe are highly subjective and can lead to diametrically opposite conclusions, there has been less than total or enduring support for either: Americans do not all feel equally threatened by any of these situations.

One way to think about the ongoing debate surrounding security is by focusing it on the psychological sense of security. The Washington consensus on the threat during the Cold War has remained largely in place even since the end of the Cold War and the end of the threat on which the consensus was based. During the 1990s, defenders of the Cold War paradigm fought a rear guard action maintaining that the policies remained important because of the supposed danger of communist resurgence. The supporters were conceptually losing that intellectual battle, but were revitalized by the emergence of a new, physical threat in the form of terrorism, apparently providing the same kind of physical threat base Soviet nuclear weapons posed. The result has been, in a sense, to "white out" the Cold War communist base of the Cold War paradigm and to insert Middle East terrorism in its place. As the apparent threat posed by groups like Al Qaeda has appeared to become less plausible as a physical threat to the American homeland, this modification of the Cold War paradigm has become progressively strained. The result has been to throw the political debate over national security more into the psychological dimension of security, where there is much more disagreement and dissent than when that debate can be moored in a direct, physical threat that must be countered.

This intellectual debate occurs within the context of a considerable institutional structure that arose and matured during the consensus supporting the Cold War paradigm and which feels threatened and potentially dispossessed depending on the outcome of any intellectual dissection of the previous consensus. The heart of this structure is the national security establishment. Its components include the national security structure within the government consisting of entrenched elements such as the Department of Defense (including the military) and related edifices such as the array of intelligence apparatuses associated with the government. It also includes supportive institutions and individuals in the Congress and the elite population of defense analysts, academics, and commentators, all of whose prosperity is tied to the paradigm and its perpetuation. Outside the formal structure of government is a whole range of direct interests from defense industries and contractors to local communities where armed forces are based or weapons are manufactured. Cumulatively, these influences are often aggregated as the *military-industrial complex*, a term first popularized by President Eisenhower, who warned against its pernicious potential influence. The various individuals and institutions that are part of this entrenched complex are certainly supporters of national security. Their involvement goes beyond a pure, abstract interest in the debate or its outcomes, since they are personally involved in that process and its outcomes: they are self-interested.

Self-Interest

The other concept is thus self-interest. If national interest is in some measure subjective, it raises the question of what other influences may affect how one defines the national interest. One of the possible influences is *self-interest*, the extent to which individuals and groups profit (in one sense or another of that term) from different depictions of the national interest and policies to ensure it. This is a subject that is extremely controversial and explosive, and it is at the heart of the basic cleavage about the future of American national security policy.

Discussions about self-interest are controversial and tend to create a very emotional, occasionally vituperative and conspiratorial tone. The controversy arises primarily from the alleged levels of influence that those in the military-industrial complex (hereafter MIC) have on defense policy and from the extraordinary amount of national resources (mainly money) that is involved in national security policy implementation. It is emotional because so much of the debate is grounded in the subjective dimension of security and how that translates into policy directions and resource allocation in which the MIC has a direct and tangible stake. The debate is vituperative because each side accuses the other of impure, even unpatriotic motives: defenders of the Cold War paradigm accusing critics of seeking to undermine basic American safety, and critics accusing the MIC of venality and self-interested greed rather than patriotic purposes. It is conspiratorial in that critics often attribute support for policies with personally enriching outcomes to conspiracies among elements of the MIC.

The arguments about self-interest arise because of the amount of national resources involved in national security and the consequences of national security decisions. The American response to the perceived dictates of the Cold War paradigm was to create an enormous edifice of governmental mechanisms and private sector institutions that supported and implemented that set of institutions. During the 1950s (before the development of and rise in spending on entitlement programs that began in the 1960s), defense spending constituted roughly half of what the government spent, and this enormous bite created Eisenhower's warning that the intertwined governmental and private institutions who created the consensus and implemented it were becoming too large and too powerful. Eisenhower issued his warning in 1960 as he witnessed the development of an increasingly large, powerful, and entrenched set of defense institutions and supporting rationales as they had developed to that point. In the ensuing half-century plus, those interests have become even more a part of, and many would argue obstacle to, responsible national security policy.

The existence and nature of the MIC has always been a point of disagreement and controversy. Roughly speaking, the MIC refers to the relationship between large defense industries who provide and promote the equipment and support for the armed services, the armed services themselves, and those political figures in the executive and legislative branches of government who provide the resources which defense industries use to equip and supply the armed forces. The relationship between the elements of the resulting "iron triangle" is controversial in two basic ways: the rotation of personnel among its various parts, and the influence of those who have personal interests in outcomes on the shape of the problem that confronts the country and which the MIC "services."

The rotation of personnel is an obvious case of potentially compromising self-interest. The problem is that members of each set of institutions can and do move from one part of the MIC to the other, often to great personal advantage. A retiring military officer, for instance, may accept a position in a defense industry whose activities he might have monitored while in uniform; a staff member of a congressional committee overseeing national security or an assistant secretary within the Pentagon might accept a job lobbying on behalf of a defense industry; or an official in a defense industry might accept a position within a presidential administration, knowing he or she will return to industry after completing his or her government assignment. The rationale for this rotation is that the individuals who engage in the rotation have expertise accumulated to help them do their jobs: the officer knows the industry he formerly monitored, the congressional staffer has accumulated knowledge about national security, and the industry official knows what his or her industry can contribute to national security implementation. The insidious influence is that the jobs are often quite lucrative and competitive, meaning that those who move from arena to arena may be compromised knowing that their ability to profit personally may depend on how supportive they are of the potential employer.

The process also influences the shape and content of the national security policy it purports to serve. The great lubricant of the process is the considerable amount of money that it generates, and those who benefit from the funds generated have a vested interest in making that "pot" and their part of it as large as possible. The major recipients of benefits are defense industries, and they rely on government (including the military) to direct funding to the particular products they produce—notably weapons systems of various kinds. Since their prosperity depends on a maximum transfer of funds from government coffers to their corporate pockets, they thus have a vested interest in maximizing the "demand" for their services, and the chief vehicle for stimulating and sustaining that flow is the perception of a robust national security threat that requires vigilance in terms of large government investments in their products. It is thus no surprise that those who are part of the MIC support and promote the existence of a "strong" national defense as a response to the direst possible assessment of the threats facing the country.

In his farewell address, Eisenhower, who was Supreme Commander Allied Expeditionary Force (SCAEF) during World War II, warned of the insidious influence of the MIC. The heart of his entreaty was based in the inflated demands that the MIC made on scarce national resources, a particular concern of the thirty-fourth president. "Ike" believed the key element in national security was a sound economy, which he equated with a balanced budget, a goal excessive defense spending demands threatened. His warning has particular resonance in the current debate in which involvement in DWICs is a costly component. One obvious way to help rein in runaway government deficits is to reduce expenditures on defense. Many who favor deficit reductions also favor continued robust defense expenditures, and critics see the fingers of the MIC heavily influencing this apparent contradiction to Eisenhower's conclusions.

The question of self-interest comes down to the amount and degree of influence that those who have personal stakes in defense spending levels should have on the outcomes or a process from which they personally profit. Critics tend to argue that the influence is incestuous and invidious, and that it pollutes a more objective analysis of defense problems. Unsurprisingly, these critics argue that a more "objective" analysis (one conducted by people like themselves lacking self-interest in the outcomes) would result in reduced defense spending, an outcome they favor. Defenders, equally unsurprisingly, argue that the MIC is largely an analytical fiction and that the various components of what critics label a conspiracy represent an indispensable expert base whose advice and counsel is necessary to keep the country safe. Since these individuals and the institutions of which they are members have been in place for decades, theirs is the "establishment" view.

There is considerable disagreement about which of these positions is correct or even responsible. The MIC is, for instance, the key mechanism of Bacevich's Washington rules, and thus the dynamics it represents are at the heart of his calls for reform, a sentiment shared by many, generally liberal, reform advocates. The establishment, on the other hand, can argue that the generally conservative path (erring on the side of overpreparation, for instance) has served the country well through the Cold War and beyond, and that any wholesale dismantling of the MIC would have potentially devastating national security consequences, such as underpreparedness should serious threats arise. This latter position has greatest resonance with those who profit from the ongoing relationship and more generally from many defense-minded conservatives.

The question of self-interest is not a black-or-white matter. No one, of course, defends the notion that people should profit simply because of their positions, a clear violation of federal law and ethics, and those who defend the current system would argue that self-aggrandizement is not a major outcome of a working system, the purpose of which is to serve the national defense. The simple fact is that both sides in the debate have a point. Self-interest is clearly involved in any system in which the decisions have private profit as a consequence, and trying to guard against abuse in the exercise of self-interest is a legitimate concern. At the same time, those who are part of the MIC establishment do have or develop considerable expertise in the areas in which they work and from which they profit. There is clearly a synergism involved in the two poles. Those who seek to avoid decisions dominated by self-interested greed do not want to lose the expertise of those within the process who have useful knowledge and perspective on problems, which dismantling or removing all of the profit motives would likely endanger. At the same time, most members of the MIC have patriotic, defensible arguments for what they advocate, even if profit is a byproduct or motivation. It is difficult to cull the advantages from the dangers.

One consequence of the existence of a robust, influential MIC has been to give a strong status quo loading to the process and its outcomes. Members of the various elements of the MIC tend to share or to develop similar views on national security matters. As noted earlier, there is a strong natural conservative bias among those who make policy in this area because of the potential consequences of being wrong, and this translates into the institutionalization of attitudes and pre-dilections to rely upon "tried-and-true" solutions to problems and to develop intellectual cases for those solutions. The Cold War paradigm, for instance, offered an assessment of the military threat and prescribed "heavy" military solu-tions in the form of armed forces equipped with large stocks of generally large, lethal, and expensive weapons systems. Many of these weapons platforms, some-times in modified forms, remain in the inventory and are justified at least partly because they apparently worked during the Cold War. As these weapons age and are threatened with obsolescence (or simply wear out), it is a natural position of those manufacturers and architects of plans using these weapons to believe that more advanced and more capable replicas are the solution, even if the problem may be different. Is their advocacy honest or disingenuous, the result of seeking to reinvigorate security or to perpetuate past profits? Do, for instance, aerospace manufacturers see the need for new aircraft of various kinds as the result of objective defense needs or because they want to make large profits manufacturing them? The answer probably has elements of both: you are likely to promote what you believe in and also what you profit from. The question is where to draw the line between the purely national security and profit motivations. The status quo loading comes into play because those who have devoted a lifetime to traditional solutions are not likely to promote solutions that deny the continuing relevance of what they have favored for a long time and, coincidentally or not, from which they have profited.

The heart of the industrial aspect of the MIC contributes, directly or indirectly, to the expansionist bias that was a major characteristic of the Cold War paradigm.

The paradigm sought to prevent the expansion of communist domain and to increase that part of the world that opposed communism. Certainly part of the motivation was the underlying missionary zeal of a competition between Western values and "godless, evil" communism, but part of it has to be associated with a productive system that thrived from an expanded competition that required ever larger, newer, and more capable military equipment to conduct the competition successfully. A static, passive competition would likely have been "bad for business" in the sense that it would have required lesser expenditures on military wherewithal and thus have suppressed the profits that accompanied a very lively military competition between the two sides seemingly ever in need of nourishment.

Was this expansionism necessary for the country or a matter of self-aggrandizement for those who were part of the MIC? The answer is not as easy as partisans on either side of the issue portray it, and it undoubtedly contained elements of both. The military-industrial complex membership is, generally speaking, composed of people who share common values that have either caused them to seek positions within its various institutions or of people who have adopted those attitudes if they did not originally possess them. One of the core values is a commitment to maximizing the security of the country, and it provides its adherents with a conservative bias that suggests a basic continuation of present practices until or unless the situation is unalterably and unambiguously changed. Dysfunction is the major perception that can foster change, but there is a bias to minimize the belief in environmental change as illusory and aimed at (or having the consequence of) reducing vigilance in a setting that members are predisposed to see as dangerous and threatening. From this predisposition, a maximum effort to protect against a hostile environment seems the only realistic, responsible action, and entreaties to the contrary are likely rejected as weak, deluded, even suspicious.

The result, a commitment to perpetuating a very robust national security state, is self-aggrandizing for those who are part of the industrial base that "feeds the beast." But what motivates those who profit? Is it the wealth they accumulate from the effort? Or is it patriotism? It is a question that can be asked of a wide variety of people involved in various parts of the MIC. It is most obvious to ask the question of those who reap the profits from defense expenditures like the CEOs of defense supplying companies, but it extends down the chain to communities that house defense industries or military bases and whose prosperity is partly dependent on a robust defense effort. It also affects both uniformed military whose career paths through the ranks partially relies on a large military establishment with ample opportunities for promotion and to defense analysts and so-called "defense intellectuals" who would have less to think or write about in a more restricted national security environment.

Whatever the source or reasons that underlay it, the impact of the MIC is to resist change, including a needed modification of attitudes and practices surrounding American involvement in internal conflicts in developing countries. The Washington rulers whose base is in the Cold War setting and paradigm are firmly committed to a process that is weighted toward a static, status quo–loaded view of the world, and they find much of their sustenance in the support of the traditional elements of the MIC: defense decision makers who rotate among its parts and whose credibility is largely measured in the orthodoxy of their views, military officers whose futures within and outside the uniformed services are defined by the structure of how things are done, and the defense industrial base that provides the fodder that nourishes the system. Their endurance and resiliency in the policy process are most clearly demonstrated by their continued sway physically and conceptually over two decades after the nurturing environment of the Cold War has utterly disappeared. They are under some siege in the current environment of economic austerity and reaction to the debacles of Iraq and Afghanistan, but the question is whether their hold can be loosened enough to allow for the entrance of a newer cast with different perspectives that reflects the twenty-first century's concerns, such as those surrounding DWICs.

Intermestic Intersection: Geopolitical Folly or Ike's Rejoinder

Virtually all national security concerns have both *inter*national and do*mestic* aspects and consequences, and it is from that combination that the notion of *intermestic politics* was born (the idea is discussed at some length in Snow and Patrick J. Haney, *American Foreign Policy for a New Era*). This intermestic phenomenon is a simple reality of the contemporary world, and it means that virtually any international action will have some domestic consequences, and that many apparently internal decisions will have reverberations beyond American borders as well. The intermestic condition is particularly true for the United States, since this country, as part of its post–World War II evangelism and activism, has an interest in what happens virtually everywhere and which, because of that universal concern, means the rest of the world has to be concerned about what America thinks and does.

American policy toward DWICs is certainly intermestic. Whenever domestic violence flares or the political condition of other countries becomes problematic, there will be Americans who view the situation with alarm and who will advocate some kind of American remediation to resettle that situation to one of which the United States more greatly approves. For some Americans, this impulse will be motivated by humanitarian concerns, since horrendous civilian suffering is usually associated with these situations. For others, the sentiments may be an extension of the underlying conviction of the Cold War paradigm that the United States must act wherever its interests, however minor, may be threatened. Given the American stature as arguably the world's remaining superpower, keeping the world order has been a self-appointed role for some Americans. American policy has been activist and aggressive enough in this regard that much of the world now expects American reaction and leadership everywhere. Some, of course, anticipate our responses positively and some dread them, but the expectation of some American reaction is a virtual given.

The American ability to order or change international conditions, particularly by force, has become increasingly bounded. One of the reasons is that there are situations in which American preferences for outcomes and those of the indigenous populations where conflict arises are in contrast and the indigenous population is capable of resisting American solutions to its problems. The DWICs are prime examples of this limitation. The United States is simply not capable of imposing a *Pax Americana* on places where the indigenous population does not want it. Whether this truth represents a regrettable decline of the United States as a world power or a simple recognition of the characteristics of the environment and adaptation to it is an interesting question. Nonetheless, it is a fact to which policy must adjust. The calls to avoid future Vietnams, Iraqs, and Afghanistans may, to paraphrase the old Vietnam conclusion, amount to a call for "no more windmills (quixotic quests)."

The intermestic influence comes from the expense that American adventurism has created and its negative effect on the American domestic situation. Acting effectively as the world's policeman has been very costly, and involvement in unwinnable wars has been one of the gaudiest examples of American resources expended in large amounts for dubious purposes and with minimal positive results. In an era where private, businesslike values have been a resurgent goal within the American body politic, these kinds of involvements can hardly be characterized as anything but bad business. Ironically, of course, these otherwise bad business decisions have been very good business for those with a vested interest in the MIC, and that countervailing influence helps explain partly why conservative, pro-business interests also support national security policies that are utterly bankrupt within their more familiar terms of reference (investment returns).

The costs of interventions in developing world conflicts are numerous and diverse, from the expenditure of precious human lives to lost opportunities to invest resources in other, more productive ways, both domestically and internationally. In the current economic climate, however, it is the direct costs of such involvements on government budgets and thus the health of the overall economy that is the most obvious area of impact, and it is a concern that will endure until the point of a total recovery of the American economy from the impacts of the recession of 2008. The basic question is "can we afford any more wars like those in Iraq and Afghanistan?"

The answer, of course, depends on one's perspective. From the vantage point of the Cold War paradigm, the basis for assessing opportunities is largely geopolitical. The bulk of traditional arguments suggests that the United States must remain activist to maintain its position in the international scheme of things, but does not necessarily mean an uncritical acceptance of continued American intervention in wars it cannot possibly win. The geopolitical perspective may have as one of its built-in blinders an aversion to assessing the "can't do" side of potential situations, but it nonetheless cannot fail to acknowledge that quixotic adventures detract from rather than enhance America's prestige in the world.

From the Cold War vantage point, the question is more properly, "can the United States afford *not* to assert itself in troublesome situations in the world?" If

American interests are essentially universal and the country does not act decisively to protect those interests, does it lose its claim to being the preeminent power in the world? The answer is not as obvious as its strongest defenders might suggest. Rather, one can raise the question of whether American involvement in the world's troubles should be universal or selective. Phrasing the question in that manner suggests the added concern of the bases for selection. The likely ability of the country to succeed in its pursuit of self-interest has to be at least one of those concerns. Most Americans would agree that supporting losing causes does not enhance national prestige, however meritorious the failed cause.

This kind of calculation may not have been so important during the Cold War, when the perceived geopolitical consequences of inaction seemed so severe. It was assumed that important, even vital, American interests were at stake whenever a potential "breakout" of the containment line presented itself (which most DWICs appeared to do), making some sort of virile response mandatory. One consequence may have been an implicit assumption that American important interests were always engaged, thereby muting concern over the likelihood of success. An important environmental change from the Cold War is that the question of necessity has become more abstract: rather than a potential advantage for the Soviet Union, the perception of necessity is likely to be made in terms of more abstract notions about the American role as superpower. The answer to the *need* for the United States to "do something" has changed. Proposed involvements in the future are more likely to be in wars of choice, not necessity, and rephrasing the situation that way makes the other intermestic consideration of affordability more important.

The second perspective is more clearly economic and domestic, and arises from a sentiment more closely associated with Eisenhower's entreaty as he left office. If American security depends as much on the health of the American economy and that health requires something like a balance in governmental expenditures and revenues, is continued American activism, especially in DWICs, sustainable or even responsible? The expenses of DWICs are, of course, only a part of the negative budgetary calculus with which the country has been faced since 2008, but they are nonetheless significant symbolically. When critics of the current economic malaise view its causes in the early twenty-first century, one of the major factors in turning the Clinton budget surpluses of the late 1990s into the runaway stream of red ink since 9/11 has been American unfunded participation in Iraq and Afghanistan. The exact extent of that monetary expense is highly political (supporters want to make it look as small as possible, detractors as large as possible), and expenditures have been secreted in many government budgets, so that reaching a reliable tally is virtually impossible. A combined tab of a couple trillion dollars is probably as good an estimate as any, and as long as the effort continues in Afghanistan, the meter keeps running.

Political posturing notwithstanding, there are four possible outcomes to the current economic malaise. First, the government can effectively ignore it (which is what it has effectively done for the past four years), but that ultimately satisfies no one entirely and only works if a growing economy creates enough added revenues to erase the deficit. Second, it can decrease expenditures but not raise taxes, or vice versa. That is the partisan solution, but it is plagued by the dual problems that it would require massive majorities for one party or the other to get passed (which is unlikely), and it probably would not be enough to solve the problem. Third, the system can continue to try work at the margins of reform to expenditures or receipts while hoping for economic activity to "grow us" out of the recession. This is the traditional way in which government has recovered from economic downturns, and it was reflected in the assumptions of both party platforms for the 2012 election. The problem is that projections of growth are essentially "pixie dust," more or less pure guesses the accuracy of which is impossible to specify in advance. Fourth, government can engage in *both* reduced expenditures and higher taxes to reduce the gap. This, of course, is the most clearly adult solution to the problem, but it may also be the least likely because it requires governors of all political stripes to engage in hated loss allocation.

Whether one can defend the proposition that national security spending should be exempt (or participate less than other sectors) from cuts depends on the national security paradigm under which one operates. Defenders of the enormous defense budget that the United States currently has are at least implicitly arguing that the size and shape of the military effort is necessitated by a very threatening world condition that requires an activist U.S. policy to contain. In such a worldview, adventures like Iraq and Afghanistan may be justifiable, and certainly should continue to be considered. If, on the other hand, one argues that the presumptions of the Cold War paradigm no longer hold, then such an activist national security policy and stance may be less needed or justified.

More to the point, the ongoing economic crisis raises the additional question about American involvement in DWICs, "Can we afford it?" Engaing in DWICs in the past may have been geopolitical folly because it placed the United States in untenable situations where it could not prevail. That folly—effectively wasting resources—may have been tenable when resources were plentiful or the perceptions of necessity seemed great, but neither of those circumstances clearly applies today. President Eisenhower would have had an answer to this situation, and it would have involved pulling back on defense expenditures, which in turn would entail reducing the situations in which the United States becomes directly involved with its armed forces. If a healthy economy is the prerequisite to national security, then the search for an alternative set of guidelines to guide when the United States uses its armed forces seems all the more imperative.

Bibliography

Allison, Graham T., and Philip Zelikow. *Essence of Decision: Explaining the Cuban Missile Crisis* (2nd ed.). New York: Pearson Longman, 1999.

Bacevich, Andrew C. *Washington Rules: America's Path to Permanent War*. New York: Metropolitan Books, 2010.

Brodie, Bernard, and Fawn M. Brodie. *From Crossbow to H-Bomb: The Evolution of Weapons and Tactics in Warfare* (Revised ed.). Bloomington, IN: Indiana University Press, 1973.

Clark, Ronald W. *The Greatest Power on Earth: The International Race for Nuclear Supremacy from Earliest Theory to Three Mile Island*. New York: Harper and Row, 1980.

Drew, Dennis M., and Donald M. Snow. *Making Twenty-First Century Strategy: An Introduction to Modern National Security Processes and Problems*. Montgomery, AL: Air University Press, 2006.

Franks, Tommy (with Malcolm McConnell). *American Soldier*. New York: Regan Books, 2005.

George, Alexander. *Presidential Decisionmaking in Foreign Policy: The Effective Use of Information and Advice*. Boulder, CO: Westview Press, 1980.

Haney, Patrick J. *Organizing for Foreign Policy Crises: Presidents, Advisors, and the Management of Decision-Making*. Ann Arbor, MI: University of Michigan Press, 2002.

Hartung, William D. *Prophets of War: Lockheed Martin and the Making of the Military-Industrial Complex*. New York: Nation Books, 2012.

Janis, Irving L. *Groupthink: Psychological Studies of Policy Decisions and Fiascoes* (2nd ed.). New York: Cengage, 1982.

Ledbetter, James. *Unwanted Influence: Dwight D. Eisenhower and the Military-Industrial Complex*. New Haven, CT: Yale University Press, 2011.

McCalla, Robert B. *Uncertain Perceptions: U.S. Cold War Crisis Decision Making*. Ann Arbor, MI: University of Michigan Press, 1992.

McMaster, H. R. *Dereliction of Duty: Johnson, McNamara, the Joint Chiefs of Staff, and the Lies That Led to Vietnam*. New York: Harper Perennials, 1998.

Mann, James. *Rise of the Vulcans: A History of Bush's War Cabinet*. New York: Viking, 2004.

Mintz, Alex, and Karl Derouen Jr. *Understanding Foreign Policy Decision Making*. New York: Oxford University Press, 2010.

O'Hanlon, Michael E. *Defense Strategy for the Post-Saddam Era*. Washington, DC: Brookings Institution Press, 2003.

Pincus, Walter. "High Cost of a Defense Label." *Washington Post* (online). August 7, 2012.

Robinson, William I. *Promoting Polyarchy: Globalization, U.S. Intervention, and Hegemony*. New York: Cambridge University Press, 1996.

Shafer, Mark, and Scott Crichlow. *Groupthink versus High-Quality Decision Making in International Relations*. New York: Columbia University Press, 2010.

Snow, Donald M. *National Security for a New Era* (5th ed.). New York: Pearson, 2014.

——*The Shadow of the Mushroom-Shaped Cloud*. Columbus, OH: Consortium for International Studies Education, 1979.

Snow, Donald M., and Patrick J. Haney. *American Foreign Policy for a New Era*. New York: Pearson, 2013.

Swanson, David (ed.). *The Military-Industrial Complex at 50*. New York: David Swanson, 2011.

Turse, Nick. *The Complex: How the Military Invades Our Everyday Lives*. New York: Metropolitan Books, 2009.

Wilson, James Q. *Bureaucracy: What Government Agencies Do and Why They Do It*. New York: Basic Books, 1989.

7

THE WAY AHEAD

What should the future direction of U.S. personal involvement in military interventions be? More specifically, should the United States continue to contemplate and occasionally undertake direct, personal interventions in DWICs, the major source of opportunities and temptations for military action in the contemporary world? What is the way ahead for American policy?

It is an important question, because military intervention in DWICs is one of the most prominent potential uses of American military force in the years ahead. An aggressive positive answer suggests an activist military employment pattern in the future. A more cautionary answer implies a much more constrained pattern of U.S. force usage, if not necessarily a less active overall American role in the world. In his address to the graduating cadets at the U.S. Military Academy (West Point) in May 2014, President Obama suggested the latter pattern.

This volume also counsels restraint. Part of that restraint is based on analysis of the past record, which has not been exemplary. Part of it also arises from dual concerns about whether DWICs merit U.S. military involvement and whether such interventions can succeed. After reviewing these questions, the narrative concludes with five criteria by which future interventions might be judged.

DWIC situations hardly ever approach intolerable infringements on truly vital American interests, meaning even the worst outcomes do not endanger fundamental American values or interests. If true, this assessment means that intervention is largely going to be in what are wars of choice for the United States, not involvements of necessity. The U.S. government must ultimately defend its dispatch of forces to the public, which is much more highly likely to be supportive when the United States must be involved because vital interests are at stake, rather than when it simply chooses to do so. One of the lessons of American involvement in DWICs is that support wanes in situations where the most important American interests are not clearly engaged. One reasonable future filter may be the level of interests involved.

The other aspect of symbolism is the choice of instruments to achieve success in these endeavors. The large "heavy" forces that dominate the U.S. military are inherently large, blunt, and fairly indiscriminate instruments meant to smash into smithereens whatever they are used to destroy. They are neither subtle nor highly selective in their application, and they are best suited to contests with similar opponents. DWICs, on the other hand, more accurately reflect what Galula, in his classic 1965 work, *Counterinsurgency Warfare,* called the "war of the fleas," where subtle and very flexible force is more appropriate. The United States has made considerable efforts to adapt to this change, but it has not succeeded entirely.

The United States has, in effect, been bludgeoning fleas in its involvement in places like Vietnam, Iraq, and Afghanistan. It is in danger of doing the same thing in the future unless it comes to grips with the incongruity of this approach and adopts a more sensible attitude toward the developing world internal wars that have been an all too familiar siren's call in the past.

All of this has been happening in unsettled political times in which American interventions are less and less acceptable and increasingly controversial. American domestic politics is polarized at levels that have not been seen in a long time, generations even, and continued American foreign policy activism is one of the myriad issues where that polarization is showcased. Partisan issues cloud judgments and undermine support.

The center of operational national security concern has gravitated increasingly toward developing world conflicts, and the question is what role the United States should play in these kinds of disturbances. The answer is clouded by considerations that include those voiced in these pages. The domestic and international issues converge at the intermestic intersection of what kinds and levels of involvement the United States can afford given its own domestic, budget-driven difficulties and the additional strains on the domestic consensus that potential international activism requires.

The growing recognition that the terrorism-inspired interventions in Iraq and Afghanistan have not worked out to American net advantage adds to the poisoned political atmosphere of the moment. With the life-and-death consequences of advocacies during the Cold War removed, the question of America's role in the world has resurfaced in ways not dissimilar to the 1970s, the last time such a debate occurred. At the end of the Vietnam War, the United States faced the realities that it had made an enormous investment of blood and treasure in the name of a cause that had not succeeded. The expenditure particularly of young American lives and the apparent "defeat" of the country provided a great national shock, and occurring alongside the Watergate scandal that brought down Richard Nixon, undermined much of the American consensus behind those who governed the country. As the shock wore off, it also created a debate over whether the future included a diminished American role and stature in the world because of its failure in Southeast Asia. In the wake of these traumatic events in the first half of the decade of the 1970s, an obscure Southern governor and peanut farmer was propelled into the White House in 1976 on a promise to bring about needed change. Sound familiar?

The dual traumas of Iraq and Afghanistan have not been as strong as those of Vietnam. For one thing, Vietnam was a much more personal event for those Americans who lived through it, largely because it was fought by reluctant friends and neighbors drafted into military service. For another, the fall of Saigon and the declaration of a united, communist Vietnam in 1975 was a dramatic, concrete event that could not be denied or entirely ignored (although we tried). The situation is not so dramatic today. The wars of the 2000s, for better or worse, have been fought by volunteer, professional American soldiers, insulating much of the American population (and especially those with the greatest political influence) from the direct consequences of the fighting. At the same time, there has been no dramatic symbol of American futility like the fall of Saigon in Iraq and Afghanistan. Both countries may be drifting toward post-war outcomes that do not meet American objectives, but there has not been a dramatic symbolic event to punctuate the finality and totality of American futility. Such an event may or may not occur: if it does, American public outrage will be maximized; if it does not, the reaction will be more subdued.

As the United States moves away physically from its "wars on terror" in Iraq and Afghanistan, the international scene is littered with other alternatives for American activism for which there is no paradigmatic guidance for the country's appropriate response. Libya blew up as a political and humanitarian disaster, with a limited American response. Egypt convulsed with far less violence, and the Americans stayed on the sidelines. The Syrian regime declared war on its own citizenry, and the United States joined the rest of the world in condemning the bloodshed but showed enormous reluctance to do much about it. Iran continues to work on nuclear weapons in a much more concrete way than Saddam Hussein was accused of doing a decade ago, and very few other than the most fervent supporters of Israel's militant regime call for an American intervention. The opportunities are there; guidelines for responding are largely missing.

What the United States should be doing in these kinds of situations has become part of what passes for an American political debate on national security policy. The direction of that debate is oblique: it has not centered on the advisability of American activism or passivity in particular situations so much as on general propositions about American leadership in the world and what decisions about specific situations mean for global perceptions of American leadership. During the months leading to the 2012 American presidential election, for instance, some of the minimal discussions about foreign policy centered on the slaughter in Syria and what the United States should do about it. Criticisms of an apparent hands-off policy by the Obama administration came from two directions. One was humanitarian: how could the United States stand by and allow the Assad regime to murder its own citizens? The other was geopolitical: how could the United States remain passive and still claim relevance as a world leader? The two arguments intermingled: criticism of apparent passivity (or at least the lack of military activism) was seen as evidence of general American decline in the world.

The imputation was clear: the United States should "do something" to save the Syrian people from their own government. What should be done was not so clear. Minimalist advocacies said the country should arm and train the rebels—at least once someone figured out who the "good" ones were. While the administration quietly pursued such a restrained form of involvement, others suggested more assertive actions like no-fly zones and air operations to restrict the mobility and effectiveness of Syrian military actions against rebel strongholds that happened to be located in urban centers (an evidence of the asymmetrical nature of the rebellion).

None of the focus in the American debate was about ultimate U.S. policy toward the Syrian rebellion. There was virtual unanimity (eerily similar to policy toward Iraq a decade earlier) that Bashar al-Assad must be removed because of his actions toward his own people, a sentiment with broad international support. That consensus did not, however, extend far past the general goal of Assad's departure; certainly it did not contain any general agreement on what should be done to hasten the end of the regime or any assessments about who would replace him and how they would represent an improvement. This vagueness was also present in the advocacies of those Americans who favored greater activism, suggesting they had not absorbed much from the Iraq experience.

The disagreement about what to do about Syria would likely have been much more pointed had it, like virtually all other aspects of foreign policy, not been thoroughly overshadowed by domestic concerns, most pointedly the continuing American internal economic crisis. Economic considerations like job creation were a much more potent campaign issue than the virtual abstraction of involvement in Syria or elsewhere (Iran, for instance). There was some irony in the simultaneous campaigns of both presidential candidates about Afghanistan, with both essentially arguing who could get American troops out of that country first but responsibly, while at the same time not ruling out categorically an involvement in Syria that could turn out to be very similar to Iraq and Afghanistan. The primary leavening influence was intermestic: the United States had spent a bundle on Iraq and Afghanistan, both of which shared part of the blame for the economic crisis, and the American people were clearly not in the mood for opening up their wallets for more of the same during economic bad times.

As the post-election dust settled, the United States found itself at a familiar crossroads regarding its national security policy toward the world. American forces have been gone from Iraq for well over four years. The internal political situation in Iraq has certainly not followed the course the United States would have preferred, but neither has it deteriorated so completely as to offend greatly any residual American concern for its trajectory. Should the Shiite ruling regime too closely fall into the Iranian embrace or should Sunni-Shiite-Kurd violence seriously break out, as it did in 2014, that situation could change. The American (and allied) withdrawal from Afghanistan continues its ineluctable march, and when it is completed, that country will begin an evolution largely free of American influence and likely in a direction not in total harmony with American preferences.

If the Vietnam experience is some harbinger of the future, the United States will breathe a long sigh of relief when it is finally extricated from these engagements and will pay scant attention to the vicissitudes that follow. Saigon fell, all of Vietnam was communized, and, despite impassioned, shrill, and dire warnings by war advocates, the outcome really made little geopolitical difference to the United States. The same is likely to be true after America leaves two wars on Iran's borders. Those absences of large consequences speak to the importance of becoming engaged in the first place. If the United States had never sent a single G.I. to Vietnam, would the American situation in the world have been greatly affected? It is hard, with forty years perspective, to argue convincingly that it would have. If one asks the same question about Iraq and Afghanistan after some interval, would the answer be pretty much the same?

The 1970s precedent is cautionary for the present and future. In the aftermath of "losing" in Vietnam, Americans learned that it was best for the United States to avoid similar future imbroglios in the future, and then promptly forgot those lessons when the Cold War monster was replaced by a newer scourge. Studies similar to this one were crafted after Vietnam, were read, and were heeded for awhile, and then they were discarded. Will we do the same thing again? It is a depressing possibility, but it is also an avoidable fate.

A possible reason that the good lessons of the Southeast Asian experience did not take hold was that they were planted in a Cold War intellectual seedbed with which they were incompatible. The Cold War taught the need for and virtue of military readiness and military solutions to problems. America's activism therein and the universality of American power and reach were in strong contradiction to the cautionary lessons of the Vietnam experience. "No more Vietnams" counseled caution and selectivity of involvement in a culture of "can do" omniscience, and those in power identified with and promoted the Cold War paradigm over a Vietnam experience which contradicted it. By the time the Cold War ended and the entreaties of the Cold War paradigm were largely overcome by events, the caution of the Vietnam experience had largely been swamped. Muddling through without a clear paradigmatic mandate ever since, the activists have continued to hold sway.

Although the reaction is less dramatic, the misbegotten Iraq and Afghanistan experiences offer a challenge to the existing consensus not unlike that provided in the wake of Vietnam, but with one hopeful difference. In 1972, the activist consensus was firmly in intellectual and political control, largely because of a geopolitical environment in which it still appeared to make pragmatic sense. Today there is no equivalent of the Soviet threat to buttress that activism; the crusade against terrorism is a less-than-convincing substitute. The result is a conceptual void. Filling that vacuum with an organizing concept is one major task that faces the United States national security community. While many of those who will influence the fashioning of a new set of ground rules are still part of the activist past for a variety of reasons, they do not have the "comforting" backdrop of the anti-communist crusade to absorb criticism. The sheet of paper on which a new paradigm can be laid out may not be a *tabula rasa*, but neither is it a tablet on which virtually all the space has been filled in. Advocates of a new concept that includes counsel of caution about intervention in DWICs do not face as steep intellectual and political odds as they did a generation ago.

The rest of the chapter begins the process of laying out what such an approach might look like. It begins by reviewing the problems already identified: the predictable failure of intervention in civil conflicts in the manner the United States has chosen to follow and the inexplicable surprise that the United States has experienced when failure happens, the often tragic consequences for the state in which intervention occurs, and the "target-rich environment" of potential enticements for the United States. It concludes with a plea for a more restrained approach that includes a series of five cautionary questions for viewing future candidates for American force and the call for a new, post-Cold War concept.

The Horns of Dilemma: Activism and Failure

The activist legacy of the Cold War paradigm and its national security structure and predilections regarding the use of force has left the United States in a quandary that befuddles thinking about the future. The core legacy of this past has been a belief that the United States has interests it must physically defend with armed force everywhere if it is to maintain its position in the world. This belief builds upon several Cold War suppositions of varying credence and continuing relevance. Regardless of the general virtue of the activist argument, an unfortunate consequence is to predispose the country to consider ill-advised involvements in DWICs it might not otherwise consider.

The presumption arose from the global nature of the Cold War competition, which magnified mischief and instability anywhere to inclusion in the global conflict, whether the projection was warranted or not. Sometimes this supposition had validity and sometimes it did not, but its effect was to elevate the importance of events in places where American interests by any other metric were not very important. A second presumption that flowed from the first was that America's universal interests meant that unfavorable outcomes to disputes anywhere harmed the United States. As a result, the United States had to take action in places it might otherwise not consider because not to do so harmed America's global interests and national reputation. When the communist half of the competition evaporated and the United States was the unchallenged "king of the hill," a third presumption was that the United States must act, or be prepared to act, because it was the only power that could do so. The United States, in other words, must be active everywhere in order to be relevant anywhere.

The national security enterprise is naturally tilted toward this kind of reasoning. The heart of that concept is, after all, the identification and nullification of threats to American security. As a result, those in the national security business naturally see the world through "threat-colored glasses," and one consequence is to interpret events in terms of the threats they may pose. There is nothing inherently wrong with this perspective being represented in decision-making forums, as long as it is counterbalanced by other perspectives as well. The enterprise is further influenced by the very large set of institutions and incentives that threat-based decisions may produce. The military-industrial complex has a built-in self-interest in a threat-based assessment, since activism can lead to responses from which its members benefit.

The often grotesque nature of events in DWICs reinforces the predilection to activism, even among those with little vested interest in promoting activism. It is a simple fact of the modern world that man's inhumanity toward his fellow man is now very public. Atrocity around the world is probably no worse than it has ever been, and probably is less so because those contemplating terrible things must know their atrocities may become public knowledge. Today, one can do very little that may not appear on social media and potentially on global television. When atrocity occurs, there is a natural emotion to, in veteran U.S. diplomat Ryan Crocker's phrase (captured in a *Newsweek* profile of Crocker by Leslie H. Gelb), "just do something." The problem is that such manifestations of the "do something syndrome" can result in what Crocker rightly calls "ill-conceived military intervention abroad."

Why are such responses "ill-conceived"? The analysis here suggests two basic responses, each of which should be, but have not always been, sufficiently cautionary to squelch such actions. One objection is that most of these responses occur in places where there are not sufficient American interests involved to warrant an American military response. Put in useful realist terms, most developing world situations do not challenge basic, *vital*, U.S. interests in which a negative outcome is intolerable for the United States. The only way they reach such importance is to assume that the failure to act everywhere undermines American relevance everywhere and is intolerable. As noted particularly in Chapter 4, each of the cases of major American interventions in developing country conflicts included an assertion of the vitality of U.S. interests, and in each case, that assertion proved specious. The dominos fell in Southeast Asia, and it really did not matter; the claim in Iraq of weapons of mass destruction and congress with terrorists turned out to be untrue; and Afghanistan lacked terrorists to expunge after their 2001 eviction. Stripped of the protective veil of vitality, each was a war of choice, not of necessity, and Americans turned against it. The fact that the places were not vital to American interests eventually manifested themselves in the loss of resolve the country had toward "staying the course" in each contest.

A major reason that resolve weakens is that these contests are much more important to the indigenous parties than they are to the intervening Americans.

Asymmetry of importance transforms the war into a contest of comparative cost-tolerance—which side has the highest resistance to the pain inflicted by the other and thus which side will persevere. The vitality of the outcome is the distinct feature of determining relative cost-tolerance: the side to which the outcome is most important will almost always have a higher threshold of pain tolerance. For the American intervener, the only way to prevail in this context is to defeat the opponent so thoroughly and quickly that the opponent will have to quit. The whole purpose of an asymmetric approach is to avoid such a decisive conclusion. For the indigenous opponent, their path to success involves prolonging the action and inflicting enough pain on the American interveners to convince them to decide further sacrifice is not worth it. Unable to attain decisive military victory and progressively convinced the effort is not worth it, the intervener's cost-tolerance is exceeded and the intervener quits. Until the United States can find an antidote to these human dynamics, interventions will continue to be frustrating.

The second objection flowing from this point, of course, is thus that these interventions are destined to fail. There is often a central and stunningly simple explanation of why failure occurs. When a large country intervenes in the affairs of a smaller and weaker country that has not been able to settle its own disputes, the intervening party tends to take over the action. Usually this occurs unintentionally and without much forethought. Iraq is the most dramatic example. As best that can be gleaned from the public record, prewar "planning" assumed that once the Saddam Hussein regime collapsed, an alternative Iraqi regime would magically emerge and take over in a short period of time. This would allow the Americans to wash their hands and leave to the adulation of a grateful population. When this outcome did not occur, the United States was left to run Iraq, a contingency for which it was almost totally unprepared. The ensuing chaos has been well recorded in the literature on the war, but underlying it is a dynamic identified by Crocker, who asserts sanguinely that the United States government should not "entangle us in running someone else's country, which we cannot do." In Vietnam and Afghanistan, rather than taking over, the United States tried to influence the regime to act in ways of which the Americans approved but Vietnamese and Afghans did not, and both resisted. In both cases, American advice was probably sound and would have worked with a population that shared American values and goals. A lot of Vietnamese and Afghans did not share those values, resisted "helpful" advice, and violently rejected a continuing presence. In the end, they won, which was probably the appropriate outcome given it was their countries involved.

Why any of this surprises anyone when it happens is hard to understand. Ignoring these truths requires a certain level of willful arrogance regarding the power and centrality of the United States in the world. The already stated notion that the United States must be decisively intrusive everywhere to be relevant anywhere is certainly a part of this willful self-delusion, because it seems to create a mandate for resolving sources of instability that are not otherwise any (or much) of our business. But if American national security interests are global, America's status as the world's superpower requires American intrusiveness and intervention everywhere. That the places intervention may occur also generally feature humanitarian disasters that make American action more apparently benign and noble is an added bonus, but the core is still the self-assertion that American activism is necessary for a world order in which the United States retains its vital centrality. This perception, which pops up whenever violence (usually internal) breaks out anywhere, is the major legacy of the Cold War period. It is an assumption that must be challenged and supplanted.

The Pottery Barn Tragedy

To this point, the analysis has emphasized the inadvisability of intervening in developing world conflicts, but the way these conflicts end and their aftermaths are important considerations as well. There have been no happy endings to these conflicts for the Americans, and in the end, this country has been faced with a withdrawal on the best, most face-saving terms it can devise. Those terms generally bear little resemblance to the objectives the United States envisaged achieving when it became involved, and they are often outcomes that leave matters as bad or worse for all or some of the population of the country where intervention has taken place. Those members of the indigenous population that cooperated with the intervention may suffer the worst fate. What, if any, obligations does the United States incur when it faces unfortunate, unhappy exit realities?

Former Army General and Secretary of State Colin Powell offered this quandary as a cautionary note in what he described as the "Pottery Barn analogy." If one drops and breaks a piece of pottery in a Pottery Barn store, one has to buy it; if a country intervenes in another country and destroys the status quo, one must, he argued, adopt a similar obligation: if you break it, you own it!

Disruption of the ongoing status quo is, after all, a major purpose of intervention in the first place. If intervention is on the behalf of a beleaguered government (e.g., Vietnam, Afghanistan), there must have been some underlying reasons a movement was seeking to overthrow those on whose behalf intervention was undertaken, and government reform of some kind is almost certainly part of the American intent. In Vietnam, the thrusts of that reform tended to be land reform and purging corruption; in Afghanistan, reducing the levels of rampant corruption and brutality have been major objectives. If the intervention is against the government (e.g., Iraq, the potential in Syria), the open and clear purpose is to tear down and replace an existing governmental structure. In either case, the intent is to "break" the status quo.

Part of the problem, of course, is that the intervener's goals will almost never be identical to those of the parties for or against which intervention occurs. A beleaguered government may desire outside military assistance for fear of losing otherwise, but it almost always will treat the accompanying demands for change as gratuitous and unwelcome. South Vietnam's president Ngo Dinh Diem, for instance, was not interested in land reform, which was aimed at distributing land controlled by large, usually absentee landowners to landless peasants, because those large landowners formed much of his political base. Hamid Karzai did not wholeheartedly embrace American entreaties to clean up corruption in Afghanistan at least partly because members of his family were involved in it. The advice the interveners offer may be sound in a general, abstract sense, but it does not always coincide with the interests of those to whom it is offered. Saddam Hussein did not want his government overthrown and his life extinguished at the end of a hangman's noose, and Bashar al-Assad did not want to be toppled from power. The ability of the side being supported may in fact make achievement of the intervener's goal more difficult if not impossible, yet another sense of the frustration and futility of intervening in the first place.

An added piece of this puzzle is what the intervener can or proves willing to do to bring about the change it desires and promotes. For interventions to be ultimately successful, the old edifice needs to be brought down or modified extensively, and something must be put in its place. Intervener military force may or may not be effective in tearing down the old status quo that caused the problem, but it almost certainly is incapable of building a new and better successor order that creates the sense of order and stability the intervener prefers. That task is the province of *state building* (sometimes known as *nation building*), and it an economic and political exercise intended to produce a more prosperous and stable future that the people will embrace. It is a necessary exercise without which the post-intervention situation may be little improvement over the pre-intervention condition. It is also a controversial exercise in the contemporary environment, even though it is an integral dynamic within any intervention strategy. State building has become a pejorative term in the American political dialogue, and the question is why this is the case.

State building is, in essence, another way of saying economic and political development. As such, the need for state building is virtually universal in the developing world, and especially in the more volatile, unstable regions and countries. Some people suffer deprivation, and this situation creates the underlying conditions that can turn violent and be the reason an outside intervention can seem necessary.

The development problem has been identified for a long time, and during the Cold War period, it was the subject of a great deal of study within both academic and governmental circles that has produced a large literature on the subject (Michael Latham provides a good, comprehensive overview in his book, *The Right Kind of Revolution*). The basic assumption of the developmental theorists was that both economic and political development—at least implicitly defined as emulating the institutions and performance of the Western democracies—is the necessary condition for developing world countries to achieve stability. This imperative is particularly important in countries where stability has already broken down to the point of violence, and it is especially necessary in places where intervention has occurred and where whatever level of development that preexisted has probably been "broken." Thus, no intervention is likely to be ultimately successful unless it is accompanied by some sort of developmental program that improves the conditions of life to above pre-intervention levels and thus creates a sense of hope and progress that will lead to and sustain the stability that is always part of the pre-intervention rationale for intrusion in the first place.

The concept of state building has become politically toxic in the United States. At a superficial level, the reason is related to the general American disagreement about the proper function and role of government. For those who have a general opposition to government's role in society, state building smacks of the taint of the "nanny" state and thus engenders opposition on that ground. This argument lies in the background whenever the United States government proposes to come actively to the assistance of a developing world state—including one the U.S. has invaded, occupied, and from which it is withdrawing—and is buttressed by at least two other objections to state building.

The first objection is that nobody has really fully demonstrated that state building will work. Most of the arguments favoring state building are theoretical and have never been entirely or wholeheartedly tested or implemented, so there is no solid, indisputable evidence that proposed state-building proposals will succeed. The apparent exceptions were the programs to rehabilitate the Axis powers after World War II and the massive infusion of assistance into South Korea after the Korean War, but these were exceptional cases. Most of the state building that has occurred has been on a scale smaller than advocates would hold is necessary for success. As a result, there are no "models" against which to compare proposed efforts that would in any sense "guarantee" that the desired outcomes would hold. Whether this is evidence that state building is a futile exercise or one that has been inadequately or inappropriately undertaken is arguable enough that both sides can be and are taken.

The situation poses a quandary. While most observers agree that improvement in the life conditions of the target population is a necessary condition for creating post-intervention stability, there is insufficient evidence that the process works well enough to create a satisfactory post-intervention condition. In terms of the Powell analogy, it may be necessary to repair whatever piece of pottery one has broken, but it is not clear that repair efforts will work. If they do not, what is the impact on ownership?

This question becomes less than academic in light of the second objection, which is whether the United States has the will to "stay the course" of state building in countries where it has had a long involvement. As the Vietnam, Afghan, and Iraqi examples offer testimony, the United States is almost certain to tire of its involvement before any definitive outcome is achieved, and certainly before any consensus supporting a state-building effort has developed and been agreed to. Rather, the desire to extricate the country from a long and indeterminate intervention is likely to emphasize the vast amounts of money that have already been expended in the futile effort. From that perception, the idea of investing further large amounts of funds (and state building is likely to be very expensive) on concluding the conflict is likely to be derided as throwing more money "down a rat hole." Advocating more expenditure is likely to be opposed on the grounds that the billions being pumped into a place like Afghanistan are needed far more in the United States.

The result is a dilemma. The military act of intervention has not been successful in achieving the original goal, and public frustration is mounting to terminate the intervention. If the United States accedes to the demands to leave, it will likely not achieve any of its goals, and the only chance for redemption is some sort of act that will improve the situation in the target country enough so that the pre-intervention condition of the country is better than it was previously. The only remaining response may be state building, which if successful, could ameliorate many of the negative feelings the intervention has produced both within the host country and the United States. The dilemma is that the American public is likely either indifferent about or hostile to anything other than getting out, meaning political expediency militates toward actions that will, almost as a self-fulfilling prophecy, guarantee a maximum negative outcome. The result is a set of devil's choices: none are good.

If history is any guide, the likely response will be essentially to "cut and run." No one in a decision-making position will frame the response this way, of course, and the cover for "folding our tent" is normally some fairly cosmetic process of turning over responsibility gradually to those in the host country that have been supported while knowing full well that this assistance will ultimately prove inadequate. The prototype for this solution was "Vietnamization," where the United States gradually trained South Vietnamese forces to supplant and replace American combat forces. In the process of this effort, the United States was aiming at "peace with honor" (Richard Nixon's 1972 election year slogan) where the United States left its allies with a "reasonable chance" to prevail, while privately knowing all along that those chances were slender indeed. The same process has played itself out in Iraq, with unfolding but almost surely long-term negative consequences, and the process of "Afghanistanization" has begun. As an aside, those who propose these losing strategies of extrication generally seek to cover the inevitability of their failure by blaming it on an imperfect implementation of their recommendations. In the cases of Iraq and Afghanistan, that cover has been that they recommended leaving some American forces in country after disengagement to continue to aid "our" side, and the rejection of these recommendations is what eventually undermined (or will undermine) the exit strategy. Such rejoinders should be taken with a considerable grain of salt.

The inevitable withdrawal leaves behind it shards of the broken pottery, and the question is what obligations the intervening state has toward easing the post-intervention situation. What will, in Crocker's terms, the "consequences of a swift withdrawal" be? At a minimum, those indigenous individuals and groups who supported the intervention are likely to suffer retribution when the United States is gone. Those who can will likely flee into exile somewhere else. Many will be left behind, and they may well be treated as quislings and suffer the same fate (death) as the Norwegian prime minister who invited the Nazi occupation of his country in 1940. At the same time, the success of whoever opposed the American action is likely to enhance their popularity, meaning the act of withdrawal may actually make the failure of American objectives even more likely than it otherwise would have been.

The track record of the United States in its other misadventures does not offer reassurance in terms of the likelihood the United States, as part of its departure, will do "the right thing." Like broken shards of pottery at the Pottery Barn, the United States has not cleaned up its mess when it has left in the past. Usually, there is some assurance that the physical departure of American armed forces will be followed by resources (e.g., funds, expertise) to help rebuild the country better and to assure that a "better state of the peace" results from the action. That never happens in fact: when the decision to leave and its implementation occurs, the American people want to wash their hands completely of the experience, and policy makers prove more than willing to accommodate that preference. Promises of post-intervention assistance are effectively written on "flash paper," and once the United States departs, those promises quickly burst into flames and become ashes.

How the United States terminates interventions thus makes a difference, and one that Crocker suggests probably should have been considered before the intervention occurred. As he puts it, "If you don't think it through thoroughly before getting in, for God's sake think it through carefully before you pull the plug. The consequences of withdrawal can be as great or greater than the consequences of intervention." There is, of course, one way to avoid the Pottery Barn tragedy and its consequences, and that is to avoid the Pottery Barn.

Siren's Call on the Horizon: Can and Will We Resist?

As the country debates how much of its prior commitment to national security spending will have to be sacrificed at the altar of budget balancing and debt reduction, preparation for and intervention in developing world internal conflicts will, or certainly should, become part of the discussion. Potential opportunities for the United States to become physically active in numerous places will not disappear. In some of these instances, events are designed to provoke the United States into physical responses in which the country cannot prevail and which will further alienate indigenous populations from the United States. There are other potential venues for the United States to stage conceptual reenactments of the failures in Vietnam, Iraq, and Afghanistan—Iran is the most prominent and most frightening—and the question is whether constraint will prevail or not.

There is a countervailing element in the debate. It is ideological in the sense of representing different worldviews about the world and America's place in it. One side represents the tradition of the Cold War paradigm. As suggested and reiterated in these pages, this tradition emphasizes the need for American active participation in some way in any international crisis as part of the American "mission" in the world, and that activism is not limited to non-lethal means. Regardless of whether this position is heartfelt or self-serving (or some combination of both), it leads to an advocacy of large defense budgets that include provision to prepare and carry out military interventions in developing world contingencies.

The activists are opposed by the old-fashioned realists. The realists share the nurturing background of the Cold War, but they take different lessons from that experience. The realists also possess a general support for a vibrant national security capability, but their advocacy contains a greater degree of nuance than does the position of the activists. Realists are generously represented in, among other places, the military, and this colors the nature of their conservatism in the national security arena. For one thing, realists are likely to view themselves as believers in the idea that military force should be an instrument of last resort *and* that its use should be reserved for situations where truly vital interests are at risk; in other words, they support wars of necessity and eschew wars of choice. They generally reject the activist-implied contention that the United States must be prominent everywhere to retain relevance. The old-fashioned realists also are much more likely than the activists to support the Eisenhower position that national security requires a sound American economy, and along with the inherent sense of service the realists (particularly those in the military) hold, they are much less likely to support expenditures on, preparations for, and participation in military adventures in the developing world. The realist position, in other words, leads to opposing the promiscuous use of American military force and tends to define intervention in DWICs within its definition of promiscuity.

Both of these positions resonated in the 2012 election cycle. All sides agreed that deficit reduction was a priority mandate, but they disagreed on the application of that principle to defense spending. National security activists argued that defense spending should largely be exempt from the budgeter's axe on traditional grounds of continuing and projected threat. Defense, in other words, should take a much smaller "hit" than other budget elements, and the capacity for developing world intervention thus remains relatively inviolate. Realists, on the other hand, saw the mandate of budget reductions as a way to rein in the promiscuous use of force by denying the resources to encourage such contingencies. In their view, defense should "man up" and take its share of cuts in the name of national security.

Events in the Middle East reinforced this divide. Most of the signs of instability spinning off from the Arab Spring of 2011 were internal in nature yet had some impact on the United States and its interests broadly defined—the cauldron in which interventions in the past have been brewed. The continuing Syrian slaughter offended Americans (and most of the rest of the world) on humanitarian grounds and activated the "do something syndrome" in some Americans. The assassination of the American ambassador to Libya J. Christopher Stevens at the consulate in

Benghazi, Libya, ignited a debate over the ongoing American role in the world, among other things.

The potential for more disturbances analogous to those that partially infected the already toxic presidential campaign transcends the American electoral cycle. The jagged edges and uncertain "progress" of the series of movements associated with the Arab Spring will continue to produce incidents that can be construed as harmful to American interests and prestige. This is particularly true in the Near East, which has also been the crucible for so much American activism over the past generation. Anti-Americanism has been one of the arguable outgrowths of American actions in the past: whether it is the intrusion of Americans physically in Iraq and Afghanistan, the huge continuing American military footprint in the oil-rich Persian Gulf region, the spotted history of American interference in Iran, or the use of American attack drones over the sovereign territory of countries like Pakistan or Yemen. The inevitable result of regional dynamics will almost certainly produce situations where advocacy for virile responses will arise again, as they have in the past. The major question is how to respond to those provocations when they do pop up. The siren's calls are not likely to disappear. It does mean they should be viewed very critically.

Five Hard Questions

To avoid repeating past mistakes, I propose a set of five questions that should be asked and adequately answered before the idea of a future intervention moves from broad, strategic contemplation to an operational, tactical level where military action is seriously proposed. They are questions I have asked elsewhere: explicitly in my 1993 and 1997 editions of *Distant Thunder* and, in slightly different construction, in my 2000 *When America Fights*. They were good questions then, and they still are. Individually and cumulatively, they help define both the worth of potential intervention to the United States and the prospects for achieving American goals. If they can be answered positively, then intervention may be considered. If not, it should probably be avoided. Like most good questions, they are simple to state but more difficult to answer.

The questions and their answers are sequential. This means that it is necessary to answer one question before moving to the next, because the inability to provide a satisfactory answer to any given question makes it impossible or, at best, problematic, to be able to answer subsequent questions positively. For that reason, a negative—and possibly even an ambiguous—answer to any question makes moving beyond that point dubious.

What Is Wrong Here?

When any country contemplates involvement in another country's instabilities, it is normally because instabilities have boiled over into violence. The first reaction when viewing these situations is to their human tragedy, especially in the contemporary world, where the human side of suffering is almost always displayed in vivid electronic terms that are widely distributed and difficult to avoid. Something is clearly wrong wherever these outbreaks happen, and the relentless publicity surrounding the death and destruction is graphic and evokes visceral responses. "Why is this happening?" may quickly be drowned out by emotional entreaties that ask, "What can we do alleviate the suffering?"

These kinds of reactions have been building as the electronic revolution has spread more inexorably around the globe, but it has reached a kind of crescendo in the past decade or so. Even during the 1990s, when international concerns first congealed around humanitarian interventions, the landscape was neither so graphic nor apparently compelling. When news photographs of Bosnian prisoners peering out from behind barbed-wire, prisoner-of-war enclosures looking like Nazi victims of the Holocaust were made public, world opinion was outraged and action ensued. Far bloodier and more hideous mayhem occurred during the ethnic rampage in Rwanda in 1994, but because the worst was not electronically recorded and instantly beamed around the world, the world was able to avert its eyes, registering its horror only after the worst was over. Today, there is scarcely anyplace that a Rwanda or even far lesser horror can happen without global publicity. That something is wrong is very clear, and it acts as a stimulus to want to "do something" about it. That instinct, in turn, can have two deleterious effects in assessing the basic question.

One problem is that the outward manifestation often obscures a deeper understanding of the underlying problem from which the public atrocity arises. Drawing from one of the analogies in the last section, violence and atrocity are likely the symptoms of some more fundamental malaise. In a similar vein, Saddam Hussein's tyranny was a precipitant of action against him, but the reason for that tyranny and the violence that flowed from it was deeper, imbedded in the ethnic hatreds of an artificial state. The bloody suppression of the Syrian population is a form of suffering that can be alleviated by depriving the government of the ability to attack and savage its own population, but doing so does not in itself resolve the deep divisions between minority Shiite Alawites and majority Sunni Arabs from which much of the division ultimately derives.

The other problem is geopolitical and affects how one can and does respond to problems in terms of its own interests. During the Cold War, of course, this function was served through the colored lens of the competition with communism, and interest was assigned—rightly or wrongly, in different cases—to the Cold War consequences of different outcomes. In that light, not all terrible events had equal prescience. In the rampage by the Khmer Rouge in Cambodia, where upward of one-third of the population was killed in the name of ideological cleansing, both the killers and those who sought to end the killing were communists (the Khmer Rouge aligned with China, Vietnamese interveners with the Soviet Union). It was not viewed as an American problem and was one we ignored. The fact that knowledge of the atrocities were verbal rumors rather than graphic electronic footage made it easier than it would be today. Ties to international terrorism now form a bond of interest parallel to that of communism; without such a bond, would there be any meaningful, compelling rationale for American continued involvement in Afghanistan after 2001?

The developing world situations in which outsiders may become interested are complex, and cursory geopolitical or humanitarian assessments do not adequately capture the entirety, or even the essence, of the problems that are involved and that may be encountered when outside involvement is contemplated. The horrific nature of circumstances makes calm, reasoned assessment both of the causes and cures more difficult, and the deferment of judgments while such determinations are being made appear weak, even pusillanimous. Yet, unless the layers of the onion are peeled away and the nature of the problem thoroughly understood, the chances of making informed decisions that have more than a random chance of being responsive to what is wrong are not guaranteed.

How Do You Come Down on the Side of the Angels?

The idea that one should come down "on the side of the angels" is a florid way of saying that one should identify and support the side in an internal conflict that is truly worthy of support. The phrase itself was coined by British prime minister Benjamin Disraeli as a rhetorical critique of Darwin's theory of evolution where Disraeli contrasted Darwin's idea of man evolving from primates to biblical interpretation and said he preferred to come down "on the side of the angels." The phrase caught on and was broadened, in the words of *Dictionary.com*, to refer to "supporting the good side."

The core of the concept is that one should support the side in a conflict that represents good and right, at least as one sees the meaning of those terms. Because Americans view themselves as being a highly moralistic people, being on the angels' side has particular importance, and moral virtue is indeed one of the characteristics of a "good" political objective in war. The failure to be on the virtuous side will inevitably help subvert American support for any war effort.

Coming down on the righteous side in developing world conflicts is not always easy, for several reasons. One is the definition of what constitutes virtue, and that is subjective and has changed across time. During the Cold War, for instance, the profession of fervent anti-communism trumped all other definitions of virtue, and the result was that the United States was sometimes saddled with leaders of questionable rectitude beyond their anti-communism. Some of these leaders more recently joined the anti-terrorist campaign with equal enthusiasm, and an American crusading anti-terrorism policy made this embrace by otherwise questionable "angels" acceptable. Egypt's former president Hosni Mubarak was a caricature of this genre of leader, and the United States has paid a price for its close association with him. The United States would prefer to embrace honest, pro-democratic leaders, but they are often scarce in DWIC-prone countries.

A second reason is that there may be little difference qualitatively between the sides in a civil conflict, at least as measured by Western standards of goodness. The criteria of honesty and democratic adherence are exemplary. Most developing world countries lack political traditions that fundamentally reflect either of these characteristics in a Western sense. In many developing world settings, for instance, the collection of bribes or side payments is simply presumed to be part of holding office, a way to make a living, and it is most unusual to find anyone who has had any substantial government experience who is not in some way tainted. At the same time, the lack of a democratic tradition is almost universal, and while professing democratic values may be a necessary way for a politician to appeal to the Americans, it is not a familiar or comfortable political position domestically. The Karzai regime in Afghanistan has been a clear example. The Karzai family is apparently deeply involved in traditional forms of governmental corruption (bribery and connections to illicit drug production and trafficking, for instance), and while President Karzai purported to stand for Westernizing principles, he does so in a society in which these values are not well rooted.

The heart of this problem arises from ignorance (or only a partial level of knowledge) of the political players and realities in a target country. There are usually some experts either in the government or in places like academia who have, or purport to have, expert knowledge about a possible target country, but what they know may not comport with what those who have become interested in intervention want to hear. As an example, Senator McCain advocated an active military interference in the slaughter in Syria during the summer of 2012, but there is no reason to believe that his calls for the United States to aid in the overthrow of Bashar al-Assad were leavened with any particular knowledge or understanding of those who might succeed him, leading to a third problem.

The third problem is how one knows who the angels are. One of the difficulties is that the United States often has incomplete or conflicting understanding of foreign leaders in countries with which it has not had long and intimate relationships. The result may be that one lacks a real understanding of whether different political actors are "good" or "bad," and must rely on the sometimes contradictory views of people who may have a stake in one actor or another. While proposed interventions usually have some noble goal, the articulation of that goal may be part of a broader geopolitical or humanitarian concern and not be based in any clear idea of who or what forces within the country can be promoted to lead toward the goal. Iraq is a prime example: the underlying goals for overthrowing Saddam Hussein were geopolitical (creating an Iraq that was a stabilizing influence in the region and would pose less of a threat to Israel in the neo-con vision) or humanitarian (to end Hussein's bloody suppression of portions of the population). Lacking any real knowledge of any successors who might be a real improvement and eschewing the counsel of most experts that the whole mission was a pipe dream given the realities of Iraqi politics, the advocates turned to dubious, obviously self-interested, and shadowy characters like Ahmed Chalabi for advice, and the result was certainly not to identify and promote an alternative leadership that met many observers' definition of "angels."

The fourth reason is a kind of conundrum: if one party is clearly more virtuous than the others, why does that person's own population not recognize this virtue? If it did, would the leader require outside assistance to remain in or gain power? For that matter, would there be an armed movement against him that had some chance of success without an outside interposition? Put another way, if the leader does require outside assistance, is this not an indirect way of suggesting that his or her virtue may not be above reproach and that that individual may not in fact be on the side of the angels? The counter-argument tends to be that intervention may be necessary either for geopolitical reasons (such as removing terrorist sanctuaries) or because opposing forces have invested so heavily on the "dark side" that opposes our angels that they must be countered. That is not always an easy sell.

The point is that it is sometimes difficult to come down on the side of the angels for one or both of two reasons. One may not know enough about a situation to know who the angels are, or there may be ambiguity or disagreement about the rectitude of any and all sides—at least by standards with which the United States can identify. During the 1960s and 1970s, the U.S. government dismissed Nelson Mandela as a mere communist stooge, after all. This problem is made even more difficult because there may be no viable force in the country that can adopt the virtuous stance upon which our intervention might be premised. It has been difficult, for instance, to typify Hamid Karzai as a clear representative of the angels, but is he as close to it as has been available in Afghanistan? If one cannot identify angels with whom to align, what should one do?

Does Your Side Have a Reasonable Chance of Succeeding?

If one can correctly identify the detailed nature of the problem in a developing world conflict, determine it is important enough to consider for possible action, and further identify some worthy individual or group behind whom to place support, the next question is whether assistance can ensure one side's success. It is an important consideration both because the pursuit of "impossible dreams," while arguably noble, is not how countries organize and conduct their foreign policies, all other factors being equal. Engaging in quixotic military quests is a particularly questionable idea given the enormous human costs that military involvements entail and the likelihood of adverse public reaction to failures.

Causes to champion are not always or entirely chosen because they are "winners." One may engage in military campaigns of which the outcome is uncertain for one of two basic reasons. One is situations where the outcome is so vitally important that you have no choice: wars of absolute necessity that cannot be avoided regardless of the costs. American interests in developing world countries rarely reach that level of vitality; certainly they did not in Vietnam, Iraq, and Afghanistan, although an effort was made to portray each in that light, as pointed out. The problem here is trying to achieve a justifiable balance between acting because "it is the right thing to do" (Bill Clinton's aphorism for American engagement in the Balkans) and the probability of success.

The other reason is because one may assess the prospects of success incorrectly. This has clearly been the major problem faced by the United States in those military situations where it involved itself and failed. One major cause of mis-calculation is overestimation of one's own capabilities and underestimation of the capabilities of the opposition. For the United States, the underlying, distorting assumption is that the power of the American military machine is so overwhelming that it cannot be successfully resisted. The problem is that the invincibility of American power is a matter of perspective. Matched against a similar opponent fighting European-style, the United States is clearly the "heavyweight champion"; fighting against someone who does not fight that way, the United States is not necessarily supreme. That is a lesson the United States has had a great deal of difficulty understanding and accepting.

The other part of miscalculation is overestimation of the appeal and strength of those one seeks to assist. A fundamental corollary of this section's first question ("What is wrong here?") is the admission that if some group or government cannot succeed without outside help, it probably means there is something wrong that has provided the impetus for someone seeking to take it down. Those who seek to justify siding with one side or another will always emphasize the vagaries and shortcomings of their potential opponents. In developing world situations, there is almost always an impressive list of valid charges that can be made against movements or governments under siege. It is not hard to find good reasons to oppose the Taliban or the Bashar al-Assad regime, for instance. Indeed, such assessments, if taken to their logical extreme, can raise the question of why *anyone* beyond the most self-interested (Syrian Alawites, for instance) or politically fanatic (supporters of the Taliban and its religious excesses) support such groups. Shaking one's head in disbelief, however, is not an answer.

While criticisms of the opposition may be entirely valid, that assertion begs the question of why such a movement or government has been successful against those the United States proposes to assist. It is a conundrum of sorts: if the balance of virtue between those opposed and those favored is starkly weighted toward "our" side, should this not be obvious to the people in the affected country? In other words, if our side is indeed that of the angels, should those angels need our military help? On the other hand, if they indeed do need that help, what does that say about their comparative virtue and appeal in the population's estimation? Are they angels or devils in disguise?

The assessment of the relative virtue of and prospects for success in a civil conflict should be more cautionary than it always has been. Was the government of South Vietnam's Ngo Dinh Diem somehow better than what Ho Chi Minh offered to the Vietnamese? The answer was apparently not, as the United States eventually abandoned Diem and did not intervene to save him when he was assassinated and replaced by a string of unappealing generals. Saddam Hussein was certainly a villain by almost any measure (except among his Sunni base), but have his successors proven to be improvements? Given the fanaticism of the Taliban, why have the Afghan people not rallied behind the government of Hamid Karzai in much greater numbers than they have? If one cannot answer these kinds of questions convincingly, it probably makes sense to rethink the virtue of and prospects for intervention.

Do You Recognize the Limits on Your Ability to Affect the Outcome?

There is only one viable reason to intrude into a DWIC, and that is the belief that one's action will be decisive in helping to reach an acceptable, desired outcome. The situations in which intervention is contemplated generally reflect conditions either of stalemate or impending defeat of the side one seeks to assist without active participation. The question is whether that interference can in fact tip the scales in the preferred direction.

Assuming that the United States does not seek to engage itself in purposely quixotic adventures, this is a calculation which must be answered positively in the decision process leading to action. There is, however, the danger that such a calculation will be tainted either by solipsistic reasoning or by hubris or both. In any case, the unfortunate result can be to overestimate the extent and degree to which one can influence an outcome and thus to plunge into hopeless tasks.

One problem is solipsism. The root of the term is the belief that self is the only object of real knowledge, and its practical application—acting in a solipsistic manner—is self-centered behavior that assumes whatever it is that one believes is superior to the belief of others and that others should see that wisdom and react accordingly. In the current context, solipsistic reasoning suggests that if the United States shares its vision with the world, the world should respond by recognizing the virtue of that image and emulating it. In terms of intervention, the United States sometimes believes that it is spreading the true message of the American way, and that if those with whom the vision is shared are rational, they will respond by accepting and embracing it. American forces may thus enter and occupy another country or place believing that doing so is an act of liberation from an inferior to a superior way of life. An oft-quoted supposed statement by an American soldier returning from Vietnam (that may be an urban legend) captures the dynamic. "Here we were," he purportedly said, "a great people trying to help a lesser people, and they didn't even appreciate it." It is simply a part of the American psyche to intervene in a situation to do something good; that those who are beneficiaries of that beneficence might not see it that way is simply beyond our comprehension. The expectation can, however, critically predispose us to overestimate the positive impact of our actions.

It may also predispose us to assume that solutions we propose, which inevitably reflect our own values and our view of their problems, will be more appealing to others than they in fact are to them. Afghanistan and Iraq offer contrasting examples. As noted, the American view is that Afghanistan stability will be best served by a strong, preferably democratic central government, since that has been our general experience. How strong a central government that should be, of course, is a matter of some current contention within this country, but that does not diminish the perception that a strong authority in Kabul will maximize stability basically defined as the ability to control the country well enough to keep out Al Qaeda. This construct, of course, violates basic values held in much of the Afghan country-side, where Kabul is viewed with historically justified suspicion. Our solutions are so obvious to us from our perspective that we cannot understand why they are not equally obvious to the Afghans.

The American preference for democracy in Iraq, while mostly associated with the neo-cons, is similar. Iraq may have no democratic tradition, but that is a remediable flaw that emulation of the United States will fix. The vehicle for this conversion was an American presence and assistance to the Iraqis in Americanizing their political system (e.g., helping to draft an Iraqi constitution which a large number of Iraqis reject). Never mind that democratic values and institutions differentially cause advantage and disadvantage to groups within Iraq in fundamental and unacceptable ways; the United States is the beacon, and if they will follow our lead, the result will be peace and tranquility.

The problem associated with this self-centered arrogance is in believing it to the point of overestimating the influence on outcomes one can have. Promoting peace and democracy may be received well by the American public, but the implications, even content, of that entreaty may not sit so well with those subject to our help. Moreover, the American armed forces are not necessarily the best instrument for convincing people to follow our enlightened leadership. Indeed, it has been a central part of the argument here that the introduction of foreign interveners is always resented, creates as many problems as it solves, and becomes a part of the overall problem. Intervention in fact is almost always more complex and problematic than it appears in the abstract.

Indeed, the level of outside involvement and the ability to influence outcomes are inversely related. The more public and intrusive the intervention and the more obviously dependent the government or group receiving that assistance is on it, the more resentment is likely to be created in the target population. Opposition propaganda will be fueled by that resentment, adding to its appeal to the mutual center of gravity. As events do not transpire in the way the intervener prefers, the reaction may be to "double down," increasing the level of assistance. In the process, two bad outcomes already raised may occur: increased assistance may be viewed as further evidence of government weakness, and the stake for the intervener may be increased so that it becomes harder to pull out. It may in fact be true that doing less is the proper direction, but this is a hard path to adopt, because it seems to risk all. Unfortunately, outside intervention may simply make problems like insurgency worse, creating a kind of intervener's contradiction.

Do You Have a Viable Politico-Military Strategy?

This question has two related aspects. The first is about attainability; does the United States have a realistic, attainable political objective that it seeks to achieve in any given situation? And is the military plan associated with that objective viable to achieving the political objective? The second is whether that plan is acceptable to the American population, a factor that includes elements both of the importance and viability of the objective.

Adopting a viable politico-military strategy must take into consideration both audiences. The precipitator for any action by the United States reflects conditions within a target developing world country, and for American action to succeed, it must produce outcomes those in the target country can embrace. At the same time, the United States uses armed forces primarily in pursuit of its own interests, and the outcomes must thus ultimately be justified in terms of whether the United States, in addition to the target country, is better off for the intervention.

Although it is seldom recognized at the time, the sets of interests of the target country and the United States often do not coincide. In the heat of an emergency situation where American help may be desperately needed to avert a humanitarian or political disaster, the differences may be not seem important or be capable of deferment (e.g., dealing with Syria to stop the slaughter but not resolving concern about what a post-Assad Syria would be like). Those differences may become more obvious as an intervention protracts and is reflected in questions in the intervening country over the worth of its involvement and in the target country about the dubious impact of clashing objectives in the battle for hearts and minds. When cleavages appear, whose interests should be paramount? Should they be those of the intervening country whose blood and treasure have been sacrificed to avert a disastrous outcome? Or should they be the interests of the people in the country involved, whose people will have to accept an eventual outcome for it to be viable? When the interests of both the intervener and the target country coincide or overlap enough so that one outcome can satisfy both, the answer is simple. If the two sets of objectives are far apart, then the answer is not simple and affects both the outcome and what people think about it.

This leads to the second concern, which is the viability of a strategy to the American public. This concern also has multiple aspects. One is a reflection of the paradigm problem that affects U.S. national security policy. Crises in the developing world pop up periodically at different places, and the United States appears not to have a clear policy direction that says which kinds of conflicts are most-to-least important. Because of petroleum access and terrorism, the Near East has drawn the most automatic attention, but it is not clear where else a problem will bring an American response. Thus, the public is not conditioned to consider whether a conflict in any one place is important or not. The result is that determinations of level of interest and importance must be made virtually *ad hoc*, rather than as extensions from a well-thought-out and articulated strategic ordering.

The paradigm problem also manifests itself in terms of the content of responses the United States should entertain in different circumstances. Admitting a rigid formula cannot be applied in all circumstances, there is no agreement on what appropriate responses should be. When, for instance, is a situation adequately important that the United States should contemplate the insertion of American ground forces in significant numbers rather than some more limited response? During Arab Spring conflicts like those in Libya and Syria, the lack of a doctrinal consensus meant appropriate responses were debated publicly, leaving a residue of apparent lack of consensus that would plague any decision the United States might reach. Moreover, the United States has clearly not developed a clear and workable military doctrine to implement actions that uniformly produce favorable outcomes or a paradigm that places contemporary situations in priority. A new paradigm will not answer all questions, since the range of possibilities is great and to some extent unpredictable. If a new paradigm were simply to clarify general orientations toward these kinds of conflicts and to develop something like lists of criteria that should be applied to determining the wisdom of different approaches, it would be a step forward.

Part of the reason that hard guidelines have not been drawn is the implicit acknowledgement or recognition of the kinds of dynamics that have been highlighted in these pages. A robust policy of activism in developing world instability, which is one principle around which a paradigm might be crafted, means involvement in what can become a long and protracted list of engagements of indeterminate length and difficulty. In these kinds of situations, the opponent will inevitably look for the Achilles' heel of American military determination, which is public support. The only obvious inhibitor to exceeding cost-tolerance is swift and decisively successful forms of interventions, which are the very kind that are both infrequent and which probably do not require outside assistance anyway: if they can be solved by waving force like a magic wand, they are probably inconsequential in the first place.

Finding criteria for conducting operations that do not activate the democratic contradiction may be the single most important and difficult task in developing a post-Cold War paradigm for dealing with the volatile developing world. In the absence of paradigmatic response on which the public and its representatives agree in advance, possible involvements have to be handled on an *ad hoc*, situation-by-situation basis in which champions of involvement in effect have to trick the public into supporting policy actions on which that public will eventually turn by having their cost-tolerance exceeded. Those supporting intervention are left rolling the dice, hoping the United States can get in and out before public ire is raised. There has to be a better way to organize and conduct the use of military force than that.

The Capulets and the Sharks: Lament of the Recidivists

In the aftermath of the Vietnam War, there was a somber assessment of that experience. The war and its effect on the American people was an enormous tragedy in many ways, and the country would clearly have been better off had that war not occurred. The war divided Americans deeply, and the fissures that opened are still with us, if expressed sometimes in different forms and forums. These fissures included a generation gap in which members of the "Vietnam generation" were polarized over whether they served in or opposed the war and other symbols of "patriotism" that included the flight overseas of some of the most opposed to avoid involuntary participation in a war they opposed. Before the Vietnam War, drugs were scarcely seen on American college campuses; within a year or so of the American active takeover of the war with a conscripted army, the campuses became drug-infested battlegrounds, of which the 1970 confrontation and shootings at Kent and Jackson State Universities became the most dramatic symbols.

The Vietnam War was a bitterly divisive wedge politically in other ways. The war was so large, with over a half-million American servicemen "in country" at its physical apex in 1969, that only the extensive use of conscripted forces compelled more or less unwillingly to serve could meet the needs, and the result was bitter resentment against the political symbols behind the war. Chants of "LBJ, LBJ, How Many Kids Did You Kill Today?" haunted President Johnson in the White House and ultimately helped cause him not to seek reelection in 1968. Public delusion grew as the Nixon administration, which had promised "peace with honor," presided instead over what seemed a war without end. In 1973, the last American combat troops left the country, and in 1975, South Vietnam fell to the communists whose triumph the Americans had deferred for a decade. In 1974, President Nixon resigned in disgrace over the cover-up of misdoings by his reelection campaign in 1972; in combination, public disgust with the Watergate scandal and the Vietnam War triggered the enormous alienation between the public and the government that remains a central part of contemporary American politics.

The bitter reaction to Vietnam left another legacy that is infrequently raised but which is part of why others will look askance at American offers of aid in the future. Once the United States physically extricated itself from Vietnam, we physically abandoned the country and distanced ourselves from those Vietnamese we had befriended. Peter Beinart has captured the phenomenon of American help, using Iraq as his example (see, for example, *The Icarus Syndrome*). After the United States intervenes, "the tyrants flee; some other folks take over, and they seem like a big improvement at first. Then the locals grow unhappy with our presence; they begin killing U.S. soldiers in attacks that shock Americans and prompt an angry debate about getting out, which America eventually does. And then it's done. The curtain goes down, the show is over, and barely anybody in America pays any attention … anymore." The scenario seems almost certain to replay itself in Afghanistan. President Karzai's successors, beware! More to the point, future leaders who might otherwise look toward American assistance should be forewarned about what happens if the United States fails in situations where it cannot win and probably should avoid in the first place.

The reaction to Vietnam was a post-mortem that zeroes in on why the United States failed. Most of this reexamination took place within the military and especially the army, because the military and its major ground component felt the most tarnish from the experience. The result was an intense reexamination of the unconventional, guerrilla warfare the country had faced and had not been able to defeat. There was disagreement over why the effort had failed, including recriminations about levels of commitment to the forces in the field, but there was agreement that the United States had to come to grips with this apparently new (but really very old) form of warfare. The lessons were engraved in new military manuals and in the elevation of segments of the military establishment like Special Forces. These lessons were not fully articulated until 2006 when, under the direction of General Petraeus, they were combined in the joint Army/Marines manual on counterinsurgency.

The real lessons and tragedies somehow got lost along the way. Part of the reason was that the end of the Cold War caused such a sigh of relief that those lessons did not seem so important, especially as the United States emerged during the 1990s as by far the premier military power in the world. Partly, it was also the result of the fact that the post-Vietnam military was an all-volunteer force. What that meant was that the major weakness in the American armor, the Clausewitzian trinity's weak point, public support, was no longer so important. The next wars, no matter where they were fought, would not involve dragging American youth involuntarily into service, and that removed a major stumbling block to gaining acquiescence for conducting hostilities.

But that was not all. With the response to the international terrorism symbolized by Al Qaeda as the banner under which to justify renewed activism in the very kind of politico-military maelstroms that the Vietnam retrospective had counseled against, the United States plunged into quixotic quests in Iraq and Afghanistan. Like variations on the Romeo and Juliet story from Ovid to Shakespeare to Arthur Laurents (who wrote the adaptation on which *West Side Story* was based), the story continues to be repeated, and one has to wonder why? Can tomorrow's Sharks learn from yesterday's Capulets? One hopes so.

The only real basis on which to ignore these apparent lessons of the past is to deny their relevance to particular settings. That is the heart of the recidivist's lament: what seem like obvious variations on common themes are illusions because of the uniqueness of each event. It is at least arguable that no two events are identical and will differ in some ways. That does not, however, mean that they cannot be variations that reflect in structure and dynamics other events and that their comparison cannot yield useful insights, including admonitions, about what to expect from current and future events based on how similar events have played out in the past. Indeed, it is a fundamental tenet of education that its intent is vicarious experience: learning from the accumulated experience of others so that one does not have to discover all things, good and bad, entirely on one's own. We do not, after all, have to stick our hands in the fire to find out that fire burns; others have done that for us and passed along the experience. Why is it not the same for involvement in unwinnable wars?

Bibliography

Art, Robert J., Peter Feaver, Richard Fontaine, Kristin M. Lord, and Anne-Marie Slaughter. *America's Path: Grand Strategy for the Next Administration.* Washington, DC: Center for a New American Security, 2012.

Bacevich, Andrew C. (ed.). *The Short American Century: A Postmortem.* Cambridge, MA: Harvard University Press, 2012.

Beinart, Peter. *The Icarus Syndrome: A History of American Hubris.* New York: HarperCollins, 2010. (The quote is from an August 2012 *Newsweek* online article).

Brzezinski, Zbigniew. *Strategic Vision: America and the Crisis of Global Power.* New York: Basic Books, 2012.

Carafano, James J., and Paul Rosenzweig. *Winning the Long War: Lessons from the Cold War for Defeating Terrorism and Preserving Freedom.* Washington, DC: Heritage Books, 2005.

Chandrasekaran, Rajiv. *Imperial Life in the Emerald City: Inside Iraq's Green Zone.* New York: Alfred A. Knopf, 2007.

Clark, Wesley. *Winning Modern Wars: Iraq, Terrorism, and the American Empire.* New York: Public Affairs, 2003.

Galula, David. *Counterinsurgency Warfare: Theory and Practice.* Westport, CT: Praeger Publishing Classics of the Counterinsurgency Age, 2006 (originally published in 1965).

Gelb, Leslie H. "A Statesman Bows Out: America's Top Diplomat on Iraq, Afghanistan, and the Taliban Weakness." *Newsweek*, September 12, 2012, 15–17.

Haass, Richard N. *Wars of Necessity, Wars of Choice: A Memoir of Two Iraq Wars.* New York: Simon and Schuster, 2009.

Jones, Seth G. *In the Graveyard of Empires: America's War in Afghanistan.* New York: W. W. Norton, 2009.

Kaplan, Robert. *The World America Made.* New York: Alfred A. Knopf, 2012,

Latham, Michael E. *The Right Kind of Revolution: Modernization, Development, and U.S. Foreign Policy from the Cold War to the Present.* Ithaca, NY: Cornell University Press, 2011.

Mandelbaum, Michael. *The Frugal Superpower: America's Global Leadership in a Cash-Strapped Era.* New York: Public Affairs, 2010.

Obama, Barack. "Transcript of President Obama's Commencement Address at West Point." *New York Times* (online), May 28, 2014.

O'Hanlon, Michael. *The Wounded Giant: America's Armed Forces in an Age of Austerity.* New York: Penguin Books, 2011.

Orwell, George, *Burmese Diaries: A Novel.* London: Seeker and Wartburg, 1986.

Packer, George. *The Assassin's Gate: America in Iraq.* New York: Farrar, Straus, and Giroux, 2005.

Polk, William R. *Understanding Iraq.* New York: Harper Perennials, 2005.

Ricks, Thomas E. *Fiasco: The American Military Adventure in Iraq.* New York: Penguin Press, 2006.

Snow, Donald M. *National Security for a New Era* (5th ed.). New York: Pearson, 2014.

——*What After Iraq?* New York: Pearson Longman, 2009.

Zakaria, Fareed. *The Post-American World.* New York: Current Affairs Press, 2008.

INDEX

Page numbers in italics refer to figures.